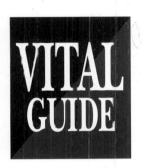

BOMBERS OF THE 20TH CENTURY

JIM WINCHESTER

Airlife

Copyright © 2003 Airlife Publishing Ltd

First published in the UK in 2003
by Airlife Publishing Ltd

British Library Cataloguing-in-Publication Data
 A catalogue record for this book
 is available from the British Library

ISBN 1 84037 386 5

Printed in Hong Kong

For a complete list of all Airlife titles please contact:
Airlife Publishing Ltd
101 Longden Road, Shrewsbury, SY3 9EB, England
E-mail: sales@airlifebooks.com
Website: www.airlifebooks.com

Zeppelin-Staaken R-planes

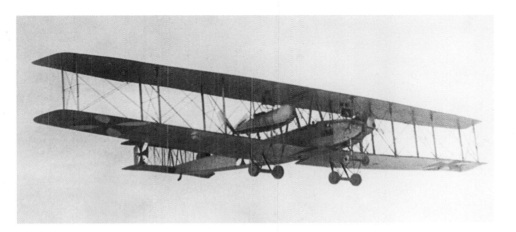

The German Imperial Air Service's series of Reisenflugzeug or giant aeroplanes originated with designers Baumann, Hirth and Klein at the East Gotha Experimental Works, or V.G.O When the development moved to the Zeppelin airfield at Staaken in summer 1916, the resulting 'R-planes', or simply 'Giants', became known as Zeppelin-Staakens. The first model appeared on 11 April 1915 as the V.G.O.I with three Maybach engines, but was soon lost.

The one-off V.G.O.II and V.G.O.III were retrospectively redesignated **R.II** and **R.III** when the similar **R.IV** flew in 1917. The wingspan of the R.IV and its predecessors was only a few feet shorter than a B-29 Superfortress, and they had an extraordinary arrangement of six 230-hp (172-kW) Mercedes engines. Two were mounted side-by-side in the nose, driving a single two-bladed propeller, and the remaining four were fitted in two nacelles between the wings, driving tractor and pusher propellers. There were stations in the nacelles that could be occupied in flight by mechanics, who were also armed with some of the seven machine-guns. The two pilots sat beside each other in an open cockpit.

The **R.V** had five Maybach engines. this time only one in the nose. The **R.VI** was the only model produced in quantity and was graced with an enclosed pilot's cabin. It could carry up to 18 220-lb (100-kg)

An R.VI is manhandled at the factory. Note the paired engines and the lozenge camouflage pattern. (Philip Jarrett collection)

An R.IV in flight shows its large engine gondolas (containing gunners and mechanics) and the anti-tip-over nosewheels. (Philip Jarrett collection)

bombs internally. or a smaller number of large bombs. As well as four mainwheels, a twin nosewheel unit allowed for a level landing attitude, after which the aircraft would settle back on its tail skid.

All but the first R.VI were built by one of three sub-contractors and 17 of the 18 R-planes built saw active service. In 1916 two giant aeroplane squadrons were sent to the Russian Front. In September 1917, one squadron was ordered to Belgium to bolster the Gotha force in its attacks on England

Three or four R-planes could lift the load of 15 Gothas and only small numbers were despatched alongside their smaller counterparts. The R.VI made its first raid on London in February 1918, hitting St Pancras Station. A raid by five Giants that month saw the first 2,205-lb (1000-kg) bombs dropped on England. Between December 1917 and May 1918, 11 raids were carried out by Zeppelin R-planes and 60,000 lb (27,190 kg) of bombs were dropped. No R-planes were lost to enemy action over the UK, but two were shot down over the Western Front.

At least two examples of the R.VI were built in seaplane configuration for naval use. Surprisingly, some Giants remained in German service after the armistice and saw action against the Bolsheviks in 1919.

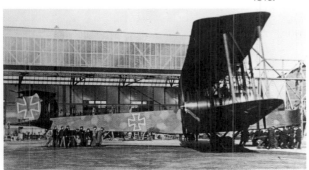

Specification: Zeppelin-Staaken R.VI
Type: four-engined heavy bomber
Crew: seven
Powerplant: four 245-hp (183-kW) Maybach Mb IV 6-cylinder in-line pistons
Dimensions: span 138 ft 6 in (42.2 m); length 72 ft 6 in (22.1 m); height 20 ft 8 in (6.3 m); wing area 3,595 sq ft (332 m²)
Weights: empty 17,426 lb (7921 kg); max. take-off 26,066 lb (11848 kg)
Performance: max. speed 84 mph (135 km/h); service ceiling 14,170 ft (4320 m); endurance up to 10 hours
Armament: four Parabellum machine-guns; bomb load up to 3,960 lb (1800 kg)

Handley Page O/100 and O/400

United Kingdom
December 1915

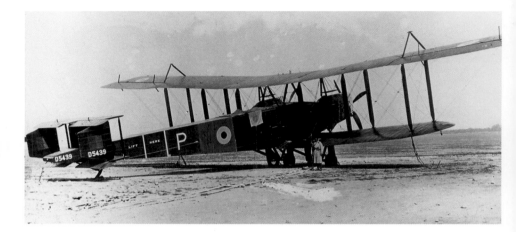

The origins of the Handley Page 'giants' of World War I and beyond can be traced back to the L/200, a large single-engined aircraft designed in 1913 to win the prize for the first Atlantic crossing. The outbreak of war in August 1914 quashed that plan, but Handley Page had solved many of the structural problems of large aircraft and when the Admiralty's Commodore Murray Sueter requested in December a 'Bloody Paralyser' to attack the German Navy, the company was ready to respond. Frederick Handley Page and George Volkert redesigned their transatlantic machine as the twin-engined **O/100** and powered it with two of the new 250-hp (186-kW) Rolls-Royce Eagle engines.

Unusually for the time, the nacelles, crew cabin and windscreens were given a degree of armour protection. A bomb load of up to sixteen 112-lb (51-kg) bombs could be carried vertically within the centre-section. The bombs fell tail-first onto spring-loaded doors, pushing them open. The unequal-span three-bay wings with huge ailerons could fold backwards to allow hangar stowage. The fuselage was essentially a cross-braced box girder and the tail was a biplane structure with a central fin and two rudders. The elevators overhung the tailplane noticeably. The nacelles initially had side-mounted radiators, and they contained most of the fuel supply in long extensions.

One year after the initial proposal, the prototype flew on 17 December 1915. The armoured cockpit enclosure was soon dispensed with but production aircraft introduced defensive armament in the form of nose, dorsal and ventral gun positions.

D5439 was one of a batch of 50 O/400s built by the Birmingham Carriage Company. It is seen in Africa sometime after WWI. (Philip Jarrett collection)

In December 1916 the first four O/100s were despatched to the front. Unfortunately, one landed at an enemy aerodrome by mistake. Joined by four more in April, the huge bombers were at first employed on anti-shipping patrols. Although they crippled a German destroyer, one was lost to anti-aircraft (AA) fire and the mission was changed to night attacks on rail targets, dockyards and industry. One aircraft was flown from an Aegean island on attacks against Constantinople, Turkey.

A version with a new fuselage fuel system and compressed air starting was tested in September 1917, and entered production as the **O/400**. Various engines were used, including the Sunbeam Maori, Fiat A.12bis and Hispano-Suiza. Most retained Eagles. O/400s equipped the new Independent Force of the RAF (which formed in April 1918). They were used in small numbers until 14 September when 40 were despatched against six targets. Three were lost and nine returned early. Production totalled 663 O/400s (107 built in the USA) and 46 O/100s.

This view of an Eagle-engined O/400 shows the much greater span and overhanging ailerons of the upper wing. (Philip Jarrett collection)

Specification: Handley Page O/400
Type: twin-engined heavy bomber
Crew: four
Powerplant: two 250-hp (186-kW) Rolls-Royce Eagle II, V-12 pistons
Type: span 100 ft (30.48 m); length 62 ft 10 in (19.15 m); height 22 ft (6.71 m); wing area 1,648 sq ft (153 m²)
Weights: empty 7,894 lb (3580 kg); max. take-off 14,020 lb (6359 kg)
Performance: max. speed 85 mph (137 km/h); service ceiling 7,000 ft (2134 m); endurance 8 hours
Armament: four or five 0.303-in (7.7-mm) machine-guns; bomb load up to 1,800 lb (816 kg)

Sopwith 1½ Strutter

United Kingdom
December 1915

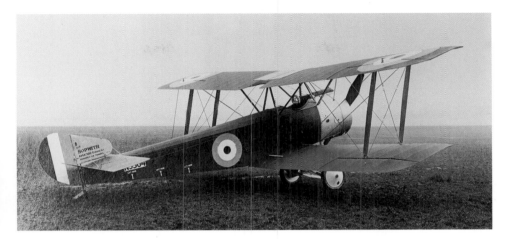

The Sopwith Two-Seater was more commonly known as the **1½ Strutter,** a reference to the length of the members of the W-shaped supports for the centre wing section. Designed to meet an Admiralty requirement for a fighter/reconnaissance aircraft, the **Type 9400** Strutter was a neat two-seat biplane with equal-span staggered wings. The **Type 9700** was the single-seat equivalent, the pilot flying from the rear cockpit position.

The Strutter first flew in mid-December 1915 and deliveries began to the Royal Naval Air Service (RNAS) in February 1916 when they were put into use on the Western Front as light bombers. Most were soon transferred to the Royal Flying Corps' (RFC's) bombing squadrons and from October operated alongside French Breguet bombers. The Strutter could be described as the first fighter-bomber as it was the first British aircraft to be equipped with a synchronised forward-firing machine-gun and was effective in the air-to-air role. The top Strutter ace was Geoffrey Cock who destroyed 13 enemy aircraft. The Strutter's observer had a Lewis gun, initially on a Scarff pillar mount, later on a Nieuport ring and then on the famous Scarff ring mounting. The 1½ Strutter had several innovative features including a type of airbrake in the trailing edges of the lower wingroots and a tailplane that was adjustable in flight.

The Strutter was initially used by naval units. This is a line up of No. 3 Wing RNAS single-seat bomber versions. (Philip Jarrett collection)

Strutter N5504 was a single-seat bomber. About 130 of the 1,315 British-built Strutters were this model. (Philip Jarrett collection)

The Strutter became popular with the French and eight manufacturers produced 4,500 single- and two-seat variants from 1916 to April 1918 as follows: the **Sop. I A2** (two-seater scout), the **Sop. I B2** (two-seater bomber) and the **Sop. B1** (single-seater bomber). The two-seaters could carry up to 130 lb (59 kg) of bombs on external racks, but with the observer's position replaced by a 12-cell compartment, the single-seat bomber could lift 224 lb (102 kg) of small bombs. Even this was not a great deal and by the time the French aircraft reached the front in summer 1917 they were basically obsolete. Even so they equipped most of the day bombing squadrons. In early 1918 they were withdrawn and used for training duties. Clerget and Le Rhône engines from 80 to 135 hp (60 to 100 kW) were used.

The Strutter was the first British ship-borne aircraft, with RNAS aircraft flying from platforms atop the gun turrets of battleships. The US Navy also flew Strutters briefly from the battleships *Texas* and *Oklahoma.* The US Army Air Service acquired 518 Strutters (130 of them single-seaters) from France in spring 1918. They saw some action but were mainly used as trainers.

Many Strutters were exported during and after the war, including to Belgium, Romania, Japan and Latvia. Japan is said to have used them against the USSR.

Specification: 1½ Strutter Sop. B1
Type: single-engined light bomber
Crew: one
Powerplant: one 130-hp (96-kW) Clerget rotary piston
Dimensions: span 33 ft 6 in (10.21 m); length 25 ft 3 in (7.69 m); height 10 ft 3 in (3.12 m); wing area 346 sq ft (32.12 m²)
Weights: empty 1,305 lb (592 kg); max. take-off 2,149 lb (975 kg)
Performance: max. speed 100 mph (161 km/h); service ceiling 15,000 ft (4570 m); endurance 3 hours 45 minutes
Armament: one 0.303-in (7.62-mm) Vickers machine-gun; bomb load up to 224 lb (102 kg)

Gotha Bombers

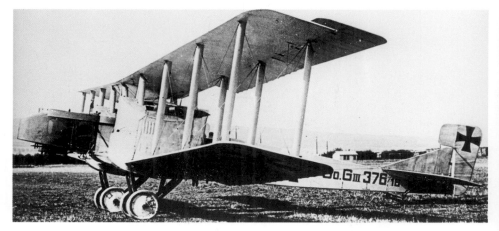

The name Gotha, a contraction of Gothaer Waggonfabrik AG, became a generic term for all large German bombers because of the success of the raids by these aircraft from early 1917. Although they caused little damage of military significance, civilian casualties were relatively heavy, and the effect on morale and public order caused severe headaches for the authorities.

The Gotha **G.II** of early 1916 was a short-range bomber of which only eight of the 10 built saw service. It was a medium-sized (77 ft (23.5 m) span) three-bay biplane housing three crew. Designer Hans Burkhard revised the design into the **G.III**, which had more reliable Mercedes D.IVa engines and a changed tail design. The type had a limited career, partly because of unreliable Mercedes D.IV engines, but achieved success by destroying a rail bridge over the Don on the Romanian front. By September 1917 all G.IIs and IIIs had been sent to training units.

The **G.IV** appeared in the autumn of 1916 and 30 were issued to Heavy Bomber Squadron No. 3 or F 3 in Belgium in the spring of 1917. The G.IV was powered by Mercedes D.VIa engines driving pusher propellers. There was a cut-out in the trailing edge of the lower wing to allow propeller clearance. The fuselage was an internally braced wooden structure skinned in plywood. The main fuel tank was aft of the wing, occupying the full width and preventing intercommunication between the crew. The three-bay wings were made of two panels on the top wing and

The G.III had some concessions to streamlining such as the engine cowlings with frontal radiators and pusher props. (Philip Jarrett collection)

three on the lower. The fabric-covered wings were slightly swept with slight dihedral. There were ailerons on all four surfaces.

The G.IV had a unique tail gun position from which the gunner could fire upwards, directly aft and also downwards through a tunnel in the fuselage, although he had to lie prone to do so. This tail 'stinger' was successful in driving off many interception attempts. The bomb armament was carried on a variety of external racks. The G.V was a refined version and the G.Vb had an extra pair of wheels at the nose to avoid nosing over, particularly in night landings.

Despite their slow climb rate (it took 52 minutes for a G.IV to reach its maximum altitude) the Belgium-based bombers were able to fly above effective AA and fighter defence by the time they crossed the Channel. The British response was to withdraw valuable squadrons to England and develop an early-warning network. The arrival cf better fighters such as the Sopwith Camel began to take their toll on the Gothas. After suffering increasing losses (in total 24 in combat, 37 in accidents), the Gothas switched to night raids from September 1917 to May 1918.

After relatively ineffective raids by Zeppelins, bombers such as this G.III taxed Britain's defences from 1916. (Philip Jarrett collection)

Specification: Gotha G.IV
Type: twin-engined heavy bomber
Crew: three
Powerplant: two 260-hp (194-kW) Mercedes D.VIa 6-cylinder inline pistons
Dimensions: span 77 ft 10 in (23.7 m); length 38 ft 11 in (11.86 m); height 14 ft 1 in (4.3 m); wing area 967 sq ft (89.5 m²)
Weights: empty 5,280 lb (2400 kg); max. take-off 8,013 lb (3635 kg)
Performance: max. speed 87mph (140 km/h); service ceiling 21,320 ft (6500 m); range 305 miles (491 km)
Armament: three Parabellum LMG14 machine-guns; bomb load up to 1,100 lb (500 kg)

Airco DH.4 and DH.4A

United Kingdom
August 1916

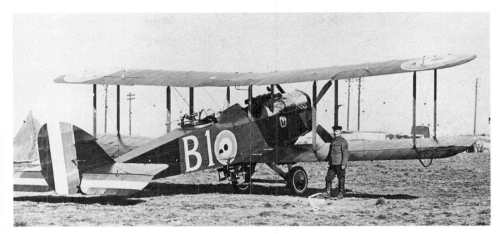

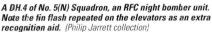

Designed by Geoffrey de Havilland and A E Hage, the Airco **DH.4** was the first purpose-built light day bomber. De Havilland himself made the first flight in his creation in mid-August 1916. The first aircraft used the 250-hp (186-kW) Beardmore-Halford-Pullinger (BHP), but delays with this engine saw initial production models appear with the Rolls-Royce Eagle of the same power. The DH.4 was a fairly conventional biplane with a two-bay wing that had slight dihedral on each surface. After official testing in late 1916 and immediate large orders, the first DH.4s were sent to France in March 1917.

The reliable Eagle engine allowed the DH.4 to climb above the effective altitude of enemy fighters. For the time it was fast and easy to fly. As well as bombing missions, it was used for artillery spotting and photoreconnaissance. It is regarded as one of the most versatile aircraft of World War I. However, owing to the vulnerable location of the petrol tank between the crew members, the DH.4 acquired the nickname 'flaming coffin'. The pilot was situated between the engine and the fuel tank and was too far from the observer/gunner for effective communication.

In 1918 DH.4s formed part of the Independent Force, a strategic branch of the RAF dedicated to attacking targets in Germany, alongside Handley Page

Eagle-engined DH.4s of No. 8 Squadron are seen lined up with their bombs in front of a canvas Bessoneau hangar.
(The Aviation Picture Library)

A DH.4 of No. 5(N) Squadron, an RFC night bomber unit. Note the fin flash repeated on the elevators as an extra recognition aid. (Philip Jarrett collection)

O/400s and other large bombers. A total of 1,429 DH.4s were built in the UK.

Three manufacturers in the USA built nearly 5,000 **DH.4A**s, also known as the Liberty Plane, powered by the 400-hp (298-kW) Liberty engine. Dayton-Wright alone built 3,100. Nearly 1,900 were shipped to France, the only American-built aircraft to see combat (from August 1918) on the Western Front. Fifteen Dayton-Wright-built DH.4s also saw US Naval Air Service (USNAS) use in France.

The plywood-skinned **DH.4B** was in US production at war's end, incorporating many DH.9A improvements such as the relocated fuel tank and pilot's cockpit. Boeing rebuilt many as the **DH.4M** (modernised) with welded tube frames. Those redelivered to the US Navy (USN) in 1922–5 were **OB-1**s and **O2B-1**s with fabric covering. Some United States Marine Corps (USMC) DH.4s were used in action in Nicaragua in 1929. The US Army's DH.4s were used for a myriad of tasks including photography, border patrol, air ambulance and airmail delivery. The very first US refuelling trials were carried out by DH.4Bs in October 1923. The last US Army DH.4s were retired in 1932. Other countries to use the DH.4 included Australia, Canada, Greece, Japan, South Africa and Spain.

Specification: Airco DH.4
Type: single-engined light day bomber
Crew: two
Powerplant: one 375-hp (275-kW) Rolls-Royce Eagle VII, V-12 piston
Dimensions: span 42 ft 5 in (12.92 m); length 30 ft 8 in (9.35 m); height 11 ft (3.35 m); wing area 434 sq ft (40.3 m²)
Weights: empty 2,387 lb (1083 kg); max. take-off 3,472 lb (1575 kg)
Performance: max. speed 143 mph (230 km/h); service ceiling 23,500 ft (7163 m); endurance 6 hr 45 min
Armament: 2–4 machine-guns, bomb load up to 460 lb (209 kg)

Breguet 14 and 16

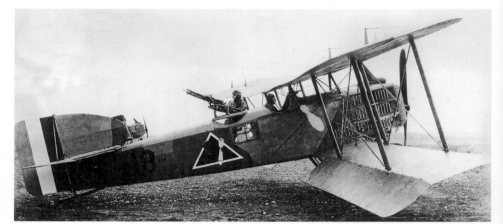

After a small number of relatively unsuccessful Breguet-Michelin pusher-configuration bombers were produced, Louis Breguet turned to a conventional tractor layout for a private-venture project called the **AV 1** in March 1916. Breguet himself flew the first prototype on 21 November 1916 and flight trials were completed by January 1917. The Aviation Militaire was at that time seeking a day bomber, a reconnaissance aircraft and a two-seat fighter. The AV 1 and **AV 2** reconnaissance model were selected for these first two roles as the **Breguet 14** or Br.14.

The Br.14 used a 220-hp (164-kW) Renault 12Fb engine behind an angular cowl with prominent cooling louvres. The wings had slight back stagger and sweep back and the upper wing, which mounted the ailerons, was slightly longer than the lower one. Transparent panels allowed the pilot and observer to view the ground. It was one of the first aircraft to make much use of duralumin, for spacers and longerons.

In March 1917 orders for 150 reconnaissance and 150 bomber versions were received, soon followed by many more, divided roughly equally. Five sub-contractors built between 220 and 330 aircraft each. The **Br.14A2** reconnaissance version could carry a camera, a radio and four small (11-lb/5-kg) bombs. The **Br.14B2** bomber could carry 32 11-lb (5-kg) bombs on its increased-span bottom wing to which sprung flaps were added. Transparent side panels provided light for the observer to view the bombsight.

Some Br.14s were fitted with Fiat A-12bis engines

Breguet Br.14B2 of the 96th Aero Squadron, US Air Service, about to set off from Amanty on 29 July 1918. This was the first US unit to bomb Germany (Philip Jarrett collection)

with underslung radiators, and others in colonial service had Lorraine-Dietrich 8Bd engines. In the 1920s China was supplied with 70 Lorraine 12Da-powered models. Two **Br.14B1** single-seat bombers were modified for a raid on Berlin that did not take place. The **Br.14E2** was a trainer version. The **Br.14S** air ambulance saw a little service in the war and more in colonial service afterwards.

The US Air Service was given 290 used machines, which equipped their first bombing unit in 1918. They had little success and suffered many losses in accidents. Belgian squadrons also flew Br.14s. In service a Lewis gun was added to the top wing and a gun hatch to the underside.

About 5,500 of the 8,000 Br.14s were produced during World War I, with output continuing until 1926. Finland, Poland, Spain and Romania bought Br.14s after the war. In France they were widely used as mailplanes into the 1930s. The **Br.16** was an enlarged derivative that was too late for wartime service. The **Br.16BN2** two-seat night bomber was used by France and Czechoslovakia up to the late 1920s.

This is a later Br.16BN2 night bomber. The Br.16 lacked the fuselage side windows of the Br.14. (Author's collection)

Specification: Breguet Br.14B2
Type: single-engined medium bomber
Crew: two
Powerplant: one 300-hp (224-kW) Renault 12Fcx piston
Dimensions: span 47 ft 2 in (14.36 m); length 29 ft 2 in (8.87 m); height 10 ft 10 in (3.33 m); wing area 540 sq ft (50.2 m²)
Weights: empty 2,242 lb (1017 kg); max. take-off 3,900 lb (1769 kg)
Performance: max. speed 121 mph (195 km/h); service ceiling 20,341 ft (6200 m); endurance 2.75 hours
Armament: one 7.7-mm (0.303-in) Vickers and two or three 7.7-mm Lewis machine-guns; bomb load up to 782 lb (355 kg)

De Havilland DH.9 and DH.9A

United Kingdom
July 1917

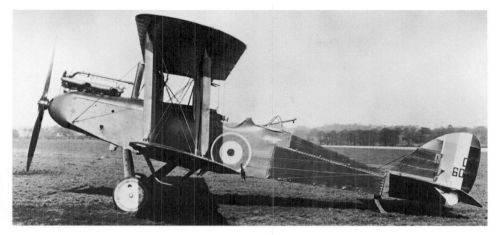

F ollowing heavy German bombing raids on England in May 1917, the British defence establishment and Cabinet agreed that both Home defence and offensive bombing squadrons of the RFC be substantially strengthened. Seven hundred DH.4s were ordered, but it was argued that a longer-range version could be produced with only seven weeks' delay to deliveries. The Air Board agreed to substitute this new **DH.9** for the DH.4s on order. By July, the prototype (a modified DH.4) was flying. It featured a re-shaped nose with the radiator relocated to a retractable position between the undercarriage legs and the pilot's cockpit repositioned further aft. The engine was the 230-hp (172-kW) BHP (or Galloway Adriatic), which was an unfortunate choice. Despite many problems, mass production had begun (as the Siddeley Puma) and it was too late to prevent the first batches being delivered with this underperforming motor.

When the DH.9 reached the Western Front in early 1918 it was inferior to the DH.4 it replaced. Unable to fly high with a full bomb load, 54 were lost to enemy action and 94 otherwise written off between May and November. In the Middle East they were more successful against Turkish forces without air cover.

A few DH.9s were supplied to the US, and others went to Belgium, Canada, New Zealand and South

The DH.9A had a long post-war career. This aircraft of 4FTS Abu Sueir, Egypt was part of a batch ordered in 1925. (Philip Jarrett collection)

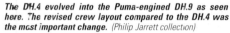

The DH.4 evolved into the Puma-engined DH.9 as seen here. The revised crew layout compared to the DH.4 was the most important change. (Philip Jarrett collection)

Africa the latter modified as the **Mpala** with Jupiter engines. Tests with different engines produced varying results, the Napier Lion proving the best, but the 'Lion-Nine' did not enter production.

American interest in producing the DH.9 with the 400-hp (298-kW) Liberty engine led to the DH.9A. Initial machines were built by Westland in the UK. The **DH.9A** had larger wings and returned to the frontal radiator design. The pilot had a synchronised Vickers gun and the observer one or two Lewis guns. Although suffering some teething troubles on its mid-1918 combat debut, the 'Nine-Ack' soon proved its reliability and suffered proportionally fewer losses than the DH.9 in its brief combat career.

In the 1920s many were refurbished and the type mainly served in the colonial policing role in the Near and Middle East. In many situations the appearance of an aircraft was enough to quell local unrest. From 1929, the DH.9As gave way to the Westland Wapiti.

DH.9s and DH.9As were supplied to several countries as 'Imperial Gift' aircraft, helping establish the air arms of Australia, New Zealand and Canada. As well as military duties, they made numerous route proving survey and airmail flights into the early 1930s. DH.9As, often modified with new fuselages, became the pioneering equipment of many airlines.

Specification: DH.9A
Type: single-engined day bomber
Powerplant: one 400-hp (298-kW) Liberty 12A V-12 piston
Crew: two
Dimensions: span 46 ft 0 in (14.02 m); length 30 ft 0 in (9.14 m); height 10 ft 9 in (3.28 m); wing area 488 sq ft (45.36 m²)
Weights: empty 2,800 lb (1270 kg); max. take-off 4,900 lb (2223 kg)
Performance: max. speed 114 mph (183 km/h); service ceiling 16,500 ft (5029 m); endurance 5.75 hours
Armament: one 0.303-in (7.7-mm) Vickers and two 0.303-in (7.7-mm) Lewis machine-guns; bomb load up to 450 lb (204 kg)

Vickers Vimy

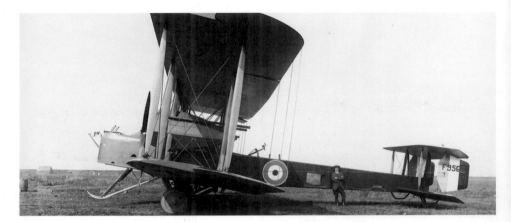

This Vimy was built to replace an early example used for engine trials. Note the prominent skids and the transparent window in mid-fuselage. (Philip Jarrett collection)

On 30 November 1917, only four months after the Air Board issued an urgent specification for a new heavy night bomber, the prototype **F.B.27** or **Vimy** made its first flight. Vickers' R K Pierson designed a large equal-span two-bay biplane with engines mounted between the wings. The square-section fuselage had an open gun position at the front and a box-like biplane tail at the rear.

The first aircraft was powered by two 200-hp (149.2-kW) Hispano-Suiza inline engines with a two-bladed propeller and later by 260-hp (194-kW) Salmson radials. The second, called the **Vimy I**, had 260-hp Sunbeam Maoris and the third, the **Vimy II**, had 300-hp (223.8-kW) Fiat A-12s. Production of this model began in 1918, followed quickly by the **Vimy IV** with the Rolls-Royce Eagle VIII. With such small engines, the performance was hardly exhilarating, although good for its time. The maximum speed was only 103 mph (166 km/h). With bombs it was more like 81 mph (130 km/h). It took 22 minutes to reach 5,000 ft (1525 m).

The first available aircraft were rushed to the Western Front, but only a handful (sources vary between one and seven) had arrived by the time of the Armistice on 11 November 1918 and they saw no action. All contracts were then cancelled, but reinstated later to equip the post-war bombing force.

Delays with engine production kept Vimys out of full squadron service until 1920, initially overseas. They were mainly used in the Middle East, particularly in Egypt, with four active units and a training school. Two bomber squadrons and one flight were equipped with Vimys in the UK from 1922.

A version for civilian use was built as the **Vimy Commercial**. This had a larger diameter fuselage and served as the basis of the **Vimy Ambulance**, which could take four stretchers or eight sitting passengers. The **Vernon** of 1921 was a bomber/transport version along similar lines with a bulbous fuselage and domed nose. This was the first purpose-built troop transport aircraft and 55 were built. The RAF operated some on the Cairo–Baghdad airmail service until 1927.

The Vimy's claim to fame is its use in several long distance record-breaking flights. Using a modified Vimy IV, James Alcock and Arthur Whitten Brown flew from Newfoundland to Ireland on 14/15 June 1919 in a flight taking 16 hours 47 minutes. Brothers Ross and Keith Smith and two crew made the first England–Australia flight in October/November 1919, taking nearly a month. A Vimy also attempted the first England–South Africa flight.

The Vimy was mainly retired from front-line service in 1924–5, although one squadron in Northern Ireland retained the aircraft until 1929.

The Vimy was more famous as a pioneering long-range record setter than as a bomber. The bomber versions saw most use in the Middle East. (Philip Jarrett collection)

Specification: Vickers Vimy IV
Type: twin-engined heavy bomber
Crew: three
Powerplant: two 360-hp (269-kW) Rolls-Royce Eagle VIII V-12 pistons
Dimensions: span 67 ft 2 in (20.47 m); length 43 ft 6.5 in (13.27 m); height 15 ft 3in (4.65 m); wing area 1,330 sq ft (123.56 m²)
Weights: empty 7,104 lb (3222 kg); max. take-off 12,450 lb (5647 kg)
Performance: max. speed 103 mph (166 km/h); service ceiling 10,000 ft (3048 m); range 910 miles (1464 km)
Armament: two 0.303-in (7.7-mm) Lewis machine-guns; bomb load up to 2,476 lb (1124 kg)

Handley Page V/1500

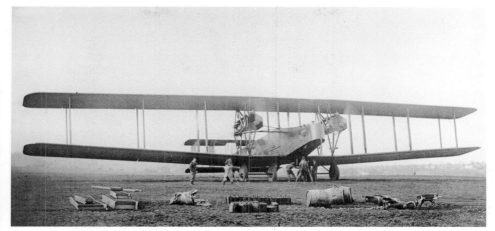

The first true strategic bomber, the Handley Page V/1500 was Britain's answer to the German 'Giants' and was built with the intention of raiding Berlin direct from English bases.

Designed by George Volkert, the V/1500 was intended to be powered by two 600-hp (448-kW) Rolls-Royce Condor engines, but delays in their development necessitated the use of four Eagle VIII V-12 engines in back-to-back layout. The engine configuration was modelled on that of the German R-planes. The tractor engines drove an enormous two-bladed propeller while the pusher engines each had a four-bladed unit. The prototype had a single radiator for all four engines, but the production aircraft had a hexagonal radiator for each pair. To handle the great weight of the V/1500 the steel tube undercarriage had independent shock absorbers on the four wheels.

Of the same general layout as the O/100 and O/400, the V/1500 was of similar length but had over a third greater span. The centre-section was perpendicular, but the long outer sections were gently swept back. Rearward-folding wings allowed the V/1500 to be stowed in the standard Bessonneau canvas hangars of the day. Defensive armament comprised single or

The V/1500 prototype shows the original tail with the top plane near the fuselage. On later aircraft this gap was increased. (Philip Jarrett collection)

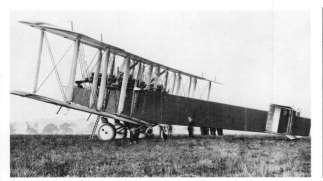

A V/1500 prepares for a flight. Note the characteristic hexagonal radiator faces and the uncowled engines. (Philip Jarrett collection)

twin 0.303-in (7.7-mm) Lewis guns in nose, dorsal, ventral and tail positions. The warload of up to 32 250-lb (113-kg) bombs was stowed internally.

The prototype flew in May 1918 but crashed the following month. Contracts were issued with Harland and Wolff of Belfast for 200 aircraft, but the majority were cancelled at the Armistice and only 20 were completed. Three V/1500s were issued to No. 166 Squadron at Bircham Newton in Norfolk and were prepared for their first raid on Berlin in November 1918. Bad weather frustrated the mission and the Armistice was called before it could be carried out.

One aircraft (named *Old Carthusian*) made the first England–India flight in December 1918 via Rome, Malta, Cairo, and Baghdad to Karachi (then in India), taking 17 days. During unrest in Afghanistan in May 1919, this aircraft was called to make a bombing attack on Kabul. The four bombs that fell on the Amir's palace caused him to sue for peace. This is the only known combat mission for the V/1500.

In 1919 one V/1500 was shipped to Newfoundland with the intention of making the first Atlantic air crossing. Before the V/1500 was ready, Alcock and Brown's Vimy achieved the crossing and the attempt was abandoned. In general the V/1500 saw little post-war service before being replaced by the Vimy.

Specification: Handley Page V/1500
Type: four-engined strategic bomber
Crew: up to seven
Powerplant: four 375-hp (280-kW) Rolls-Royce Eagle VIII V-12 pistons
Dimensions: span 126 ft 0 in (38.40 m); length 64 ft 0 in (19.51 m); height 23 ft 0 in (7.01 m); wing area 3,000 sq ft (278.70 m²)
Weights: empty 17,600 lb (7983 kg); max. take-off 30,000 lb (13608 kg)
Performance: max. speed 99 mph (159 km/h); service ceiling 11,000 ft (3355 m); range 1,300 miles (2092 km)
Armament: four to eight 0.303-in (7.7-mm) Lewis machine-guns; bomb load up to 8,000 lb (3629 kg)

Vickers Virginia

Work began in 1921 to design a replacement for the Vimy in the RAF's bomber fleet. R K Pierson of Vickers designed a large twin-engined biplane, taking account of some new advances in powerplants and structural design. In general the configuration was very similar to the Vimy, although the Virginia had a lowered front gunner's 'pulpit', giving the pilot a better field of view. The chosen 450-hp (335.7-kW) Napier Lion engines had almost twice the power of the engines on the original Vimy and the wingspan was 20 ft (6 m) greater with 9 ft (2.7 m) more fuselage length. The sole gunner had a single Lewis gun. Twin wheels were mounted under each engine nacelle.

The Virginia first flew on 24 November 1922 and began service trials in December. Accepted with minor modifications, the first **Virginia I** squadron was equipped in late 1924. Early models (the **Virginia II, III, IV, V** and **VI** had straight wings with dihedral on the lower wing only, but thereafter, beginning with the **Mk VII**, had swept outer wing panels and slight dihedral on both upper and lower wings. The rear fuselage gunner, introduced with the Mk III, was relocated to a 'dustbin' turret in the tail. Many earlier aircraft were converted to Mk VIIs. The major production model, the **Mk X** of 1924, had a composite structure of duralumin and steel, covered in fabric, aluminium and plywood in different areas as opposed to the wood and fabric construction of earlier models. Fifty of the 126 Virginias were Mk Xs and the type was the most numerous RAF bomber up to 1934. Virginias played an

Virginia Mk III J7130 is seen at an Empire Air Day with a Vernon transport in the background. (The Aviation Picture Library)

important role in early aerial refuelling trials. From 1930 various successful tests were made with a trailing hose system, the nozzle being grasped with a hooked stick by a crewman in the receiving aircraft. This was not adopted for service.

As the years wore on, the ponderous performance of the Virginia pushed it into obsolescence. Accidents took a toll of 81 of the fleet. The last few were retired from parachute training and photography in 1938.

The Vickers Victoria was a transport version along the lines of the Vimy Commercial, with a greatly enlarged fuselage with capacity for 22 troops. It could also be used as a bomber. Some of the 94 built had Pegasus radial engines, as did the refined Valentia. Valentias were converted from Victorias and 28 were built new. Some had four wheels on each undercarriage unit. In 1932 they were used to threaten Iraqi Kurdish tribesmen by loudspeaker of impending bombing attacks in the Middle East as late as 1943.

J7566 was built as a Virginia VI and like most of the type was rebuilt several times to later marks. (The Aviation Picture Library)

Specification: Vickers Virginia Mk X
Type: twin-engined heavy bomber
Crew: four
Powerplant: two 580-hp (432.7-kW) Napier Lion VB inline pistons
Dimensions: span 87 ft 8 in (26.77 m); length 52 ft 3 in (15.93 m); height 18 ft 2 in (5.54 m); wing area 663.85 sq ft (202.34 m²)
Weights: empty 9,650 lb (4377 kg); max. take-off 17,620 lb (7993 kg)
Performance: max. speed 108 mph (173 km/h); service ceiling 15,500 ft (4725 m); range 985 miles (1585 km)
Armament: three 0.303-in (7.7-mm) Vickers machine-guns; bomb load up to 3,000 lb (1360 kg)

Boulton-Paul Sidestrand & Overstrand

United Kingdom
December 1926

In response to a 1924 specification for a twin-engined medium-range day bomber, John North of the Boulton-Paul company designed a streamlined biplane with long, equal area, slightly swept wings called the **Sidestrand I** (named after a Norfolk village). The Sidestrand was the company's first significant design, although it had built many other manufacturers' designs under licence during World War I. The construction was mostly aluminium tube skinned with wood. The pilot and navigator/bomb-aimer sat in open tandem cockpits with a gunner's position in the streamlined nose. A rear gunner operated Lewis guns in both a dorsal position and a ventral gondola. An unusual feature was the rudder trim tab mounted on struts of some length behind the tail itself.

Only one squadron (No. 101) operated Sidestrands receiving them from April 1928. In fact, the aircraft was ordered especially for this unit. The production version was the **Mk II**, with 425-hp (317-kW) Bristol Jupiter VI radials. These were later updated to **Mk III** standard with 460-hp (343-kW) Jupiter VIIIs and refinements including a hinged bomb-aiming window.

The Sidestrand was extremely manoeuvrable for its size, and could be looped and rolled, helped by the Handley Page slots in the wings. The top speed of 140 mph (225 km/h) was somewhat better than the Virginia heavy bomber of the day. The bombing

The Overstrand was a developed version of the Sidestrand with a powered turret and enclosed cockpit. (Philip Jarrett collection)

Only No. 101 Squadron flew the Sidestrand. Most of the Sidestrand IIs were converted to Sidestrand IIIs with Jupiter engines. (Philip Jarrett collection)

accuracy was the best of any RAF bomber to date.

Seeing a need for frontal protection, a fully enclosed power-operated nose turret was designed for the Sidestrand. This was the first such unit to be fitted to any bomber and was powered by air from an engine-driven compressor passed through pressurised bottles. The bottles held reserves for 20 revolutions of the turret. The turreted version was ordered as the **Sidestrand V**, but delivered as the **Overstrand I**, the first of which flew in 1933. Apart from the nose turret, the main difference was the use of cowled Bristol Pegasus IIM3 motors of 580 hp (433 kW).

The Overstrand introduced a glazed cockpit enclosure and a windshield for the dorsal gunner. Despite its good qualities, more advanced metal monoplanes were in the offing and only 24 Overstrands entered service. In 1937 they were sent to gunnery schools for use as trainers. A version with a retractable undercarriage, called the Superstrand, was not built. Boulton-Paul's success with the Overstrand's turret led to the production of similar units for many other manufacturers. The only other Boulton-Paul aircraft of note was the Defiant fighter, which relied too much on its turret as its only means of attack and defence.

Specification: Overstrand I
Type: twin-engined medium bomber
Crew: five
Powerplant: two 580-hp (433-kW) Bristol Pegasus IIM3 radial pistons
Dimensions: span 72 ft (21.95 m); length 46 ft (14.02 m); height 15 ft 6 in (4.72 m); wing area 980 sq ft (91.04 m²)
Weights: empty 7,937 lb (3600 kg); max. take-off 12,000 lb (5443 kg)
Performance: max. speed 153 mph (246 km/h); service ceiling 22,572 ft (6680 m); range 544 miles (875 km)
Armament: three 0.303-in (7.7-mm) machine-guns; bomb load up to 1,600 lb (726 kg)

Keystone bombers (LB-3 to LB-14)

The Huff-Daland XLB-3 was a large double-bay equal-span biplane with a wide-track single-wheeled undercarriage built to a 1927 specification for a twin-engined bomber for the US Army Air Corps (USAAC). It was the first of what was to be known as the 'Keystone Bombers', all of which differed little other than in their powerplants. The XLB-3 itself was powered by Liberty V-1410-1 inverted V-12s. The first of many test models was the XLB-3A with Pratt & Whitney (P&W) R-1340-1 Wasp radials. No orders were forthcoming.

With two Liberty V-12 engines, the **XLB-5** demonstrated good reliability and single-engine safety and the Air Corps ordered 10 **LB-5**s (company name Pirate). A further 25 **LB-5A**s followed with twin rudders. The Huff-Daland company had changed its name to Keystone by this time. The LB-5s were armed with pairs of Lewis guns in open nose and dorsal positions, and a single gun was aimed through a lower fuselage opening.

The **XLB-6** was a converted LB-5 with new untapered wings and Cyclone radials mounted on struts between the wings. The new engines noticeably improved the climb rate and maximum speed. This prototype was followed by 17 production **LB-6** (company name Panther) bombers delivered in the autumn of 1929. Although they were issued to units in the US and Hawaii, their career was brief, with the last being scrapped by 1935.

A very similar model, the **LB-7** with P&W R-1690-3

Some 207 Keystone series bombers were built and they were the public face of the Air Corps in the Depression years. (Philip Jarrett collection)

Hornets, slightly preceded the LB-6 into service. Sixteen new-production LB-7s were delivered and six were converted from LB-6s. After being relegated to training, the last LB-7s were scrapped in 1934. One LB-7 was tested with P&W R-1860-3 radials as the **XLB-8** and another with Wright R-1750s as the **XLB-9**. Yet another became the **LB-12** with P&W R-1860s.

The **LB-10** reverted to single-rudder configuration. The production **LB-10A** was slightly smaller in wingspan and length and 63 were ordered. In 1930 the Air Corps changed its designation scheme so that the LB-10A became the **B-3A**.

Only seven **LB-13**s (later **Y1B-4** and **Y1B-6**) were ordered, although three were converted from B-3As. The final model was the **LB-14** (**Y1B-5**) with Wright R-1750s. Construction was basically the same for all models, being of fabric-covered steel tubes with plywood wing leading edges. The lumbering Keystones represented US air power for nearly a decade, although most of their actions were for show, including the destruction of an unwanted North Carolina bridge in 1937 by LB-5s.

Keystones like this LB-10 flew many demonstration flights in the 20s and 30s, and even flew airmail and in races. (Philip Jarret collection)

Specification: Keystone B-3A (LB-10)
Type: twin-engined bomber
Crew: four
Powerplant: two 525-hp (392-kW) Wright R-1750-1 Cyclone radials
Dimensions: span 75 ft (22.86 m); length 49 ft 3 in (15 m); height 15 ft 6 in (4.72 m); wing area 1,148 sq ft (107 m²)
Weights: empty 6,993 lb (3172 kg); max. take-off 13,285 lb (6026 kg)
Performance: max. speed 113 mph (182 km/h); service ceiling 13,440 ft (4097 m); range 350 miles (563 km)
Armament: five 0.30-in (7.62 mm) Lewis machine-guns; bomb load up to 2,200 lb (998 kg)

Vickers Vildebeest

K4175 seen here was ordered as a Vildebeest II, but completed as a Vincent for Far East use and was based in Singapore. (The Aviation Picture Library)

After World War I, Vickers Aviation had become known for its large aircraft – the Vimy, Virginia and Vernon for example. Its smaller aircraft were mostly unsuccessful until the Vildebeest torpedo-bomber appeared in 1928. Designed by R K Pierson and of all-metal construction, the ungainly Vildebeest was designed from the outset for torpedo-bombing, although it was to see considerable use as a general-purpose light bomber. The **Vildebeest I** was large for a single-engined biplane and had equal-span unstaggered single-bay wings. The pilot sat slightly forward of the wings, giving him excellent visibility. He had a fixed machine-gun in the cowl. The rear gunner/observer's position aft of the wing allowed him a good field of fire. The prototype that first flew in April 1928 had a 460-hp (343-kW) Jupiter, but the Mk I had a 622-hp (467-kW) Pegasus IM3. The **Vildebeest II** had a 660-hp (492-kW) Pegasus IIM3. The **Vildebeest III** had a modified aft cockpit. There were 152 Mks I to III, all with two-bladed propellers.

The **Vildebeest IV** was equipped with a Perseus sleeve-valve engine driving a three-bladed metal propeller. Offensive armament was an 18-in (45.8-cm) torpedo or 1,000 lb (454 kg) of bombs.

Of the 194 Vildebeest built 100 were still in service at the outbreak of World War II, many serving in the

This Vildebeest III of No. 36 Squadron was seen carrying a torpedo over the Singapore waterfront in 1936. (Philip Jarrett collection)

Far East. RAF Vildebeests attacked Japanese troop transport ships off Malaya and bombed enemy columns near Johore, but were soon all but wiped out on the ground or in the air by Japanese aircraft.

The Royal New Zealand Air Force (RNZAF) acquired the first of 39 Vildebeests (sometimes spelt Vilderbeeste) in mid-1935. The initial Mk Is were joined by RAF-surplus Mk IIs, IIIs and IVs in 1940–41. None were fitted with torpedo equipment. They were used for coastal patrol and for training until more modern US aircraft arrived.

CASA in Spain built 26 Vickers Type 245s, known as the **Spanish Vildebeest**. These were powered by 595-hp (444-kW) Hispano-Suiza 12Y engines and had a much cleaner appearance. With the outbreak of the Spanish Civil War, most ended up in Republican hands. Some were operated on floats, but little is known of their wartime career.

The Vildebeest served as the basis for the **Vincent**, which was designed for tropical use. A streamlined auxiliary tank between the undercarriage legs doubled the range, survival gear and a third seat was fitted, as were underwing bomb racks. Vincents were operated in Sudan, Egypt, India, and Iraq. Some of the 62 RNZAF Vincents served as late as 1944.

Specification: Vildebeest IV
Type: single-engined torpedo-bomber
Crew: two
Powerplant: one 660-hp (492-kW) Bristol Perseus radial piston
Dimensions: span 49 ft 0 in (14.94 m); length 36 ft 8 in (11.18 m); height 17 ft 9 in (5.41 m); wing area 728 sq ft (67.63 m²)
Weights: empty 4,229 lb (1918 kg); max. take-off 8,100 lb (3674 kg)
Performance: max. speed 142 mph (229 km/h); service ceiling 17,000 ft (5182 m); range 1,250 miles (2012 km)
Armament: two 0.303-in (7.7-mm) Lewis machine-guns; bomb load up to 1,000 lb (454 kg)

Hawker Biplane Bombers

Drawing inspiration from the Fairey Fox, Sydney Camm designed a sleek two-seat biplane in 1927 based around the same Rolls-Royce Kestrel V-12 powerplant. The prototype **Hawker Hart** flew in late June 1928 and had slim, staggered unequal-span wings with an elegant polished nose cowling covering the 477-hp (356-kW) Kestrel IIS motor. The RAF wrote a specification to match the Hart and began to order it in large numbers.

At the time the **Hart I** entered service in January 1940 it was 10 mph (16 km/h) faster than any serving RAF fighter. Its performance was superior to any other two-seat biplane in any air force. Harts were supplied to South Africa, Egypt, Southern Rhodesia, Estonia, Sweden and Yugoslavia. In RAF service they were widely used for policing the Empire, dropping bombs on recalcitrant tribesmen as an alternative to sending in ground troops. A total of 952 Harts were built by Hawker, Armstrong Whitworth, Gloster and Vickers, giving these firms much needed work when times were lean. Sweden built 42 under licence with Pegasus radials.

As well as 483 new unarmed dual control **Hart Trainers**, there were many conversions of other models. The **Hart India** and **Hart Special** were equipped for tropical use. The **Hart C** was a communications variant. The six **Hart Fighters** led to the **Demon**, of which 304 were made.

The **Audax** was a variant for the army co-operation role, differing little from the Hart. Over 650 were built

The Hart set the pattern for the many Hawker biplane fighters, bombers and army co-op aircraft of the 1920s and 30s. (The Aviation Picture Library)

and examples were exported to Iraq, Egypt, Persia and Canada with a variety of radial engines. The **Hardy** was basically a tropicalised Audax of which 47 were built. The **Hartbees** was built for (and in) South Africa. The last trainer models were used until 1946. The **Osprey** was a naval variant, many of which were configured as floatplanes. Some were operated by Sweden (with Mercuries) and others by the Spanish Republicans. The Napier Dagger-powered **Hector** was the last Hawker biplane to enter service, it saw some combat in France in 1940.

The **Hind** was the last major model, powered (in RAF form) by the supercharged Kestrel V engine. The bomb-aiming position and rear cockpit were revised. First flying in September 1934, the Hind entered service the following year and was exported to: Afghanistan, Iran, Kenya, Latvia, New Zealand, Portugal, South Africa and Yugoslavia. Some were powered by Bristol Mercuries. In all, 821 were built

In May 1941, the Hinds of No. 6 Flying Training School RAF fought against Iraqi insurgents backed by the Axis, helping to bring about their defeat.

With the bomb-aimer working head down in the rear cockpit, an Audax drops light bombs. (The Aviation Picture Library)

Specification: Hawker Hart I
Type: single-engined light bomber
Crew: two
Powerplant: one 525-hp (392-kW) Rolls-Royce Kestrel IB V-12 piston
Dimensions: span 37 ft 3 in (11.35 m); length 29 ft 4 in (8.94 m); height 10 ft 5 in (3.17 m); wing area 106 sq ft (32.33 m²)
Weights: empty 2,530 lb (1148 kg); max. take-off 4,555 lb (2066 kg)
Performance: max. speed 184 mph (296 km/h); service ceiling over 21,000 ft (6400 m); range 470 miles (756 km)
Armament: two 0.303-in (7.7-mm) machine-guns; bomb load up to 500 lb (227 kg)

Handley Page Heyford

United Kingdom
June 1930

A 1927 specification to replace the RAF's Virginia and Hinaidi biplane bombers led to proposals from four manufacturers. Two of these, by Hawker and Avro, were not built, but the Vickers Type 150 (later the Type 255 Vannock) and Handley Page H.P.38 reached the hardware stage.

Designed by George Volkert, the **H.P.38** prototype first flew in June 1930 with 550-hp (410-kW) Rolls-Royce Kestrel II engines and underwent successful service testing, winning the RAF order over the Vickers design. The first squadron (No. 99 at Upper Heyford, Oxfordshire) received the Kestrel III-powered **Heyford I** (company designation H.P.50) in July 1933. There were 15 of this variant, and 23 of the Heyford IA with the 575-hp (429-kW) Kestrel IIIS motor.

The Heyford was a biplane of distinctly unconventional appearance, with the fuselage and engines attached to the top wing and the undercarriage affixed to the lower wing and fuselage. The pilot and two gunners sat in open cockpits and the ventral gunner sat in a 'dustbin' turret. The lower wing was double the thickness of the upper wing, allowing for bombs to be stowed internally in the centre-section as well as on external racks. The wing structure was metal with fabric covering while the fuselage was partly fabric-covered and partly metal-

The Heyford II was aerodynamically refined but retained two-bladed propellers. Note the enclosed canopy and the wing slots (The Aviation Picture Library)

The Heyford III was the most numerous version, with Kestrel IVs and four-bladed propellers. Note the underwing bomb racks. (The Aviation Picture Library)

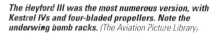

skinned. Heyfords were known as 'Express Bombers' not only for their relative speed but because they could be serviced quickly and sent back into battle. The easily accessible bomb racks in the lower wings helped the fast turnaround. Belying its looks, the Heyford was very manoeuvrable and was even said to be capable of looping. It was a favourite of the prewar Hendon air displays.

The **Heyford II** (16 built) was fitted with the 640-hp (477-kW) Kestrel VI. Reduced weight and more aerodynamic cowls improved the performance. The bomb load was increased to a maximum 3,500 lb (1588 kg), although 2,800 lb (1270 kg) was a more usual figure. The **Heyford III** also had the Kestrel VI but now driving four-bladed wooden propellers. Seventy were built up to July 1936, over half of the total production of 124 Heyfords.

Heyfords equipped 11 bomber squadrons and a number of training units. In the late 1930s, they played an important role in the development of ground-based radar by acting as targets for experimental stations. Air-to-surface vessel (ASV) radar was also tested aboard Heyfords. The last Heyfords were replaced in bombing squadrons by Wellingtons in 1939.

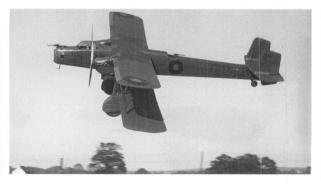

Specification: Heyford IA
Type: twin-engined heavy night bomber
Crew: four
Powerplant: two 575-hp (429-kW) Rolls-Royce Kestrel IIIS V-12 pistons
Dimensions: span 75 ft 0 in (22.86 m); length 58 ft 0 in (17.68 m); height 17 ft 6 in (5.33 m); wing area 1,470 sq ft (136.56 m²)
Weights: empty 9,200 lb (4173 kg); max. take-off 16,900 lb (7666 kg)
Performance: max. speed 142 mph (229 km/h); service ceiling 21,000 ft (6400 m); range 920 miles (1481 km)
Armament: 0.303 in (7.7 mm) Lewis machine-guns; bomb load up to 3,500 lb (1588 kg)

Amiot 140 to 143

France
April 1931

In 1928 the Armée de l'Air issued a requirement for a multi-seat combat aircraft for day and night bombing. Five manufacturers submitted designs and after an initial evaluation, the specification was widened to include reconnaissance and even escort fighter missions. In November 1933 the **Amiot 140M** was selected and 40 were ordered. The prototype of this slab-sided aircraft had flown in April 1931 powered by a pair of 650-hp (485-kW) Lorraine 12Fa radials. The extremely deep forward fuselage was joined by an equally narrow rear section with a single tail fin. The lower nose was extensively glazed, giving a grimacing appearance to the bomber's visage. The fixed undercarriage had curvaceous spats, contrasting with the angularity of the remainder of the airframe. The high-mounted wing was thick enough at the root to allow the engines to be accessed in flight.

While the 140Ms were in progress, a developed version, the **Amiot 141M** appeared. This had 700-hp (522-kW) Lorraine Orion motors and a stronger structure to carry a greater bomb load. This model also introduced gun turrets in the nose and in the middle of the rear fuselage. Neither this nor the Hispano-powered **142** entered service. The major production model was the **143M** with 138 built. This model had supercharged Gnome-Rhône 14K Mistral Major radials. From early 1934 the remaining 140M aircraft on the line were converted to 143 standard.

The first unit to be equipped with the Amiot 143M

This Amiot 143 was part of a 1936 'tour of prototypes' and is seen here alongside a Dennys 'flying flea' type. (Philip Jarrett collection)

converted in the summer of 1935 and by September 1939, five Groupes in France and one in Morocco were active with 91 aircraft. At the outbreak of the European War, Amiots were immediately engaged in leaflet raids on Germany. With the invasion of the Low Countries, they switched to night bombing missions on Germany, Belgium and France itself as the enemy advanced. In 197 sorties the 143s dropped nearly 340,000 lb (154,224 kg) of bombs for only four losses, despite their ponderous speed and complete lack of armour. On the one occasion that a daylight raid was attempted, however, against the Sedan bridges on 14 May 1940, only one of the 12 Amiots despatched returned to its base.

Two complete Groupes and a few other units continued flying 143s as bombers under the Vichy regime until May 1941, after which they were operated as transports. One of these units was sent to Tunisia where several aircraft remained in use up until the Axis defeat in North Africa. The last Amiots were grounded in early 1944.

The Amiots saw their final service as transports. This Amiot 143M was with GT III/15 of the Vichy air force in 1941/42. (Philip Jarrett collection)

Specification: Amiot 143
Type: twin-engined medium bomber
Crew: five
Powerplant: two 870-hp (649-kW) Gnome-Rhône 14K radial pistons
Dimensions: span 80 ft 6.5 in (24.5 m); length 59 ft 10.5 in (18.26 m); height 16 ft 10 in (4.85 m); wing area 1,076.4 sq ft (328 m²)
Weights: empty 13,448 lb (6100 kg); max. take-off 21,385 lb (9700 kg)
Performance: max. speed 193 mph (311 km/h); service ceiling 26,250 ft (8000 m); range 807 miles (1299 km)
Armament: four 7.5-mm (0.295-in) MAC 1934 machine-guns; bomb load up to 1,984 lb (900 kg)

Martin B-10/B-12

United States
February 1932

The egg-shaped nose turret on the B-10 was the first US aerial gun turret. Note the Wright Field marking on this early example. (Via Robert F Dorr)

The Martin **Model 123** was designed as a private venture by Martin Aircraft of Baltimore as a successor to its slow MB-2 biplane bomber. The new aircraft was as modern as the MB-2 was old-fashioned, with an all-metal structure, sleek aerodynamic form and a mid-wing monoplane layout. The Model 123 first flew on 16 February 1932 and was powered by a pair of 600-hp (448-kW) SR-1820-E Cyclone radials inside NACA-designed low-drag cowlings. The nose, cockpit and dorsal positions were all partially open to the elements and were not connected. The retractable undercarriage was manually operated. After initial US Army trials the aircraft had a hand-turned egg-shaped nose turret with a single gun fitted. This was the first turret to be fitted on an American bomber. At the same time the wingspan was increased and 675-hp (503-kW) R-1820-19 engines were installed. With these changes the Model 123 became the **XB-907A** for another round of trials. With improved performance, the USAAC purchased the XB-907A as the **XB-10** and ordered 48 more in January 1933. This was the first all-metal monoplane bomber to be accepted by the Air Corps. The first 14 built were **YB-10s**, introducing sliding transparencies over the pilot and gunner and adding a radio operator. One **YB-10A** was tested with

The B-10 was faster than US fighters of the period, the first US bomber to have that distinction. (Author's collection)

superchargers. The 34 production models from the initial contract were **B-12As** with 700-hp (521-kW) Pratt & Whitney R-1690-11 Hornet radials and an extra bomb bay fuel tank. Some of the B-12As were operated on floats for coastal patrol from 1931.

A further 103 aircraft were ordered in 1934 as the **B-10B**, mainly differing in engine intake and exhaust details. Deliveries ran from December 1935 to August 1936 and B-10Bs were issued to five Bombardment Groups, including one in the Philippines. By 1940 the B-10 and B-12 were relegated to training and support roles with the Air Corps and saw no combat with US forces. The last Philippine-based aircraft were withdrawn from service during 1941.

The B-10 had considerable export success. The Argentine Navy took 13 **Model 139Ws** and the Army 26. Six went to Siam and six **Model 139WCs** went to China. Turkey took 20, but the main customer was the Netherlands East Indies, taking 116 Model 139WHs in three subvariants, the last of which had 900-hp (671-kW) Wright R-1820Gs and a continuous 'greenhouse' canopy. The Dutch Martins fought desperate battles against the advancing Japanese in early 1942, but were all but wiped out in the air and on the ground by superior Japanese aircraft.

Specification: Martin B-10B
Type: twin-engined medium bomber
Crew: four
Powerplant: two 775-hp (578-kW) R-1820-33 Cyclone radial engines
Dimensions: span 70 ft 6 in (21.49 m); length 44 ft 9 in (13.65 m); height 15 ft 5 in (4.72 m); wing area 678 sq ft (63 m²)
Weights: empty 9,861 lb (4473 kg); max. take-off 16,400 lb (7439 kg)
Performance: max. speed 213 mph (343 km/h); service ceiling 14,200 ft (4328 m); range 1,240 miles (1996 km)
Armament: three 0.30-in (7.62-mm) Browning machine-guns; bomb load up to 2,260 lb (1025 kg)

17

Farman F 220 to F 222

The Farman **F 220** prototype flew on 26 May 1932. Like its successors it was a very large high-winged externally braced monoplane with a slab-sided fuselage and an extensively glazed nose compartment. Gunners' cockpits at the nose and dorsal positions were open, but the cockpit was fully enclosed. The engines were slung under the wings in pairs, one behind the other in tractor and pusher configuration. The undercarriage was non-retractable.

The Farman **F 221** production model had 800-hp (597-kW) Gnome-Rhône L4Kirs radials and enclosed turrets. The fixed gear contributed to the less than dramatic top speed of 185 mph (298 km/h). Twelve were built from 1933–6, equipping one squadron. They were mostly used as 20-seater transports.

The prototype Farman F 222 was created in 1935–6 by modifying the first F 221 with a retractable undercarriage. A dozen appeared as the **F 222 BN5** (for Bombardment de Nuit-Cinq-Place). While these were in production, Farman developed numerous improvements and these were incorporated in the **F 222.2 BN5**. The first batch was retrospectively designated the **F 222.1**. The **F 222.2** had a longer nose section with less glazing and sloping upper profile. The wing had considerable dihedral. A further 16 followed with Gnome-Rhône 14N engines. Production ended in May 1938, by which time Farman was reorganised as Société Nationale de Constructions Aeronautiques du Centre (SNCAC or just Centre).

Despite their ungainly appearance, the Farmans

The Farman bombers were imposing yet ungainly and angular. This is a Farman (Centre) F 222.2 night bomber.
(Philip Jarrett collection)

were of modern all-metal construction and possessed good range and lifting ability. Up to 9,240 lb (4190 kg) could be carried internally in bays in the wing, although the load was more usually 5,510 lb (2500 kg). The Farmans were briefly the only four-engined modern bombers in service outside the USSR.

Five of the F 222s were based in Senegal by September 1939. The remainder served in Metropolitan France and began night leaflet raids against Germany in December. Night bombing missions against German targets began in mid-May 1940 and nearly 300,000 lb (136,080 kg) of bombs had been dropped by the time the two operational squadrons withdrew to North Africa a month later. Only one was lost (in an accident) during this brief combat period, A single aircraft carried out the first air attack on Berlin in June. Some missions were flown against Italy by one aircraft based in southern France. After the Armistice the F 222s mainly served as transports under the Vichy flag. In 1942, some were destroyed on the ground by US Navy Wildcats.

This view of an F 221 shows its massive undercarriage and 'push-me-pull-you' engines as well as the dorsal and ventral turrets and the glazed nose. (Philip Jarrett collection)

Specification: Farman F 222.2 BN5
Type: four-engined heavy night bomber
Crew: five
Powerplant: four 970-hp (723.6-kW) Gnome-Rhône 14N 11/15 14-cylinder radials
Dimensions: span 118 ft 1 in (36 m); length 70 ft 4.5 in (21.46 m); height 17 ft (5.18 m); wing area 2,002 sq ft (185.99 m²)
Weights: empty 23,122 lb (10488 kg); max. take-off 41,226 lb (18700 kg)
Performance: max. speed 199 mph (320.3 km/h); service ceiling 26,250 ft (8000m); range 1,240 miles (1996 km)
Armament: three 7.5-mm (0.295-in) MAC 1934 machine-guns; bomb load up to 9,240 lb (4190 kg)

PZL P.23 Karas

PZL P.23B Karas light reconnaissance bomber of 41 Eskadra, Polish Air Force. (D ' Windle)

In 1931, a Panstwowe Zaklady Lotnicze (PZL) design team led by Stanislaw Prauss designed a single-engined six-seater airliner, the P.13, for the state airline LOT. The airline rejected the design but it was decided to modify it nto a three-seat army co-operation machine, using a Bristol Pegasus engine licence-built by Skoda in Poland. The Polish military showed more interest and the first prototype flew in August 1934 with the designation **P.23/I** and the name Karas (a type of carp). The P.23/I had a bomb bay but this was eliminated or the subsequent **P.23/II** and **P.23/III** prototypes, which were progressively modified to production standard. The first order, n '935, was for 40 of the P.23a, which first flew in June 1936 with a 580-hp (433-kW) PZL-built Pegasus II. This installation proved troublesome and the P.23as were issued to training units. The first operational model was the **P.23b**, which entered service in mid-1937 and eventually equipped 14 squadrons. The 210 P.23bs had 680-hp (507-kW) PZL-built Pegasus VIIIs.

The Karas was a somewhat functional-looking all-metal low-winged monoplane with fixed spatted undercarriage. The forward and centre cockpits were glazed, but the rear gunner's position was open. A ventral gondo a had a bomb-aiming window to the front and a gun position at the rear. The wings had

flaps and leading-edge slats. Production of the P.23b continued until February 1938.

One P.23b was converted to test features of the proposed P.46 dive-bomber including a twin tail unit and retractable gondola. Only a single P.46 was built, but a dozen **P.43a** Karas were built for Bulgaria in 1937. They had 930-hp (694-kW) Gnome-Rhône engines. They were followed by 42 **P.43b**s with the 980-hp (731-kW) Gnome-Rhône N.1. The last nine of these were still under construction at the outbreak of war and were taken over by the Polish Air Force.

Eleven squadrons were active at the time of the German invasion, with 114 P.23s, plus aircraft in training units. They were used to attack advancing enemy columns, but unlike the German Stukas, they were very slow and had to fly level over their targets. Without effective fighter cover they were vulnerable to Me 109s and many were shot down. Those that returned with damage could not be repaired with the time and resources available. Some 90 per cent of the P.23s in front-line units were destroyed or abandoned.

About 30 P.23s escaped to Romania and they were taken over by the Romanian Air Force, seeing action on the Eastern Front against the Russians until January 1943, being withdrawn after Stalingrad.

The Romanian P.23s saw the most action, being used on the Eastern Front until 1943. These were ex-Polish aircraft.
(Philip Jarrett collection)

Specification: PZL P.23b Karas
Type: single-engined attack bomber
Crew: three
Powerplant: one 680-hp (507-kW) Pegasus radial piston
Dimensions: span 45 ft 6 in (13.95 m); length 31 ft 9 in (9.68 m); height 10 ft 10 in (3.30 m); wing area 288.48 sq ft (26.8 m²)
Weights: empty 4,371 lb (1980 kg); max. take-off 7,771 lb (3525 kg)
Performance: max. speed 198 mph (319 km/h); service ceiling 23.950 ft (7300 m); range 782 miles (1260 km)
Armament: one 7.9-mm (0.31-in) PWU wz.33 and two 7.9-mm Vickers F machine-guns; bomb load up to 1,543 lb (700 kg)

Savoia-Marchetti S.M. 79 Sparviero

The Savoia-Marchetti S.M. 79 story began with the S.M. 79P eight-seat passenger transport of late 1934. As was fashionable with airliner designs of the 1930s (notably those of Ford and Junkers), the S.M. 79P was given three engines. These were the rather puny 610-hp (455-kW) Piaggio Stella radials. The Italian High Command was sufficiently impressed to adopt the design as the basis of a reconnaissance bomber.

The first military model was the **S.M. 79-I**, which entered service from late 1936. The cockpit was modified and the side windows deleted. A ventral gondola was added for a bomb-aimer. Engines on the initial model were 780-hp (582-kW) Alfa Romeo 126 RC.32 9-cylinder radials. The cockpit enclosure sloped upwards towards the spine. At the apex was a gun position with a single 0.50-in (12.7-mm) machine-gun. Other guns were usually fitted in the gondola and the beam window. The tail fin had a curved leading edge as did the tailplanes, which were braced by two lower struts. Officially named Sparviero (Sparrowhawk), it was also nicknamed Gobbo (hunchback) by its crews.

Tested in the Spanish Civil War, the S.M. 79-I proved itself and was ordered in large numbers. Nearly 600 S.M. 79-Is and S.M. 79-IIs were in Italian service by late 1939. An additional order for 45 S.M. 79-Is came from Yugoslavia, as the **S.M. 79K**.

The **S.M. 79B** was a twin-engined model for the export market. Three went to Brazil with Alfa 128 radials, four to Iraq with Fiat A.80s and 24 to Romania with Gnome-Rhône 14K Mistral Majors. The nose was

The S.M. 79-II was the torpedo-bomber model and had considerable success, particularly against British shipping around Malta. (TRH Pictures)

glazed for a bomb-aimer and the cockpit glazing was revised. **The S.M. 79JR** was a later Romanian version with Jumo 211Da V-12s. As well as the 24 delivered, 16 were built under licence. The Romanian S.M. 79s fought on the Eastern Front from 1941–4.

The initial models of the **S.M. 79-II** torpedo-bomber had 1,000-hp (746-kW) Piaggio P.XI RC.40 engines. Others had 1,030-hp (768-kW) Fiat A.80 RC.41s or 1,350-hp (1007-kW) Alfa Romeo 135 RC.32s. Two 18-in (450-mm) diameter torpedoes could be carried. In this role, the S.M. 79-II sank several Royal Navy destroyers and damaged a battleship and the aircraft-carriers *Indomitable*, *Victorious* and *Eagle*.

The **S.M. 79-III** had a forward-firing 20-mm cannon mounted above the cockpit and no ventral gondola. Over 1,300 Sparvieros were produced up to 1944. Some S.M. 79s fought on the Allied side with the Co-belligerent Air Force after Italy's surrender.

The **S.M. 79C** was a staff transport version that remained in Italian use until the 1950s. Three were supplied to Lebanon and saw service into the 1960s.

The final production model was the S.M. 79-III, which had a 20-mm cannon mounted above the cockpit and no ventral gondola. (TRH Pictures)

Specification: S.M. 79-I
Type: three-engined medium bomber
Powerplant: three 780-hp (582-kW) Alfa Romeo 126 RC.34 9-cylinder radial pistons
Crew: five
Dimensions: span 69 ft 6.75 in (21.2 m); length 51 ft 10 in (15.8 m); height 14 ft 1.25 in (4.31 m); wing area 664.16 sq ft (61.7 m²)
Weights: empty 14,991 lb (6800 kg); max. take-off 23,104 lb (10480 kg)
Performance: max. speed 267 mph (430 km/h); service ceiling 23,000ft (7000m); range 1,181 miles (1900 km)
Armament: three 0.50-in (12.7-mm) and one 0.303-in (7.7-mm) machine-guns; bomb load up to 2,756 lb (1250 kg)

Tupolev SB-2

When the Tupolev **SB** bomber emerged in the mid-1930s, it was superior to all others in its class and was issued in large numbers. By the time of the German invasion, however, it was obsolete and easy prey for German fighters. The first model was designed by Andrei N Tupolev during 1933 as the SB and was the first Soviet bomber with stressed-skin construction. The official requirement called for a top speed of 205 mph (330 km/h), a range of 434 miles (700 km) and a bomb load of 1,102 lb (500 kg), all good figures for the day and better than the slightly later Blenheim, for example. The SB (usually known outside Russia as the **SB-2**) first flew on 7 October 1934 and was similar in configuration to the Blenheim in that it was a twin-engined all-metal low-wing monoplane with a single fin. It differed in having only a partially retracting undercarriage, and a hemispherical glazed nose. Two 0.30-in (7.62-mm) machine-guns were aimed through vertical slits in this nose piece. The engines were Klimov VK-100 V-12s, derived from the Hispano-Suiza 12Y. The use of cylindrical cowlings and a frontal radiator gave the impression of radial engines. A glazed dorsal position mounted another machine-gun as did a ventral hatch.

The initial production **SB-2M** aircraft suffered from poor manufacturing standards and were slower than

A camouflaged SB-2M is seen undergoing field maintenance. Despite the cowling shape, this model had V-12 engines. (Philip Jarrett collection)

the prototype. Other deficiencies included a cramped cockpit and restricted fields of fire for the guns. The pilot had a poor forward and downward view.

The **SB-2bis** had an improved ventral gun mount and a mid-upper turret similar to that on the Hudson. The cowling and radiator arrangement were completely revised to give a more streamlined 'inline' look and better lateral visibility for the pilot.

The SB-2 was successful with Republican forces in the Spanish Civil War because it outpaced most Nationalist biplane fighters. Only a small number saw service in Spain because the USSR demanded full payment for them in gold. About 60 were used by Russia against the Japanese in the 1939 Nomonhan Incident in Manchuria. The Chinese Central Government was supplied with a large number in early 1938. Soviet SB-2s were effective against Finland in 1939–40. By 1941 SB-2s were obsolete and able to achieve little against the German invaders, although they stayed in front-line service until 1944.

The SB-2 was numerically the most important bomber in the world in the late 1930s. In all, 6,556 were produced. Retired bomber versions were converted to trainers and transports.

An SB-2 is loaded with bombs before a night raid on the southern front. This view shows the twin nose guns. (The Aviation Picture Library)

Specification: Tupolev SB-2M
Type: light bomber
Crew: three
Powerplant: two 860-hp (641-kW) Klimov M-100A V-12 pistons
Dimensions: span 66 ft 9 in (20.33 m); length 40 ft 3 in (12.29 m); height 10 ft 8 in (3.25 m); wing area 610 sq ft (56.67 m²)
Weights: empty 8951 lb (4060 kg); max. take-off 12 407 lb (5628 kg)
Performance: max. speed 244 mph (393 km/h); service ceiling 31400 ft (9571 m); range 777 miles (1250 km)
Armament: four 0.30-in (7.62-mm) ShKAS machine-guns; bomb load up to 1,322 lb (600 kg)

Dornier Do 17

The Dornier Do 17 was one of a small number of bombers that originated as a civil airliner. Dornier designed a sleek twin-engined, twin-tailed machine with a long circular-section rear fuselage as a fast mail carrier or six-seat passenger airliner. The prototype airliner flew on 23 November 1934. Lufthansa rejected the prototypes as being too cramped, but an Air Ministry (RLM) officer flew one and recommended more prototypes be ordered to military specification. The first production military version was the **Do 17E-1** bomber closely followed by the **Do 17F** reconnaissance aircraft. Both were combat-tested in Spain where they could easily outpace Republican fighters. The Do-17E-1 was powered by two 750-hp (559-kW) BMW VI engines. An internal bomb bay replaced the passenger cabin, but capacity was limited to 1,102 lb (500 kg). The defensive armament was light, consisting of only two 0.312-in (7.92-mm) MG 15 machine-guns, in dorsal and ventral hatches. The **Do 17F-1** reconnaissance variant was built for Yugoslavia with 980-hp (731-kW) Gnome-Rhône 14N-1/2 radials and was armed with a 20-mm cannon and three MG 15s. Some were built in Yugoslavia itself.

The **Do 17M** was a version of the Do 17E-1 with BMW-Bramo Fafnir radials of 1,000-hp (746-kW) with superchargers. The **Do 17P** designed for reconnaissance had Fafnirs and an extra MG 15.

The definitive bomber version was the four-crew **Do 17Z**, made in many subvariants, of which the **Do 17Z-2** was the most important. A new, deeper

The Do 17 was the oldest and least effective of the Luftwaffe's early war bombers, although it had been successful in Spain. (TRH Pictures)

cockpit section was topped with a large canopy (instead of a stepped windscreen), and the nose comprised multi-faceted flat panels. Six MG 15s were fitted in the cockpit and nose and in beam windows. The maximum bomb load was doubled to 2,205 lb (1000 kg). The Do 17Z was the most reliable bomber of the Blitzkrieg period, but suffered at the hands of the RAF in the Battle of Britain. The Do 17 saw action in Russia, but was withdrawn by the end of 1942.

The **Do 215B** was a Do 17Z powered by Daimler-Benz DB 601As and intended for export. Sweden ordered a batch, but all sales were embargoed on the outbreak of war. A total of 92 were built and some later transferred to Hungary. Like the **Do 17Z-10** *Kauz* (Screech owl) II, the **Do 215B-5** was converted to become a less-than-effective night-fighter with a 'solid' cannon/machine-gun nose. The **Do 215B-5** also saw action as an intruder over Britain and Sicily, and led to the similar-looking, but otherwise all-new, Do 217 night-fighter series.

The Do 215 was intended for export but evolved into a night-fighter and intruder for the Luftwaffe. (Philip Jarrett collection)

Specification: Dornier Do 17E-1
Type: twin-engined medium bomber
Crew: three
Powerplant: two 750-hp (559 kW) BMW VI V-12 pistons
Dimensions: span 59 ft 0.5 in (18.0 m); length 51 ft 9.5 in (15.79 m); height 14 ft 11.5 in (4.56 m); wing area 592.03 sq ft (55 m²)
Weights: empty 9,921 lb. (4500 kg); max. take-off 15,520 lb (7050 kg)
Performance: max. speed 220 mph (355 km/h); service ceiling 16,730 ft (5100 m); range 620 miles (1000 km)
Armament: two 0.312-in (7.92-mm) machine-guns; bomb load 1,102 lb (500 kg)

Ilyushin DB-3/II-4

USSR
1935

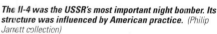

Stemming from the experimental TsKB-26 of 1935, the Ilyushin **DB-3** and its derivatives were the most important Soviet night bombers of World War II. After a long development process, the DB-3 entered service in 1937 with 765-hp (571-kW) Shvetsov M-85 engines, but they were soon supplanted by 960-hp (734-kW) M-86s. Using (then) innovative welded tube frames and L-channel construction, the DB-3 was labour-intensive and time-consuming to build. Defensive armament was light, with single machine-guns in a nose turret, ventral hatch and dorsal turret. The DB-3 was used in the Winter War with Finland in 1939–40 with heavy losses. One squadron of eight was wiped out by Fokker D.XXIs. Finland operated captured DB-3s in the Continuation War of 1943–5.

The **DB-3T** torpedo-bomber could carry a torpedo on an external mount, otherwise it was identical to the bomber version. The cold of winter often caused the torpedo gyros to fail and a version was trialled with a heated enclosed torpedo bay but not adopted. The **DB-3TM** was an unsuccessful floatplane version.

The **DB-3M** of 1938, later renamed the **DB-3F**, was a greatly refined version. Externally, only the navigator's cockpit was changed, the nose was lengthened and the manually operated nose turret removed, but the internal structure was all new with

A rare view of the original DB-3 model in flight. The DB-3 had limited nose glazing and a shorter nose than the DB-3F/II-4. (Philip Jarrett collection)

The II-4 was the USSR's most important night bomber. Its structure was influenced by American practice. (Philip Jarrett collection)

T-section components. This type of manufacture stemmed from the licence production of the DC-3 (Li-2) and greatly simplified and speeded up construction. Some batches had wooden outer wings and forward fuselages to save strategic materials, the shortage of which briefly halted production in late 1941. After March 1942, the DB-3F was renamed the **II-4** following the change in policy to designate aircraft after their designers.

The II-4 saw use as a bomber, torpedo-bomber, glider tug, transport, paratroop carrier and reconnaissance aircraft. In the bombing role it mostly operated at night and was sturdy and reliable. It could become hard to handle with a full (or overload) bomb load. An extra pair of 1,100-lb (500-kg) or one 2,205-lb (1000-kg) bomb was often carried externally. About 27 per cent of the II-4's loaded weight was fuel, a considerably higher proportion than on contemporary German medium bombers, and this gave the Ilyushin exceptional range. The II-4 is mainly remembered as the first Allied aircraft to bomb Berlin; on 8 August 1941 a force of Soviet Navy II-4s made the first of many attacks. This raid caused no great damage, but boosted Russian morale and led to Berlin being blacked out at night for the rest of the war.

Specification: Ilyushin II-4
Type: twin-engined medium bomber
Crew: four
Powerplant: two 1,100 hp (820-kW) Tumansky M-88B radial pistons
Dimensions: span 70 ft 5 in (21.45 m); length 48 ft 7 in (14.81 m); height 13 ft 6 in (4.1 m); wing area 718 sq ft (66.7 m²)
Weights: empty 12,787 lb (5800 kg); max. take-off 24,912 lb (11300 kg)
Performance: max. speed 261 mph (420 km/h); service ceiling 30,840 ft (9400 m); range 2,361 miles (3800 km)
Armament: two 0.30-in (7.62-mm) ShKAS and one 0.50-in (12.7-mm) UBT machine-guns; bomb load up to 5,952 lb (2700 kg)

Heinkel He 111

The Heinkel He 111 was a bomber developed under the guise of a civil airliner. Over a year after the **He 111a** (or **He 111 V1**) flew in secret on 24 February 1935, the Nazis revealed the third prototype, the **He 111c** (**He 111 V3**), as a high-speed mailplane/passenger transport. Designed by twins Siegfried and Walter Günter, the He 111 owed much to the single-engined He 70, with a tapering fuselage and semi-elliptical wing. The most significant early models were the **He 111B** and **He 111E** which, like the A, had a stepped cockpit and elongated nose. These models were evaluated in Spain from 1937. Power came from Daimler-Benz DB 600A engines, and a ventral 'dustbin' turret gave a measure of underside defence. Some **He 111F**s were built in Romania as the **He 111J**.

The **He 111P** with DB 601 engines introduced the characteristic glazed nose and a ventral gondola containing one or two MG 15 machine-guns. Other guns were fitted in the nose, dorsal position and in beam windows. The bombs were stowed tail-first in vertical racks, optimising space but reducing accuracy.

Developed in parallel with the P model, the main production model was the Junkers Jumo 211-powered **He 111H**, appearing in 14 new or remanufactured versions. The H-series aircraft varied mainly in having internal or external bomb loads and in specifics of defensive armament. Over 780 H and P models were in service in 1939 and they were the most important Luftwaffe bomber in the Battle of

The He 111H-23 was one of the last German models. This captured example was later displayed in the RAF Museum. (Aviation Picture Library)

Britain and the night Blitz. He 111s continued to serve as bombers, transports and n the anti-shipping role throughout World War II. Some **He 111H-11**s carried torpedoes and some **He 111H-12**s carried guided weapons such as the Henschel Hs 293 anti-shipping missile. From July 1944 a variety of He 111s were used to launch V-1 flying bombs at the UK, about 1,700 such missions being flown. In general, the He 111 was obsolete as a bomber by late 1943, although some continued to serve until the end of the war.

The final German version was the extraordinary **He 111Z** (for *Zwilling*, or twin), of which 12 were created by mating two He 111H fuselages to a new centre-section and fifth engine to produce a tug capable of towing the enormous Me 323 Gigant glider.

From 1945 to 1956, Spain built 236 **He 111H-16**s under licence as the **CASA 2.111**. Of these, 136 were **2.111A**s equipped with Jumo 211F-2 engines and 100 were built with Rolls-Royce Merlins as **2.111B**s, **2.111E** transports or **2.111D**s. Thirty-two were used in the making of the film *Battle of Britain* in 1968 and the last were retired in 1975.

An early He 111 of the Condor Legion shows the vertical bomb stowage and the 'dustbin' ventral gun position. (The Aviation Picture Library)

Specification: Heinkel He 111H-1
Type: twin-engined medium bomber
Crew: five
Powerplant: two 1,000-hp (746-kW) Junkers Jumo 211A-1 V-12 pistons
Dimensions: span 74 ft 1.75 in (22.6 m); length 54 ft 6 in (16.60 m); height 13 ft 1.25 in (4.0 m); wing area 942.9 sq ft (87.60 m²)
Weights: empty 14,859 lb (6740 kg); max. take-off 27,778 lb (12600 kg)
Performance: max. speed 270 mph (435 km/h); service ceiling 21,320 ft (6500 m); range 1,243 miles (2000 km)
Armament: five to seven 0.312-in (7.9-mm) machine-guns, later one MG 17 20-mm tail cannon; bomb load up to 4,410 lb (2000 kg)

Douglas B-18 and B-23

United States
April 1935

A B-18A of the 18th Reconnaissance Squadron shows its unusual nose contours. The Bolo saw little war service. (Philip Jarrett collection)

In May 1934 the US Army Air Corps initiated a competition for a new bomber with nearly double the load and range abilities of the Martin B-10, but a similar maximum speed. Douglas submitted the **DB-1** essentially a DC-2 wing attached to a new fuselage containing a centre-section bomb bay. The tail surfaces were similar to but larger than the DC-2 s and the wingspan was slightly less. Three gunners operated single 0.30-in (7.62-mm) machine-guns, one in the nose, one in a ventral hatch and one in a flat-topped retractable dorsal turret.

The DB-1 first flew in April 1935 powered by a pair of 850-hp (634-kW) Wright R-1820-G5 radials. In August 1935 the DB-1 was evaluated against a refined version of the Martin B-10 and the Boeing Model 299 (B-17 prototype). Although the DB-1 was inferior to the Boeing, many more could be bought with the available funds, and 82 were ordered as the **B-18** in January 1936. With R-1820-45 engines of 930 hp (694 kW) and a revised nose shape, the B-18 Bolo was delivered from November 1937.

The **B-18A** had a completely changed nose arrangement with the bomb-aimer positioned in a semi-spherical enclosure above and ahead of the gunner. This was the reverse of the contemporary practice. The first of an order of 255 B-18As flew for

The B-23 reveals its DC-2 ancestry in this May 1941 view. The fuselage and vertical fin were of new design. (Philip Jarrett collection)

the first time in April 1938. Although the RAF rejected the B-18A in 1938, 20 were ordered for Canada as the **Digby I**. These had British-calibre guns and other minor changes and were used on Canada's east coast in the anti-submarine role.

In September 1939, the Bolo was the most numerous US bomber. By December 1941, most were based outside the continental US, mainly in the Canal Zone and Caribbean. Those in Hawaii and the Philippines were almost all destroyed on the ground.

In 1942 most surviving B-18s were given nose radar and a magnetic anomaly detection (MAD) unit and assigned to anti-sub patrols as **B-18C**s. They sank two U-boats before being phased out in 1943.

The last 38 B-18As were delivered as **B-23 Dragon**s in 1938. They featured a much larger fin and rudder, a tail-gunner's position, 1,600-hp (1193-kW) Wright R-2600-3 radials and a redesigned fuselage. The armament was only four machine-guns with no turrets. The B-23 was much faster than the B-18, but by the time it entered service in 1940, new designs such as the B-25 and B-26 had appeared, offering much better performance. The B-23s were used for coastal patrol, training and test programmes. In 1942 12 were converted to **UC-67** transports.

> **Specification: Douglas B-18A**
> **Type:** twin-engined medium bomber
> **Crew:** six
> **Powerplant:** two 1,000-hp (746-kW) Wright R-1820-53 Cyclone 9-cylinder radial pistons
> **Dimensions:** span 89 ft 6 in (27.28 m); length 57 ft 10 in (17.63 m); height 15 ft 2 in (4.62 m); wing area 965 sq ft (89.65 m²)
> **Weights:** empty 16,321 lb (7403 kg); max. take-off 27,673 lb (12552 kg)
> **Performance:** max. speed 215 mph (346 km/h); service ceiling 23,900 ft (7285 m); range 1,200 miles (1931 km)
> **Armament:** three 0.30-in (7.62-mm) machine-guns; bomb load up to 6,500 lb (2948 kg)

Henschel Hs 123

Japan
May 1935

As the German Army developed its Blitzkrieg tactics in the mid-1930s they saw the usefulness of close-air support for ground troops and in particular dive-bombers. Two prototypes of new *Sturzkampfflugzeug* or dive-bombers were ordered from Fiesler and Henschel. The Fiesler Fi 98 was an old-fashioned design and was quickly rejected. The Henschel **Hs 123V1**, which was first flown on 8 May 1935 by Ernst Udet, was also a biplane, but of more modern conception. It was as streamlined as a fixed-undercarriage radial-engined biplane can be, with no bracing wires between the wings and finely shaped landing-gear 'trousers' and interplane struts. The lower wing was half the size of the top wing, making the Hs 123 a sesquiplane. The construction was all-metal except for parts of the upper wings and the control surfaces. The third prototype was equipped with armament, two 7.92-mm MG 17 machine-guns mounted above the nose and firing through the cowling. The engine was the 650-hp (485-kW) BMW 132A radial, a licence-built Pratt & Whitney Hornet.

With some strengthening of the top wing centre-section (following the loss of two prototypes for structural failure) and an engine change to the BMW 132Dc, the Hs 123 was ordered into production as the **Hs 123A-1** in late 1935 and deliveries began in mid-1936. Production aircraft could carry a 551-lb (250-kg) bomb between the undercarriage legs and two 110-lb (50-kg) bombs under each lower wing. In service the Hs 123 often had an auxiliary fuel tank instead of the

One of the early Hs 123s is seen in civil guise. The centre-section mount was often used for an auxiliary fuel tank.
(The Aviation Picture Library)

larger bomb. Anti-personnel bomblet dispensers were commonly carried on the Russian Front.

A small group of early **Hs 123A-0** aircraft was tested under combat conditions in the Spanish Civil War and given favourable reports by Legion Condor pilots. Production ended at 604 Hs 123s in October 1938. In service the Hs 123 equipped the close-support units (*Schlachtgeschwaderen*) and in the Polish campaign, the Hs 123s wreaked much havoc on the enemy's airfields and communications. Although it lacked the sirens of the Ju 87, by adjusting the propeller pitch in the dive, the Hs 123 pilot could ensure an equally terrifying noise reached the troops and civilians on the ground.

In April 1941 the one remaining *Schlacht* unit was sent to the Balkans, where it operated effectively in the rugged terrain. Thence despatched to the Soviet Union, the Hs 123 proved its ability to operate in the most austere of conditions and survive considerable battle damage. It was used for day attacks on Russian transport and night harassment raids.

Loaded with bombs, a camouflaged Hs 123 begins its attack. The 123 was one of the last biplanes to see combat.
(The Aviation Picture Library)

Specification: Hs 123A-1
Type: single-engined dive-bomber
Crew: one
Powerplant: one 880-hp (656-kW) BMW 132Dc radial
Dimensions: span 34 ft 5 in (10.5 m); length 27 ft 4 in (8.33 m); height 10 ft 6 in (3.12 m); wing area 267.5 sq ft (24.85 m²)
Weights: empty 3,316 lb (1504 kg); max. take-off 4,888 lb (2217 kg)
Performance: max. speed 212 mph (341 km/h); service ceiling 29,525 ft (8999 m); range 534 miles (859 km)
Armament: two 0.312-in (7.92-mm) machine-guns and two 20-mm Oerlikon MG FF cannon; bomb load up to 992 lb (450 kg)

Vickers Wellesley

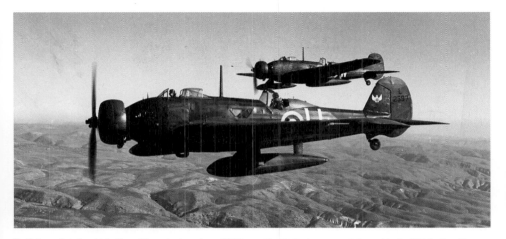

Vickers Aviation Ltd offered two designs for a 1931 Air Ministry requirement for a 'general-purpose bomber. One was the Type 253 biplane and the other the **Type 290** monoplane. The Air Ministry, ever conservative, ordered the biplane but Vickers went ahead and built the monoplane as a private venture. Designer R K Pierson employed Barnes Wallis's patented geodetic construction to create a low-wing aircraft with exceptionally long span wings with an aspect ratio of nearly 9:1. This was the first production aircraft with geodetic structure, later to be used in the Wellington. The oval-section fuselage was basically the same as the Type 253's and tapered at the nose to meet a supercharged 925-hp (690-kW) Bristol Pegasus XX radial in a Townend ring cowl driving a three-bladed propeller. The two crew sat in completely separate enclosed cockpits fore and aft of the wing. The weapons load of 2,000 lb (907 kg), usually made up of small bombs, was carried in external panniers under the wings to avoid compromising the wing structure.

The prototype Type 290 or **Wellesley** took to the air on 19 June 1935. Despite crashing in July, it was judged superior to the Type 253, which was cancelled. The Air Ministry ordered an initial 96 Wellesley Is, the first of which flew in January 1937 and entered

The Wellesley saw only limited service with Home-based bomber squadrons. These Mk Is were based at RAF Scampton. (Philip Jarrett collection)

The Wellesley was mainly used in the Middle East. Note the underwing bomb panniers on these No. 14 Squadron Mk Is. (Philip Jarrett collection)

service in April that year. Six squadrons were equipped with the type, but its front-line career with Home-based bomber squadrons was short. Lacking defensive armament and speed, the Wellesley was based exclusively in the Middle East from April 1939. Wellesleys were used by three squadrons in the East African campaign, bombing Asmara, Eritrea, in June 1940 and continuing operations until April 1941. Many were lost to Italian Fiat CR.42 biplanes, but the Wellesley's high-altitude performance often protected it from attack. Operational Wellesleys usually mounted a Vickers K gun in the rear cockpit. The pilot had a fixed gun firing through the propeller arc. The **Wellesley II** had a single canopy that covered both the pilot and observer/navigator's cockpits. Production of this version took the total to 177 Wellesleys.

In November 1938, the Wellesley achieved its greatest claim to fame when two machines (of three) of the specially created Long-range Development Flight flew 7,162 miles (11525 km) from Ismailia, Egypt to Darwin, Australia non-stop in 48 hours 5 minutes. These aircraft had a Pegasus XXII, a constant speed propeller, extra fuel tanks and a third crewman. The record stood until 1946.

Specification: Vickers Wellesley I
Type: single-engined long-range bomber
Crew: two
Powerplant: one 925-hp (690-kW) Bristol Pegasus XX radial
Dimensions: span 74 ft 7 in (22.73 m); length 39 ft 3 in (11.96 m); height 12 ft 4 in (3.76 m); wing area 630 sq ft (58.53 m²)
Weights: empty 6,370 lb (2889 kg); max. take-off 11,100 lb (5035 kg)
Performance: max. speed 228 mph (367 km/h); service ceiling 33,000 ft (10060 m); range 1,110 miles (1786 km)
Armament: two 0.303-in (7.7-mm) Vickers machine-guns; bomb load up to 2,000 lb (907 kg)

Boeing B-17 Flying Fortress

Esmerelda *was a B-17E, identifiable by its framed nose glazing. The B-17E was the first truly combat-worthy model.* (TRH Pictures)

The most famous US bomber began with a 1934 specification for a multi-engined Air Corps bomber able to attack an invading fleet. Boeing produced the four-engined **Model 299**, which was much larger than its twin-engined rivals. It flew for the first time on 28 July 1935 and was soon dubbed the 'Flying Fortress'. An order for 13 **Y1B-17** (later **B-17**) test aircraft was made in January 1936. The Fortress had a low-set wing of large area and a relatively slim fuselage tapering towards the tail. Four Wright Cyclone engines of (initially) 750-hp (560-kW) provided the power. There were gun positions in the nose, upper fuselage, waists and in a ventral gondola.

The first production aircraft were **B-17B**s (39 built) and **B-17C**s. Twenty of the 39 Cs became **Fortress I**s with the RAF, but had a short and unsuccessful career as high-altitude day bombers. Modified **B-17D**s saw combat in Hawaii and the Philippines, but the **B-17E** was the first truly combat-ready version. This had a deeper fuselage and larger fin, a tail turret and rotating top, and ball turrets instead of pivoting mounts. The RAF took 45 of the 512 built as the **Fortress IIA**, giving most to Coastal Command. Eighth Air Force B-17 s first flew combat missions from England in August 1942, but it took until May 1943 before one survived 25 missions. The **B-17F** (**Fortress II**) had a Plexiglas nose, more powerful engines and a greater bomb load.

Douglas and Lockheed-Vega built 1,105 of the

2,300 Fs under licence. Late F models had a twin-gun Bendix chin turret, incorporated on all **B-17G**s, which was the major production model with 8,680 built by three makers. Most Gs had enclosed waist positions and a new tail turret, but were otherwise similar to the F. The combat weight increased as World War II progressed until late B-17Gs were taking off at weights undreamt of by the designers. Nonetheless, the B-17's maximum bomb load of 13,600 lb (6169 kg) was restricted by bomb bay size and was much less than that of the RAF 'heavies'. A more common actual bomb load was only 4,000 lb (1814 kg).

Most subvariants were based on the B-17G. The RAF's 170 **Fortress III**s were used by Coastal Command and by Bomber Command in the Radio Counter Measures (RCM) role. Some B-17Gs were converted to **SB-17G**s (later **PB1-G**s) with large life raft containers for the Coast Guard. Brazil also flew PB1-Gs. The US Navy flew nearly 50 **PB-1W** warning aircraft into the mid-1950s. Other surplus 'Forts' became **DB-17** drone controllers and **QB-17** drones.

The RAF's experience with the Fortress I was not a happy one. AN530 of No. 90 Squadron was one of 20 used in 1941. (The Aviation Picture Library)

Specification: B-17F Flying Fortress
Type: four-engined heavy bomber
Crew: 10
Powerplant: four 1,200-hp (895-kW) Wright R-1820-97 Cyclone radial pistons
Dimensions: span 103 ft 9 in (31.6 m); length 74 ft 9 in (22.8 m); height 19 ft 2 in (5.85 m); wing area 1,420 sq ft (131.92 m²)
Weights: empty 34,000 lb (15422 kg); max. take-off 72,000 lb (32660 kg)
Performance: max. speed 295 mph (475 km/h); service ceiling 36,000 ft (10975 m); combat range 1,600 miles (2574 km)
Armament: 12 0.50-in (12.7-mm) machine-guns; bomb load 9,600 lb (4355 kg)

Junkers Ju 87 Stuka

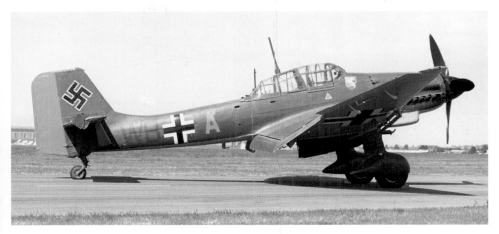

In response to an Air Ministry requirement, Herman Pohlmann designed an aircraft to replace the Henschel Hs 123 biplane. **The Ju 87 V1** flew on 17 September 1935 with a 640-hp (477.4-kW) Rolls-Royce Kestrel owing to delays with the Junkers Jumo. The Ju 87 had an angular, even brutal, appearance, with a deep chin radiator, an inverted gull-wing, square-tipped tail surfaces, a heavily framed canopy and fixed landing gear with large 'trouser' fairings. The Ju 87 was chosen as the best of four contenders, mainly because of its strength in the pull-out from a dive.

The **Ju 87A**, powered by the Junkers Jumo 210Da, entered service in the spring of 1937 and production was completed at the end of 1938 with the 262nd example. The armament was two MG 17 machine-guns in the wings and an MG 15 in the rear cockpit. A 551-lb (250-kg) bomb was carried on a cradle on the centreline that swung down to clear the propeller arc in a dive. Pairs of 110-lb (50-kg) bombs could be carried under the outer wings. Three Ju 87As were sent for evaluation in Spain. The Ju 87 acquired the nickname 'Stuka' from the German word for dive-bomber – *Sturzkampfflugzeug*. An ingenious autopilot trimmed the aircraft for its dive and pulled it out at a preset altitude. Normally the bomb was released at

This is one of the prototype Stukas with the Kestrel engine and large 'trousers' on the undercarriage legs. (The Aviation Picture Library)

This Ju 87D-3, now in the Royal Air Force Museum, shows its much refined shape compared with early models. (The Aviation Picture Library)

about 2,950 ft (900 m) and the aircraft levelled off at 1,312 ft (400 m) in a manoeuvre that could impart 6g.

The **Ju 87B** dispensed with the fairings on the undercarriage legs, fitting new spats that mounted a wind-driven 'Jericho trumpet' siren to instil fear on the ground. The Ju 87B had the Jumo 211 engine in a new cowling and a new canopy. The **Ju 87C** was intended for aircraft-carrier use and had folding wings, but the 40 built all flew from land. The **Ju 87R** was basically a B with an improved fuel system and provision for drop tanks. The B was extremely effective in the Blitzkrieg attacks of 1939–40, clearing the way for the motorised troops and tanks. In the Battle of Britain, the Stuka had initial success, particularly against radar stations but was withdrawn because of heavy losses in August 1940.

The **Ju 87D** was redesigned with a new shallow radiator and paddle-bladed propeller. The reshaped canopy had twin rear guns and from the **Ju 87D-4** had 20-mm wing cannon. The **Ju 87D-5** had longer-span wings with pointed tips, as did the **Ju 87G**, which abandoned dive attacks for low-level anti-tank work with two long-barrelled Rheinmetall-Borsig 37-mm cannon. One pilot alone, Hans Rudel, using a variety of Stuka models destroyed over 500 Soviet tanks on the Eastern Front and also sank a battleship.

Specification: Ju 87D-1
Type: single-engined dive-bomber
Crew: two
Powerplant: one 1,400-hp (1044-kW) Junkers Jumo 211J-1 inverted V-12 piston
Dimensions: span 45 ft 3.5 in (13.80 m); length 37 ft 3.75-in (11.50 m); height 12 ft 10 in (3.90 m); wing area 343.4 sq ft (31.90 m²)
Weights: empty 8,598 lb (3900 kg); max. take-off 14,550 lb (6600 kg)
Performance: max. speed 255 mph (410 km/h); service ceiling 23,915 ft (7290 m); range 954 m les (1535 km)
Armament: two 0.312-in (7.92-mm) MG 17 machine-guns, one twin MG 81Z gun unit; bomb load 3968 lb (1800 kg)

Fiat BR.20 Cicogna

N amed after its designer Celstino Rosatelli, better known for his biplane fighters, the Fiat **BR.20 Cicogna** (BR – Bombardamento Rosatelli, Cicogna – Stork) was developed very quickly and was the backbone of the Italian bomber force at the beginning of World War II. On 10 February 1936, six months after design work began, the first BR.20 flew, and service deliveries began that September. When it appeared it was the most advanced bomber of its day, despite its mix of metal and fabric skinning. The BR.20 was a low-winged bomber with widely space twin tail fins with external bracing. The engines were two 1,000-hp (746-kW) Fiat A.80 RC.41 18-cylinder radials. There were relatively large windows in the fuselage, and dorsal and ventral gun positions mounting 0.303-in (7.7-mm) Breda SAFAT machine-guns. The dorsal turret had two guns and a nose turret mounted a fifth. The wing had a straight leading edge and strongly tapered trailing edges.

Seventy-five BR.20s were sold to the Japanese Army in 1937 when deliveries of the Ki-21 were delayed. They were used in China and during World War II as the **Yi-shiki** or **Army Type 1 Heavy Bomber Model 100**. The Allies gave it the code-name 'Ruth'. A dozen BR.20s were operated by the Nationalists to good effect in the Spanish Civil War. A further 25 were supplied after the war. Venezuela also took a number of the bombers.

The **BR.20M** (M signifying Modificato or modified)

The BR.20bis was a slightly enlarged version of the BR.20M with better armour and armament. Only 10 were built.
(The Aviation Picture Library)

had crew armour, a longer nose with a revised turret (having armoured sides) and various aerodynamic refinements. These kept the performance equal to the BR.20 despite the increased weight, which rose by over 700 lb (318 kg). There were 264 BR.20Ms, the first entering service in 1939. In mid-1940, one third of the 162 BR.20s in Regia Aeronautica service were Ms.

The **BR.20bis** had even more armour but also Fiat A.82 RC.32 radials giving 1,250-hp (932-kW) power. The length and wingspan were increased and a pair of 0.50-in (12.7-mm) guns were added to side mountings. During production it was decided to concentrate on other designs and only 10 were built.

Despite its initial success in Spain, development of the BR.20 did not keep pace with Allied designs and the Cicogna suffered badly at the hands of more modern British and Soviet fighters. The BR.20Ms saw some service over Britain as a day and later night bomber in late 1940. Half the attacking force was destroyed by Hurricanes in the only major daylight raid on 11 November and the Belgian-based force returned to Italy in February 1941.

A flight of Fiat BR.20Ms. The Cicogna was the main Italian bomber at the outbreak of war, alongside the heavy trimotors. (TRH Pictures)

Specification: Fiat BR.20 Cicogna
Type: twin-engined medium bomber
Crew: five
Powerplant: two 1,000-hp (746-kW) Fiat A.80 RC.41 18-cylinder radial pistons
Dimensions: span 70 ft 9 in (21.56 m); length 52 ft 10 in (16.10 m); height 14 ft 1.25 in (4.30 m); wing area 796.5 sq ft (74 m²)
Weights: empty 14,110 lb (6400 kg); max. take-off 21,826 lb (9900 kg)
Performance: max. speed 268 mph (432 km/h); service ceiling 29,530 ft (9000 m); range 1,864 miles (3000 km)
Armament: three 050-in (12.7-mm) and two 0.303-in (7.7-mm) machine-guns; bomb load up to 3,527 lb (1600 kg)

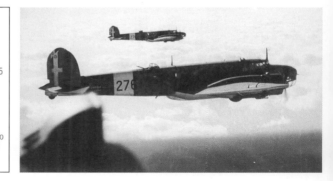

Fairey Battle

United Kingdom
March 1936

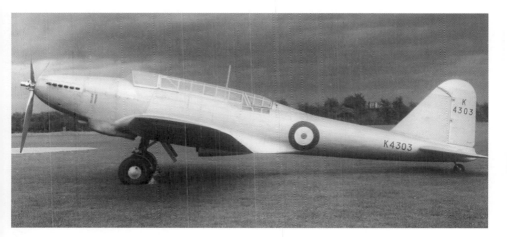

The prototype Battle looked like its successors apart from cowl and exhaust details which changed with engine mark. (The Aviation Picture Library)

Belgian designer Marcel Lobelle drew up Fairey's contender for a 1932 specification for a light day bomber able to carry a 1,000-lb (454-kg) bomb load 1,000 miles (1609 km) at 200 mph (322 km/h). A prototype was ordered, but before it flew on 10 March 1936, the RAF had already ordered 155. The competing Armstrong Whitworth A.W.29 did not progress past the prototype stage. The relative aesthetics of the Fairey **Battle** may have played a part, as it was built behind a Rolls-Royce Merlin in a close-fitting cowl and had a symmetry that the Tiger radial-powered A.W.29 singularly lacked.

The Battle was Fairey's first all-metal monoplane and the first aircraft ordered with the Merlin engine. The prototype crew consisted of a pilot and bomb-aimer/navigator, but production **Battle Is** revised this arrangement to add a wireless operator/gunner. The usual load of four 250-lb (114 kg) bombs was carried in bays inset into the wings. A single 0.303-Browning (7.7-mm) gun was fitted in the starboard wing and a Vickers 0.303-in (7.7-mm) K gun was mounted in the rear cockpit.

The main versions of Battle varied only in engine mark. The **Battle II** had the Merlin II, the **Battle III** the Merlin III, and so on to the **Battle V**. A specialised training version was the **Battle (T)**, which had a

Although relatively modern when it appeared, the Battle was underpowered and poorly armed and suffered heavy losses in 1940. (TRH Pictures)

separate dual-control rear cockpit. The **Battle TT** was a target-towing version with a prominent external winch.

By the time World War II started many of the 2,205 Battles were in service, although they were obsolescent. Despite its much greater weight and size, the Battle had the same powerplant as the Spitfire I and thus was 100 mph (160 km) slower. Belgium operated 18 locally assembled Merlin III-powered Battles. These had a revised cowling shape.

RAF Battles equipped the Advanced Air Striking Force, a component of the British Expeditionary Force (BEF) in France. In attempts to stop German forces crossing the Albert Canal in Belgium, Battles attacked the bridges. In one attack on 12 May 1940, an entire squadron (No. 12) was wiped out. Two of the three crew of one aircraft were awarded the Victoria Cross (VC) for this action. After withdrawal from France, the Battles were used for some raids on French ports and then relegated to training and other roles.

Under the Empire Air Training Scheme, 366 Battles were operated in Australian bombing and gunnery schools with RAF serial numbers. The aircraft arrived from 1941 to 1943 and the last was retired in 1949. Many more were used in Canada for Empire training. South Africa and Turkey also operated Battles.

Specification: Fairey Battle I
Type: single-engined day bomber
Crew: three
Powerplant: one 1,050-hp (783-kW) Rolls-Royce Merlin V-12 piston
Dimensions: span 54 ft 0 in (16.62 m); length 42 ft 4 in (12.90 m); height 15 ft 6 in (4.72 m); wing area 422 sq ft (39.2 m²)
Weights: empty 6 647 lb (3015 kg); max. take-off 10,792 lb (4895 kg)
Performance: max. speed 257 mph (414 km/h); service ceiling 25,000 ft (7620 m); range 1,000 miles (1609 km)
Armament: one 0.303-in (7.7-mm) Browning and one Vickers machine-gun; bomb load up to 2 000 lb (907 kg)

Armstrong Whitworth Whitley

United Kingdom
March 1936

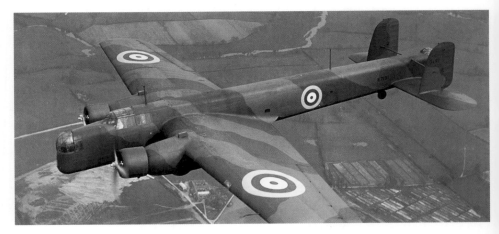

The Armstrong Whitworth A.W.38 Whitley was designed to a 1934 specification for a 'heavy' bomber (although it was only a medium bomber by later standards). Unlike previous RAF bombers, the Whitley, which first flew on 17 March 1936, had an all-metal structure and a retractable undercarriage. The Whitley did not have a bomb bay as such but carried bombs in cells in the centre fuselage and inner wings. The wing was set at a notable incidence to the fuselage, giving a distinct nose-down flying attitude. It was powered by two 795-hp (593-kW) Armstrong-Siddeley Tigers.

The initial production **Whitley I** had only two machine-guns, one in a turret at each end. After the first batch the wing was given some dihedral. The top speed was only 192 mph (309 km/h) but the Whitley had the range to reach Italian targets from the UK. The Whitley dropped the first British bombs on Germany on 19 March 1940 and was often used for both leaflet dropping and minelaying. The 46 **Whitley IIs** differed in having the Tiger VII engine of 845 hp (630 kW). Because of its slow speed, the Whitley was restricted to night missions from the beginning.

The **Whitley III** was based on the Mk II with modified weapons bays to carry larger bombs and a powered nose turret. A ventral turret mounting two 0.303-in (7.7-mm) machine-guns was added. Eighty were built.

The inadequate performance of the Tiger-engined version was addressed by installing 1,030-hp (768-kW) Merlin IVs in the **Whitley IV**. This also featured a powered four-gun rear turret and a relocated bomb-aimer's position. The speed was increased to 244 mph (393 km/h). There were 33 of this model and seven similar **Whitley IVAs**.

The **Whitley V** was the most important version with a slightly longer tail section, de-icing boots and more fuel. Fifteen of the 1,466 built were converted to freighters and agent droppers.

The **Whitley GR VII** (147 built) was a General Reconnaissance version of the Mk V for Coastal Command equipped with ASV Mk II radar and an extra crewman to operate it. A row of large aerials appeared on the rear fuselage. In the anti-submarine role from 1942, the Whitley was much more successful than it was as a bomber. With good range and a worthwhile bomb load, the Whitley destroyed many U-boats in the Bay of Biscay and elsewhere, beginning with *U-206* in November 1941. Of the 1,737 Whitleys built, 509 were lost from Bomber Command alone.

When the Whitley's operational life was over, it still gave useful service in other roles such as glider towing. (The Aviation Picture Library)

Specification: Whitley V
Type: twin-engined heavy bomber
Crew: five
Powerplant: two 1,135-hp (847-kW) Rolls-Royce Merlin X V-12 pistons
Dimensions: span 84 ft (26.5 m); length 70 ft 6 in (21.5 m); height 14 ft 0 in (4.57 m); wing area 1,137 sq ft (105.63 m²)
Weights: empty 19,330 lb (8,769 kg); max. take-off 33,500 lb (15196 kg)
Performance: max. speed 222 mph (357 km/h); service ceiling 21,000 ft (6400 m); range 1,650 miles (2650 km)
Armament: one 0.303-in (7.7-mm) Vickers and four 0.303-in Browning machine-guns; bomb load up to 7,000 lb (3175 kg)

Bristol Blenheim

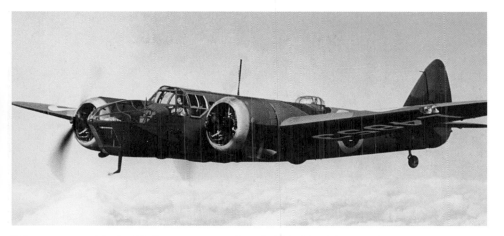

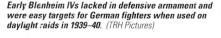

Newspaper proprietor Lord Rothermere, concerned that the RAF was lagging behind its European counterparts by persisting with biplane designs, ordered an all-metal twin-engined monoplane from Bristol Aircraft in 1935. Designed by Frank Barnwell, the **Type 142**, named *Britain First* was ostensibly a high-speed executive transport but showed obvious potential as a bomber. With its Mercury VIS engines and clean design, the Type 142, which first flew on 12 April 1935, was 50 mph (80 km/h) faster than any contemporary RAF fighter. Rothermere conated the Type 142 to the RAF for full evaluation and they ordered a very similar military version as the **Type 142M**. The wing was raised to a mid position and a bomb bay and a bomb-aimer's position were fitted as was a dorsal turret with a single 0.303-in (7.7-mm) Lewis gun. With the extra equipment and only slightly more powerful (840-hp/626.2-kW) Mercury VIII engines, performance slipped, but the Air Ministry ordered 150 as the **Blenheim I** in September 1935.

Finland, Turkey and Yugoslavia ordered Blenheims before the true prototype flew on 22 May 1936. The Yugoslavs had completed 16 licence-built aircraft by the time of the German invasion. Ski-equipped Finnish Blenheim Is saw action against the Russians in the Winter War. Fifty-two Blenheims sent to Romania also

A Blenheim IV shows its dorsal turret and rear-facing undernose guns. The extra weaponry reduced the performance. (The Aviation Picture Library)

Early Blenheim IVs lacked in defensive armament and were easy targets for German fighters when used on daylight raids in 1939–40. (TRH Pictures)

ended up fighting the Russians. The 1,330 Mk Is built by three British firms were the backbone of Bomber Command at the outbreak of war. The **Blenheim IF** (200 built) was the best night-fighter available to the RAF in 1940–41. Finland built 45 **Blenheim IIs**, basically Mk Is with some later features.

The major version was the **Blenheim IV** with a completely revised, longer nose giving the navigator/bomb-aimer better accommodation. Many had an undernose blister with a rearwards-firing 0.303-in (7.7-mm) Browning. Twin Brownings were fitted in the dorsal turret. The greater weight reduced speed to a full 40 mph (64 km/h) below that of the Type 142, although range improved. Finland built 10 unlicensed examples, but British factories produced an impressive 3,162. Large numbers were supplied to Coastal Command for anti-shipping attacks, and some as **IVF** fighters. Used initially on daylight raids, Blenheims suffered badly. Bomber Command lost 745 before they were superseded by Mosquitoes in late 1942. Mk IVs were supplied to Canada as the **Bolingbroke I** and **Bolingbroke IV** with Mercury XV engines and many equipment changes. The 942 **Blenheim Vs** or **Bisley Is** had a redesigned nose, armour and twin undernose guns.

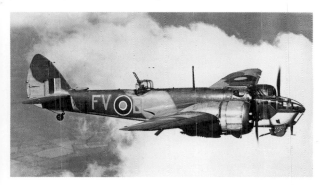

Specification: Bristol Blenheim IV-L

Type: twin-engined light bomber
Crew: three
Powerplant: two 995-hp (742-kW) Bristol Mercury XV radial pistons
Dimensions: span 56 ft 4 in (17.17 m); length 42 ft 9 in (13 m); height 12 ft 10 in (3.91 m); wing area 469 sq ft (43.57 m²)
Weights: empty 9,790 lb (4441 kg); max. take-off 14,400 (6531 kg)
Performance: max. speed 266 mph (428 km/h); service ceiling 31,500 ft (9600 m); range 1,950 miles (3138 km)
Armament: three 0.303-in (7.7-mm) Browning and three 0.303-in Vickers machine-guns; bomb load up to 2,000 lb (908 kg)

Vickers Wellington

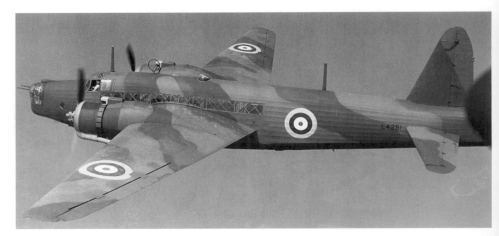

Barnes Wallis together with R K Pierson designed the Vickers 271 or **Wellington**. The Wellington was built with Wallis's patented geodetic construction method. The fuselage and wings were constructed from a grid of intersecting aluminium girders, which created a very rigid and damage-resistant structure that needed few internal bulkheads. This modern structure was fabric-covered like most earlier RAF bombers. The prototype had 915-hp (683-kW) Bristol Pegasus X radials and single 0.303-in (7.7-mm) Vickers guns in nose and tail positions and a ventral 'dustbin' turret. A feature not found on many of its contemporaries was self-sealing fuel tanks.

The prototype first flew at Brooklands on 15 June 1936. It was revised greatly before the production **Wellington I** entered service in October 1938. The Mk I had a deeper, longer fuselage, allowing for powered Vickers turrets, later replaced by Nash and Thompson units with two 0.303-in (7.7-mm) Brownings in each. The Wellington was initially used in daylight against German ports and warships, but was vulnerable to fighters owing to its slow speed, lack of armour and of beam defences. After 12 of 24 Wellingtons were lost on one raid, the RAF abandoned long-range day attacks for night raids. New Zealand Wellington pilot James Ward was awarded the VC for his actions on a July 1941 mission.

The **Wellington Ic** had beam guns, no 'dustbin' and new hydraulics and electrics. It was the most numerous model with 2,685 built. The **Mk II** was

The Wellington's geodetic structure and fabric covering are evident in this view of the first Wellington III. (The Aviation Picture Library)

powered by Rolls-Royce Merlins but lacked stability. The **Mk IV** had Twin Wasps but these proved unreliable. More success was had with the **Mk III**, and the similar **Mk X**, both equipped with Bristol Hercules motors, armour and four-gun turrets.

By October 1943, operational Wellingtons were concentrated in the Mediterranean and North Africa, with a few in the Far East. Coastal Command introduced the **Mk VIII** (based on the Ic) with ASV radar in April 1942. These could carry two torpedoes or depth charges but were soon replaced with the **Mk XI**, **XII**, **XIII** and **XIV**, all derived from the Mk X. Twenty-eight U-boats were claimed by Coastal Command Wellingtons and the torpedo-carriers had some successes against enemy shipping in the Mediterranean.

Three Vickers Armstrong plants built Wellingtons: Weybridge (2,514), Chester (5,540) and Blackpool (3,406). When retired from front-line use, many were sent to Operational Conversion Units (OCUs) to train new bomber crews.

Crews of No. 75 (NZ) Squadron pass by a Wellington. The unit operated Wellingtons from mid-1939 to late 1942. (Author's collection)

Specification: Wellington Mk Ic
Type: twin-engined medium bomber
Crew: five or six
Powerplant: two 1,050-hp (783-kW) Bristol Pegasus XVIII 9-cylinder radial pistons
Dimensions: span 86 ft 2 in (26.27 m); length 64 ft 7 in (19.68 m); height 17 ft 5 in (5.3 m); wing area 840 sq ft (78.14 m²)
Weights: empty 18,556 lb (8417 kg); max. take-off 25,800 lb (11702 kg)
Performance: max. speed 235 mph (378 km/h); service ceiling 18,000 ft (5486 m); range 1,805 miles (2905 km)
Armament: two 0.303-in (7.7-mm) Browning machine-guns in front and rear turrets; bomb load up to 4,500 lb (2041 kg)

Aichi D3A 'Val'

Japan
August 1936

The second prototype D3A seen here tested the Kinsei radial and longer wingspan used on production aircraft.
(Philip Jarrett collection)

For a few years in the late 1930s and early 1940s, no air arm was complete without a fleet of dive-bombers. Although initially very effective, the inherent vulnerability of this mode of attack saw specialist dive-bombing aircraft become obsolescent by the middle of World War II. The Aichi **D3A** was Japan's main entrant in the dive-bomber stakes, design beginning in 1936 for the Imperial Japanese Navy (IJN). By August that year a prototype was ready, powered by the same 730-hp (544-kW) Hikari 1 radial fitted to the earlier D1A2 biplane. The D3A was much heavier than the D1A2 and thus underpowered. Other unsatisfactory characteristics included ineffective dive brakes and instability in a tight turn. These deficiencies were corrected on the second prototype, with longer wings and an 840-hp (626-kW) Mitsubishi Kinsei 3 radial.

The D3A was a large single-engined monoplane with a circular-section fuselage, a long canopy covering two crew, and a large fin with a long fillet. The construction was all-metal apart from fabric-covered control surfaces. The pilot had two 0.303-in (7.7-mm) fixed forward-firing machine-guns and the gunner had a flexible mount for a 7.7-mm gun. The fixed undercarriage was covered in curvaceous spats.

In December 1939 the **D3A1** was ordered for production as the Navy Type 99 Carrier Bomber Model

This view of a D3A1 in flight shows the underwing dive brakes. This was the main version used at Pearl Harbor.
(Philip Jarrett collection)

11. The production aircraft had a slightly reduced span and the 1,000-hp (746-kW) Kinsei 43 radial. This version first saw combat in China and led the attack on Pearl Harbor on 7 December 1941. Of the 120 D3A1s that took part, 15 were lost, but they helped sink four battleships and many smaller vessels. The Allies code-named the D3A the 'Val' and it was much feared in the early months of the Pacific War, sinking the British carrier *Hermes* and two cruisers in April 1942, despite its meagre bomb load of one 551-lb (250-kg) bomb. The 'Val', like all naval dive-bombers, was most effective when saturating a ship's defences in conjunction with torpedo-bombers.

After 470 D3A1s were built, production turned to the **D3A2 Model 22** with a 1,300-hp (969-kW) Kinsei 54, more fuel capacity and fitted with a propeller spinner. Production of this model totalled 1,016, 201 of which were built by Showa.

The low speed and vulnerability of the 'Val' and destruction of Japan's carriers caused pilot experience levels to fall and bombing accuracy to drop. Although production continued until January 1944, with a total of 1,495 completed, the 'Val' was increasingly used on Kamikaze missions in the last year of World War II. The **D3A2-K** was a dual-control training variant.

Specification: Aichi D3A2 'Val'
Type: single-engined naval dive-bomber
Crew: two
Powerplant: one 1,300-hp (969-kW) Kinsei 54 14-cylinder radial piston
Dimensions: span 47 ft 8 in (14.53 m); length 33 ft 5.5 in (10.2 m); height 11 ft (3.35 m); wing area 375.67 ft (34.90 m²)
Weights: empty 5,309 lb (2408 kg); max. take-off 8,047 lb (3650 kg)
Performance: max. speed 239 mph (385 km/h); service ceiling 30,510 ft (9300 m); range 913 miles (1470 km)
Armament: two 7.7-mm (0.303-in) Type 97 machine-guns and one Type 92 gun; bomb load up to 815 lb (370 kg)

Mitsubishi Ki-21 'Sally'

In the mid-1930s, the Imperial Japanese Army Air Force (IJAAF) sought a modern heavy bomber to replace the Mitsubishi Ki-20 and Ki-1. Mitsubishi and Nakajima responded to the exacting specification of 300 mph (483 km/h) speed and five-hour endurance.

Like many Japanese aircraft projects, development was swift. The Army's specification was issued in February 1936 and the first Mitsubishi **Ha-5** prototype flew in December 1936. Testing was relatively protracted and it was not until November 1937 that production was ordered as the **Army Type 97 Heavy Bomber Model 1A**, or **Ki-21-Ia**. Apart from increased fuel capacity it was much the same as the prototypes. The Ki-21 had a circular-section fuselage and a tapered mid-set wing with plain flaps. A long dorsal 'greenhouse' ended in an open position with one 0.303-in (7.7-mm) machine-gun. Similar guns were fitted in the nose and ventral positions. Power came from two 825-hp (615-kW) Mitsubishi Ha-6 radials.

Mitsubishi built 143 Ki-21-Ias. Nakajima built 351 of this and subsequent models. In the Sino-Japanese conflict from 1938, the Ki-21 proved its worth, but demonstrated inadequacies in armament and armour when better quality fighters appeared. As a result of combat experience over China, the **Ki-21-Ib** was produced with a larger bomb bay, more armour and enlarged flaps. **The Ki-21-Ic** soon followed with an additional beam gun and a bomb bay fuel tank that displaced some of the payload to external mounts. In preparation for war against the US and Britain,

Type 97 Heavy Bombers of a training school fly above the Japanese homeland. Over 2,000 'Sallys' were produced up to 1944. (TRH Pictures)

Mitsubishi was ordered to increase the speed and ceiling, resulting in the **Ki-21-IIa** with 1,500-hp (1119-kW) Ha-101 radials and a larger tailplane. There were 590 built, followed by 668 **Ki-21-IIb**s with a 0.50-in (12.7-mm) gun in a rotating dorsal turret.

The Ki-21 was given the Allied code-name 'Sally' in December 1941, after Pearl Harbor. In the early war years it played a significant role in many actions and was popular with its aircrews due to its manoeuvrability and with groundcrews for its ease of maintenance. Despite the later addition of a tail 'stinger' gun, the 'Sally' was poorly armed with a limited bomb load. Production ended in September 1944 with 2,064 produced. By mid-1944 it was relegated to secondary roles. One of the last combat missions was in May 1945 when seven 'Sallys' carried commandos on a suicide attack on Okinawa. Soldiers on the two that got through to the island destroyed seven US aircraft.

An unarmed 11-seat transport version of the Ki-21 was built as the **Ki-57 'Topsy'**. From 1940–45, 406 were built, some serving with the Navy as the **L4M**.

A New Guinea-based 'Sally' tries to evade Allied fighters by flying low above the jungle. (The Aviation Picture Library)

Specification: Mitsubishi Ki-21-IIb
Type: twin-engined heavy bomber
Crew: five or seven
Powerplant: two 1,500-hp (1119-kW) Mitsubishi Ha-101 14-cylinder radial pistons
Dimensions: span 73 ft 9.75 in (22.50 m); length 52 ft 6 in (16.0 m); height 15 ft 11 in (4.85 m); wing area 748.19 sq ft (69.60 m²)
Weights: empty 13,382 lb (6070 kg); max. take-off 23,391 lb (10610 kg)
Performance: max. speed 301 mph (485 km/h); service ceiling 32,810 ft (10000 m); range 1,678 miles (2700 km)
Armament: five 0.303-in (7.7-mm) machine-guns and one 0 50-in (12.7-mm) machine-gun; bomb load up to 2,205 lb (1000 kg)

PZL P.37 Los

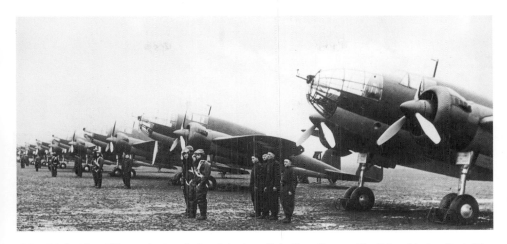

The FZL **P.37 Los** (Elk) was developed when Poland sought to replace its elderly licence-built Fokker F.VIIb-3m trimotor bombers in 1934. The new specification couldn't have called for a more different aircraft, able to carry a 4,410 lb (2000 kg) bomb load at over 217 mph (350 km/h) for 746 miles (1200 km). Jerzy Dabrowski and Piotr Kubicki of state aircraft company PZL created an aerodynamically clean mid-winged monoplane with a retractable undercarriage. The landing gear retracted into the rear of the engine nacelles and featured an unusual arrangement (for the time) of twin wheels on each leg. The nose was heavily glazed and the rear fuselage tapered gracefully to a point where it met the twin finned tailplane. Bomb bays were included in the wings and centre fuselage. The engines were Bristol Pegasus XIIB radials and the armament was three machine-guns.

Work on developing a prototype began in 1935 and on 13 December 1936 the **P.37/I** flew. The P.37/I and 10 initial production **P.37a**s had a single fin but the **P.37/II** and the **P.37a bis** and subsequent aircraft had twin tails. The **P.37/III** was the basis of the export **P.37c** with Gnome-Rhône 14Ns. There was interest from Greece, Romania, Bulgaria, Yugoslavia and Belgium, but there were no pre-war exports.

The Lotnictwo Wojskowe (Polish Air Force) ordered 124 **P.37b**s with Pegasus XX engines in 1938.

The P.37 was one of the world's most modern bombers in 1936. A relative handful were available when war broke out. (Philip Jarrett collection)

'Poland is well prepared!' said the original caption to this April 1939 photo of P.37 bombers 'of the latest type'. (Philip Jarrett collection)

Production was halted and restarted due to shifting priorities and only 104 were completed by September 1939. Only 86 front-line and reserve P.37s were available to fight the Germans. The P.37b was faster, and could carry a heavier bomb load than the Heinkel He 111, Junkers Ju 86, Dornier Do 17, Savoia-Marchetti SM.79, or the Vickers Wellington, but this was achieved by forgoing armour plate, forcing the P.37 to operate at higher altitudes where it was less accurate and more vulnerable to fighters. The P.37bs were faster than Poland's own fighters, leaving them unescorted, and attacks on German forces were made without much planning. As a result, 27 were lost in combat operations, 11 to fighters. Dispersal of the bomber force meant that spare parts were often not available to fix damaged aircraft. Forty were captured on the ground, only two in an airworthy state. Twenty-seven escaped to Romania and were impressed into local service, where they were used in the initial attack on the USSR in 1941 and thereafter as trainers. Just as Romania joined the Allies in autumn 1944, partisans blew up the survivors.

Specification: PZL P.37b Los
Type: twin-engined medium bomber
Crew: four
Powerplant: two 507-hp (680-kW) PZL Pegasus XX racials
Dimensions: span 58 ft 7 in (17.93 m); length 42 ft 3 in (12.92 m); height 13 ft 11 in (4.25 m); wing area 576 sq ft (53.50 m²)
Weights: empty 10,830 lb (4935 kg); max. take-off 19,577 lb (8880 kg)
Performance: max. speed 276 mph (445 km/h); service ceiling 19,357 ft (5900 m); range 1,616 miles (2600 km)
Armament: three 0.312-in (7.92-mm) Vickers F or PWU wz.37 machine-guns; bomb load up to 5,720 lb (2595 kg)

Junkers Ju 88

**Germany
December 1936**

The Junkers **Ju 88**, the most versatile Luftwaffe warplane of World War II, was designed by hired American engineers W H Evers and Alfred Gassner to a 1935 specification. This called for a high-speed three-seat bomber capable of over 298 mph (480 km/h). Competing designs from Messerschmitt and Henschel were not built. The **Ju 88 V1** flew on 21 December 1936 powered by two 1,000-hp (746-kW) DB 600Aa inverted V-12 engines. The **V3** prototype switched to Jumo 211A engines of the same type and output and was fitted with full military equipment. The crew was increased to four.

The 10 **Ju 88A-0** preproduction aircraft were tested operationally from March 1939 and were followed by the **Ju 88A-1**, armed with MG 15 0.312-in (7.92-mm) machine-guns in three positions. Later three more were added, all within the cockpit glazing. The Ju 88 had tapered wings, a constant-section fuselage that ended in a broad single fin, and an extensively glazed forward fuselage within which the crew were concentrated, as was German practice. The **Ju 88A-4** with Jumo 211-Js of 1,340-hp (999-kW) had a redesigned, larger wing with extra external hardpoints and more fuel. Field conversion kits allowed the A-4 to take on roles such as torpedo-bombing. The A-4 served as the basis of many further developments, and was the main version used in the Battle of Britain and in the subsequent night blitz, some fitted with large balloon cable cutters and designated **Ju 88A-6.**

The Ju 88 was the fastest and best of the German

The Ju 88 was used on all fronts and for numerous specialist roles from dive-bombing to patrol and torpedo-bombing. (Philip Jarrett collection)

medium bombers, it was adaptable to roles as diverse as maritime patrol/anti-shipping, dive-bombing ground attack and night-fighting. The **Ju 88A-7** was the dual-control trainer version. Several tropicalised versions (the **A-9**, **A-10** and **A-11**) were produced for use in North Africa. The **A-15** had a new weapons bay that could accommodate 6,614 lb (3000 kg) of bombs. Over 7,000 Ju 88As were produced from a total of 14,980 Ju 88 bombers and fighters. Ju 88As were supplied to Finland, Hungary, Italy and Romania.

After the C-series fighters came the **Ju 88D** strategic reconnaissance aircraft of which nearly 1,500 were built. The **Ju 88P** ground attacker for the Eastern Front was derived from the solid-nosed Ju 88C night-fighter. A ventral weapons tray contained a 37-mm, 50-mm or even 75-mm anti-tank gun. This high-drag tray seriously impaired performance and could be jettisoned to allow escape from Soviet fighters. Some Ju 88s were captured by the French in North Africa and some were used by Free French forces against German forces in France.

Ju 88A HM509 was captured intact when it landed by mistake at Chivenor in Devon and was evaluated by the RAF. (The Aviation Picture Library)

Specification: Junkers Ju 88A-1
Type: twin-engined medium bomber
Crew: four
Powerplant: two 1,210-hp (902-kW) Jumo 211B-1/G-1 inverted V-12 pistons
Dimensions: span 60 ft 3.25 in (18.37 m); length 47 ft 2.67 in (14.40 m); height 17 ft 5.8 in (5.33 m); wing area 565 sq ft (52.50 m²)
Weights: empty 16,975 lb (7700 kg); max. take-off 22,840 lb (10360 kg)
Performance: max. speed 280 mph (450 km/h); service ceiling 32,150 ft (9800 m); range 1,056 miles (1700 km)
Armament: three–six 0.312-in (7.92-mm) MG 15 machine-guns; bomb load up to 5,291 lb (2400 kg)

Nakajima B5N 'Kate'

Japan
January 1937

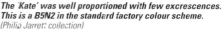

*In 1935 the Imperial Japanese Navy (IJN) issued a specification for a modern carrier-based attack bomber. Nakajima responded with a design of basically conventional appearance, but with a large wing of long span. The first Nakajima **Type K** prototype flew in January 1937 and was of modern construction, patterned after Douglas and Northrop designs of the 1930s. Power came from a 700-hp (522-kW) Nakajima Hikari 2 radial engine. Although the first prototype had Fowler-type flaps and hydraulic wing folding, these were rejected in favour of the more conservative Hikari 3-powered second prototype with non-folding wings. This was ordered into production in November 1937 as the **B5N1** or **Navy Type 97 Carrier Attack Bomber Model 1**.*

*Used as level bombers, the B5Ns first saw service over China where they were used effectively when given fighter escort. The more powerful (1,000-hp/746-kW) Nakajima Sakae 11 engine gave the **B5N2** of 1939 the ability to carry a torpedo as an alternative to bombs, of which three 550-lb (250-kg) weapons were usually carried on an external rack. Older B5N1s were converted to **B5N1-K** advanced trainers.*

A total of 143 B5N2s were involved in the Pearl Harbor attack of 7 December 1941, 40 of them armed with torpedoes and 103 acting as high-level bombers.

The Pearl Harbor attack saw the 'Kate' used as both a torpedo- and a high-level bomber, inflicting heavy damage.
(Philip Jarrett collection)

The 'Kate' was well proportioned with few excrescences. This is a B5N2 in the standard factory colour scheme.
(Philip Jarrett collection)

The torpedo-bombers scored hits on five battleships, which were also pounded by the level bombers (and D3A dive-bombers). Only five B5Ns (which the Allies soon named 'Kate') were lost.

Like the Douglas TBD Devastator, the B5N was basically obsolescent at the beginning of the Pacific War, but was the better of the two types and the best carrier-based torpedo-bomber until the arrival of the Grumman Avenger. The 'Kate' had more successes after Pearl Harbor, and was instrumental in the sinking of the US aircraft-carriers *Lexington* at Coral Sea, *Yorktown* at the Battle of Midway and *Hornet* at Santa Cruz. Better Allied fighters and anti-aircraft defences meant that the B5N's heyday was over by 1943, although it served in the front line until the Battle of the Philippine Sea in late 1944.

In secondary roles such as maritime patrol and anti-submarine warfare (ASW) 'Kates' served until the war's end. Some of the ASW B5V2s had a primitive magnetic anomaly detector (MAD) set. Many 'Kates' were expended in kamikaze attacks in the last year of the war. Production had ended in 1943 in favour of the similar-looking but completely revised B6N2 Tenzen or 'Jill'. Production of the B5N 'Kate' totalled 1,149 in three plants with the manufacturer contributing 669.

Specification: Nakajima B5N2 'Kate'
Type: single-engined naval torpedo-bomber
Crew: three
Powerplant: one 1,000-hp (746-kW) Nakajima NK1B Sakae 11 24-cylinder radial piston
Dimensions: span 50 ft 11 in (15.52 m); length 33 ft 9.5 in (10.30 m); height 12 ft 1.5 in (3.70 m); wing area 405.81 sq ft (37.70 m²)
Performance: empty 4,024 lb (2279 kg); max. take-off 9,039 lb (4100 kg)
Powerplant: max. speed 235 mph (378 km/h); service ceiling 27,100 ft (8260 m); range 1,237 miles (1990 km)
Armament: four 0.303-in (7.7-mm) machine-guns, bomb load up to 1,764 lb (800 kg)

Lioré-et-Olivier LeO 45 series

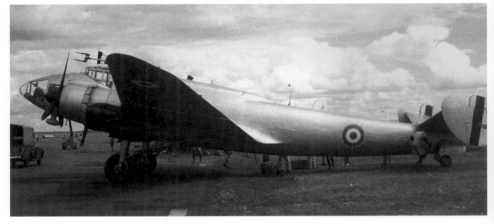

A 1934 specification was to lead to the best French bombers of World War II, but a lack of urgency was to see relatively few play a part in 1940 when they were most needed. It was not until 16 January 1937 that the first of the Lioré-et-Olivier bombers, the **LeO 45**, first took to the air. Its manufacturer was soon nationalised as SNCASE or Sud-Est. The LeO 45 could not have contrasted more with most contemporary French bombers, being curvaceous where they were angular. The LeO 45 had an extremely slender metal monocoque fuselage. Small bomb bays were fitted in the wings and fuselage. The lower surface curved up to a point at the tail. The tailplane was mounted at the top with pronounced dihedral and endplate fins and rudders. The shape of these was to change several times in the course of development of the series. The engines were 1,100 hp (820 kW) Hispano-Suiza 14AA radials, but these troublesome powerplants were replaced by Gnome-Rhône 14Ns of 1,140 hp (850 kW) during testing. This change brought about the new designation of **LeO 451** and the first of 120 flew in March 1939.

One experimental unit of 10 LeO 451s was in service in September and immediately began flying reconnaissance missions. Production was stepped up at several factories and 12 aircraft intended for Greece were reallocated to France. Orders for the type, including **LeO 451M**s for the Aéronavale and **LeO 458**s (with Wright R-2600 engines) stood at 1,267, but only about 452 were completed by May

The elegant LeO 451 was probably France's best bomber in 1939–40 but too few were combat ready to make a difference. (Philip Jarrett collection)

1940. Only 100 or so were in service and many others were destroyed by bombing while awaiting delivery. In attacks on the advancing Germans, usually without escort, losses ran to about 16 per cent. The long-barrelled 20-mm cannon in the rear turret proved to be too unwieldy for effective defence. The LeOs had more success on night raids against Italian targets from southern France.

Following the Armistice, Vichy LeO 451s fought in Lebanon, Syria and North Africa. Free French units in North Africa supported Allied forces in Tunisia until spare parts ran out. The Germans reinstated production of the type as a transport as the **LeO 451T**, using some for agent dropping. They later passed some to Italy who equipped one bomber squadron and a training school with them.

Post-war French versions included the R-1830-powered **LeO 453** refurbished from 451s and the **LeO 455**, flown before the war and produced after it for engine development and photo survey work. The last were retired as late as 1957.

The aerodynamically clean LeO bombers saw service through the war with Axis units and saw some post-war development. (TRH Pictures)

Specification: LeO 451
Type: twin-engined medium bomber
Crew: four
Powerplant: two 1,140-hp (850-kW) Gnome-Rhône 14N radial pistons
Dimensions: span 73 ft 7 in (22.5 m); length 56 ft 2 in (17.17 m); height 17 ft 2 in (5.27 m); wing area 731.95 sq ft (223 m²)
Weights: empty 17,225 lb (7813 kg); max. take-off 25,133 lb (11400 kg)
Performance: max. speed 261 mph (420 km/h); service ceiling 29,528 ft (9000 m); range 1,429 miles (2300 km)
Armament: two 7.5-mm (0.295-in) MAC 1934 machine-guns and one 20-mm Hispano cannon; bomb load up to 3,307 lb (1500 kg)

CRDA Cant Z.1007 Alcione

Italy
March 1937

Although not built in as large quantities as its contemporaries, the Cant **Z.1007 Alcione** (Kingfisher) was probably the best of Italy's trimotor medium bombers. Designer Filippo Zappata of boat builders Cantiere Navale Trestino (Cant), ater Cantieri Riuniti dell'Adriatico (CRDA), began work on a medium bomber in 1935, the design of which owed much to the Z.506 floatplane which first flew in August that year. Fittingly for a design born in a boat yard, the structure was entirely wooden. The engines were three 825-hp (615-kW) Isotta-Fraschini Asso XI radials, originally with two-bladed wooden propellers. The original Z.1007 and all later models had the same armament, although with varied locations. Two machine-guns were fitted in the belly and two in the turret. The original turret was a fixed hemispherical unit with one gun aimed forward and one aft.

The prototype was flown in March 1937, but the low power of the engines gave disappointing performance. The Italian Government had ordered a batch of 34 of this initial model for evaluation purposes. Although they equipped one unit, they did not see operational service. The first series production version was the **Z.1007bis**, which had a number of changes. The engines were changed to 1,000-hp

The Z.1007bis was lightly armed, with only four machine-guns. It was built in both single and twin tailed subvariants. (TRH Pictures)

Derived from a floatplane design, the Cant (or CRDA) Z.1007 was one of few wartime bombers built largely of wood. (TRH Pictures)

(746-kW) Piaggio P.XI RC.40 radials with three-bladed metal propellers. The fuselage was widened to permit a larger bomb load. A more efficient rotating top turret was installed on the Z.1007bis. In six out of the nine production batches the tail arrangement was changed to a twin fin layout with oval fins and a pointed rear fuselage extension. The new design gave a better field of fire for the turret.

The definitive **Z.1007ter** was an improved version of the bis with Piaggio P.XIX radials of 1,175 hp (875 kW). The speed was increased to 304 mph (489 km/h) and the ceiling to 32,890 ft (10025 m), but few ters were built of the total of 563 series production Z.1007s.

The wooden construction led to structural problems in damp conditions such as on the Channel front, so Alciones were sent to drier climates, on the Greek–Albanian front and in Africa, both as day and night bombers. They were also used in Russia, where the structure stood up surprisingly well.

A derivative, the **Z.1015**, had 1,500-hp (1140-kW) Piaggio P.XII RC.35 radials and was 40 mph (64 km/h) faster than the Z.1007ter. It was first flown as a fast mailplane design in January 1939. Plans to adapt this version for use as a bomber did not come to fruition.

Specification: Cant Z.1007bis Alcione
Type: three-engined medium bomber
Crew: five
Powerplant: three 1,000-hp (746-kW) Piaggio P.XI RC.40 14-cylinder radial pistons
Dimensions: span 81 ft 4.25 in (24.80 m); length 60 ft 2.5 in (18.35 m); height 17 ft 1.5 in (5.22 m); wing area 307.32 sq ft (75 m²)
Weights: empty 20,712 lb (9395 kg); max. take-off 30,027 lb (13620 kg)
Performance: max. speed 289 mph (465 km/h); service ceiling 26,900 ft (8200 m); range 1,087 miles (1750 km)
Armament: two 0.50-in (12.7-mm) and two 0.303-in (7.7-mm) SAFAT machine-guns; bomb load up to 2,645 lb (1200 kg)

Focke-Wulf Fw 200 Condor

Germany
July 1937

From its proposal to Lufthansa as a 26-seat airliner to its first flight, the initial development of the **Fw 200 Condor** took just over a year. Kurt Tank of Focke-Wulf promised the Lufthansa directors a four-engined aircraft capable of transatlantic range in July 1936 and the **Fw 200 V1** flew on 27 July 1937, powered by four 875-hp (652-kW) Pratt & Whitney Hornet radials. The extremely sleek design was immediately ordered by Lufthansa and two other airlines, and the second example became Hitler's personal transport. The V1 made record non-stop flights to New York and Tokyo. The Japanese ordered airliners and a maritime patrol version, and the **Fw 200 V10** was built in military configuration with more fuel, and machine-guns in a dorsal turret and ventral gondola. However, Japan never received any of its BMW-132-powered **Fw 200B**s as they, and the **Fw 200C-0**, based on the V10 with structural strengthening, were put into operation by the Luftwaffe as (initially unarmed) maritime patrol aircraft in 1940.

The production **Fw 200C-1** was armed with a cannon and four machine-guns and could carry bombs or mines in racks under the central fuselage and outer wings. This unduly stressed the airframe, and numerous Condors were wrecked on landing with rear fuselage and wing spar failures. The unarmoured underside was also vulnerable to light anti-aircraft fire. Condors based in the Bay of Biscay began patrols in mid-1940 and even made some night-bombing raids

There were many sub-types of the Condor, varying mainly in armament. A total of 262 Fw 200Cs were produced up to 1945. (TRH Pictures)

on English ports. Within three months they had sunk over 90,000 tons of Allied shipping and were almost invulnerable to fighter interception.

The **Fw 200C-3** introduced BMW-Bramo 323R-2 Fafnir engines of 1,000 hp (746 kW) and further strengthening. A turret with a 13-mm MG 15 machine-gun was installed behind the cockpit. On the **Fw 200C-3/U1** subvariant a much larger turret with a MG 151 15-mm cannon was substituted. Several different turret and gun arrangements appeared on later models. Some **Fw 200C-3/U1**s were converted to **Fw 200C-6**s to carry the Hs 293 anti-ship missile. The most numerous model was the **Fw 200C-4** with different search radar allowing blind bombing attacks.

The introduction of catapult ships, escort carriers and even heavily armed patrol aircraft like the B-24 and Sunderland reduced the effectiveness of the Condor. From early 1942, USAAF P-38s were based in Iceland and the 'Atlantic gap' was soon closed. A few transport-configured Fw 200s were used in this role and as bombers at Stalingrad in early 1943.

The Fw 200C-6 and C-8 were built to carry the Hs 293 missile. Visible here is the FuG 200 missile guidance radar. (Philip Jarrett collection)

Specification: Fw 200C-3 Condor
Type: four-engined long-range patrol bomber
Crew: six
Powerplant: four 1,000-hp (746-kW) BMW-Bramo 323R-2 Fafnir radial pistons
Dimensions: span 107 ft 8 in (32.82 m); length 76 ft 11.5 in (23.46 m); height 20 ft 8 in (6.3 m); wing area 1270 sq ft (118 m²)
Weights: empty 31,020 lb (14071 kg); max. take-off 50,045 lb (22700 kg)
Performance: max. speed 224 mph (360 km/h); service ceiling 19,685 ft (6000 m); range 2,759 miles (4440 km)
Armament: three 13-mm (0.51-in), two 7.92-mm (0.312-in) machine-guns and one 20-mm cannon; up to 4,630 lb (2100 kg) bombs

Bristol Beaufort

United Kingdom
August 1938

U rgently seeking to update Coastal Command's patrol aircraft fleet, at that time consisting mainly of Avro Ansons, the RAF ordered a Bristol (Type 156) design derived from the Blenheim directly off the drawing board There were no prototypes as such, the first aircraft flying in August 1938 as part of an initial batch for test purposes. A total of 1,014 of the initial **Beaufort I** were delivered. The aircraft was similar in configuration to the Blenheim but had a much deeper fuselage with a raised top section with a machine-gun cupola at the rear. The engines were two Bristol Mercury VIII radials of 840-hp (626.21-kW) output.

The Beaufort entered operational service in January 1940 and was capable of bombing, torpedo-dropping and minelaying. During Mk I production, many improvements were made and later incorporated in the **Beaufort II**, which also had the Pratt & Whitney Twin Wasp as fitted on DAP aircraft (see below).

Coastal Command Beauforts flew many significant missions, including bombing the cruiser *Scharnhorst* and torpedoing *Gneisnau*. Flying Officer Kenneth Campbell received the VC for the latter action in April 1941. In general, Beauforts were vulnerable to fighters and anti-aircraft fire and were replaced by Beaufighters as soon as possible.

Plans to build bombers for the RAF and Royal

This is the first of several hundred Australian-built Beauforts, used as bombers and transports throughout the Pacific theatre. (Author's collection)

Australian Air Force (RAAF) in Australia dated back to early 1939 and the Beaufort was chosen as the first suitable type. In December 1941 the Department of Aircraft Production (DAP) delivered the first of 90 **Beaufort V**s with locally built Pratt & Whitney R-1830 S3C4-G radials, which had better climb, ceiling and speed than Mercury-engined Beauforts. Another 50 **Beaufort VI**s were ordered with imported engines, but the last 10 and 60 more were built as the **Beaufort VII** with Hamilton Standard (versus Curtiss-Electric) propellers and a bigger fin. These were refitted to surviving earlier models and to 30 new **Beaufort VA**s, with locally built motors and Curtiss props. The majority of the 520 **Beaufort VIII** models built had British ASV radar and a fixed Bristol turret with twin 0.303-in (7.7-mm) Browning machine-guns. The final 140 had twin 0.50-in (12.7-mm) Brownings in an Australian-designed rotating turret.

The RAAF Beauforts destroyed many Japanese freighters and small warships around New Guinea. For many months Beauforts joined the attacks on the Japanese fortress of Rabaul, and were also used for strategic and tactical reconnaissance.

Although soon obsolescent in north-west Europe, the Beaufort was effective in the torpedo-bombing role from Malta. (TRH Pictures)

Specification: DAP Beaufort VIII
Type: twin-engined bomber/torpedo-bomber
Crew: four
Powerplant: two 1,200-hp (895.2-kW) Pratt & Whitney R-1830 S3C4-G radial pistons
Dimensions: span 57 ft 10 in (17.65 m); length 44 ft 3 in (13.47 m); height 14 ft 3 in (4.33 m); wing area 503 sq ft (46.73 m²)
Weights: empty 14,070 lb (6382 kg); max. take-off 22,500 lb (10206 kg)
Performance: max. speed 268 mph (431 km/h); service ceiling 25,000 ft (7620 m); range 1,060 miles (1706 km)
Armament: two 0.303-in (7.7-mm) and two 0.50-in (12.7-mm) Browning machine-guns; bomb load up to 2,000 lb (907 kg)

Douglas A-20 Boston/Havoc

As far back as 1936, Douglas engineers had been studying a twin-engined light bomber. The Model 7 design was dusted off and revised by Ed Heinemann to meet a 1938 US Army requirement and the **Model 7B** prototype was ready to fly by 26 October 1938. The Model 7B had a tricycle undercarriage (unusual at the time), a high-mounted wing, a single fin and a tailplane with pronounced dihedral. The nose was a glazed position for a bomb-aimer, and a radio operator/gunner was seated in the mid-fuselage. There was a single pilot and the engines were 1,000-hp (746-kW) Pratt & Whitney R-1830 Twin Wasps.

Although the US Government showed little interest, the French Purchasing Commission ordered 170 greatly revised **DB-7**s in February 1939, about half of which were delivered by the fall of France. Most of these were used against the Germans in 1940 and then by Vichy forces in North Africa. Most were destroyed by the Allies during the Operation *Torch* landings in 1942. The RAF took over the remainder of the French order as the **Boston I** and **Boston II** (the latter with 1,100-hp (821-kW) Twin Wasps). France's 200 **DB-7A**s with the 1,600-hp (1193-kW) Wright R-2600 Double Cyclone were also delivered to the UK. Many were used as **Havoc II** night-fighters, some with the unsuccessful 'Turbinlite' nose-mounted searchlight used to illuminate enemy bombers for attack by Hurricanes. The rest became **Boston III**s, some used as intruders with a 4 x 20-mm ventral gun pack.

Gun-nosed Havocs like this A-20G were used in the Pacific and by the Ninth Air Force in Europe. (Via Robert F Dorr)

The US Air Corps' equivalent of the DB-7B was the **A-20** with four forward-firing guns in fuselage blisters and twin dorsal guns. The one built was converted to the prototype **P-70** night-fighter, used in the Pacific. The **A-20A** was the low and medium altitude version.

The **A-20B** was the US equivalent of the DB-7A. Of the 999 built, 665 went to the USSR. The **A-20C** (808 built) was a standardised version for the RAF (known as the **Boston IIIA**) and the USSR. Many were used as trainers by the US Army Air Force (USAAF). In all, 3,125 A-20s were sent to the USSR.

The most important production version was the **A-20G**. This was a low-level strafer version for the Pacific with a solid nose containing four 20-mm cannon and two 0.50-in guns. Later models from a production of 2,850 had four nose guns but no cannon, and a Martin dorsal turret with two machine-guns. The **A-20J** (450 built) and the higher-powered but otherwise identical **A-20H** (412 built) were versions of the A-20G with a new, longer, glazed nose. The 413 **A-20K**s were higher-powered versions of the A-20J. A total of 7,385 A-20s were built.

RAF Bostons were used by No. 2 Group on low-level raids over Europe in 1942. These are Boston IIIs of No. 88 Squadron. (The Aviation Picture Library)

Specification: Douglas A-20G Havoc
Type: twin-engined light attack bomber
Crew: two or three
Powerplant: two 1,600-hp (1193-kW) Wright R-2600-23 Double Cyclone radial pistons
Dimensions: span 61 ft 4 in (18.69 m); length 48 ft 0 in (14.63 m); height 17 ft 7 in (5.36 m); wing area 464 sq ft (43.11 m²)
Weights: empty 15,984 lb (7265 kg); max. take-off 27,200 lb (12338 kg)
Performance: max. speed 339 mph (546 km/h); service ceiling 25,800 ft (7865 m); range 1,090 miles (1754 km)
Armament: six 0.50-in (12.7-mm) machine-guns; bomb load 3,000 lb (1364 kg)

Lockheed Hudson

United States
December 1938

The majority of Hudsons were built for the RAF and Commonwealth. Despite the US insignia, this one is probably destined for the UK. (TRH Pictures)

In the late 1930s, the RAF were desperate for a modern patrol and navigation trainer aircraft to replace the Avro Anson in Coastal and Training Commands. They turned to Lockheed, producer of a series of all-metal twin-engined airliners, and were offered a militarised version of the Model 14 Super Electra. With armament and larger engines – 1,100-hp (820-kW) Wright Cyclones – the first Model 414 **Hudson I** flew on 19 December 1938. The Hudson had mid-set wings with large Fowler-type flaps, a glazed nose for a bomb-aimer and navigator, twin fins and a large cabin with a row of small windows. At the rear of the cabin was a bulbous Boulton-Paul turret with twin 0.303-in (7.7-mm) guns. The pilot had a pair of 0.303-in guns mounted above the nose compartment. A bomb bay replaced the Lockheed 14's freight hold. Deliveries began in February 1939 and all 250 were completed by October.

There were 20 strengthened **Hudson IIs**. The **Hudson III** (428 built) had 1,200-hp (895-kW) R-1820-87s, an extra ventral gun and two beam guns. New Zealand received 54. Australia ordered 100 **Hudson IVs** with Pratt & Whitney Twin Wasps. The RAF also took most of the 409 Twin Wasp **Hudson Vs**.

About 1,500 Hudsons were purchased direct before the Lend-Lease system came into effect, after which

A Coastal Command Hudson I sets out on patrol. The type's origins as an airliner can be seen by the windows in the fuselage sides. (The Aviation Picture Library)

the US designated the Pratt & Whitney-powered aircraft the **A-28**. The RAAF took 50 as the Hudson IVA. The 410 **A-28A** (**Hudson VI**) models almost all went to the RAF and Canada. **A-29s** were **Hudson IIIAs** with Wright Cyclones. Twenty of the 394 built went to the US Navy as **PBO-1s** and 153 were impressed into the USAAF. **A-29As** went to the RAF, New Zealand and Canada. The 217 **AT-18s** and **AT-18As** were gunnery trainers with Martin turrets.

Coastal Command Hudsons were based in the UK, Iceland, the West Indies, North Africa, Palestine and even the USA for anti-submarine patrol. They also contributed to the '1,000 bomber' raids on Germany and were used as bombers in Malaya.

By May 1943 when the last of 2,941 was delivered, the Hudson was obsolescent as a patrol bomber, but became a useful life boat dropping aircraft and was used for parachuting agents over Europe. RAAF and RNZAF Hudsons were among the most modern aircraft available when the Pacific War began. They destroyed several Japanese fighters in the course of attacking Japanese shipping and shore bases up to 1944. Brazil operated 28 A-28As on Atlantic patrols, crippling a U-boat in July 1943.

Specification: Lockheed A-29 Hudson
Type: twin-engined maritime patrol bomber
Crew: four
Powerplant: two 1,200-hp (895-kW) Wright R-1820-87 Cyclone 9-cylinder radial pistons
Dimensions: span 65 ft 6 in (10.96 m); length 44 ft 4 in (13.51 m); height 11 ft 11 in (3.63 m); wing area 551 sq ft (51.19 m²)
Weights: empty 12,825 lb (5817 kg); max. take-off 20,500 lb (9299 kg)
Performance: max speed 253 mph (407 km/h); service ceiling 26,500 ft (8075 m); range 1,550 miles (2494 km)
Armament: four 0.30-in (7.62-mm) machine-guns; bomb load up to 1,600 lb (726 kg)

Douglas SBD Dauntless

United States
Early 1939

In 1935 the Northrop Corporation was part of Douglas. Jack Northrop designed the BT-1 light bomber, 54 of which were sold to the US Navy. Northrop left to start his own company before a production BT-1 was redesigned by Ed Heinemann and rebuilt as the XBT-2 with a larger Wright R-1820 Cyclone engine and a different undercarriage. This became the **XSBD-1 Dauntless** scout bomber, ordered as the **SBD-1** for the USMC and the **SBD-2** for the US Navy in April 1939. The 87 SBD-2s had more fuel and armour and twin guns, rather than the single rear guns on the 57 SBD-1s.

The SBD had a wing of Northrop multi-cellular construction without wing folding. The trailing edge had large perforated split wing flaps. The lower part dropped for use as landing flaps and the upper part also raised when needed to act as dive brakes. The main weapon was a bomb of up to 1,600 lb (726 kg) mounted on the centreline. When released in a dive attack, the bomb swung down on a cradle to keep it clear of the propeller arc, otherwise it just fell free. Two 250-lb (114-kg) bombs could be carried on pylons under the outer wing sections. The pilot had a pair of 0.30-in (7.62-mm) machine-guns mounted along the top of the cowl. The gunner sat within a rotating mount for one (later two) 0.30-in (7.62-mm) machine-guns. The Dauntless was underpowered and slow with limited combat range, gaining the nickname 'Slow But Deadly' from the initials SBD.

At the battles of Coral Sea and Midway, the **SBD-3**

This was one of the first SBD-1s for the USMC. It was destroyed on the ground during the Pearl Harbor attack in December 1941. (The Aviation Picture Library)

Dauntless with 0.50-in (12.7-mm) nose guns was the most effective strike aircraft, instrumental in the sinking of the carriers *Shoho*, *Kaga*, *Hiryu*, and *Akagi*.

There were 584 SBD-3s, plus 124 equivalent **A-24s** for the US Air Corps, followed by 780 **SBD-4s** (and 170 Army **A-24A**s) with improved electrics and propeller. Then came 2,965 of the definitive **SBD-5** and 615 **A-24B**s with the R-1820-60 engine. The final model was the **SBD-6** (450 made).

USN Dauntlesses were briefly used in European waters and in the North African *Torch* landings of October 1942. By 1943 the SBD was regarded as obsolete, but a number of SBD-3s, -4s and -5s were given to the RNZAF who used the latter in combat from Bougainville in early 1944.

Some A-24Bs were given to Free French forces in 1943 who used them in North Africa, Syria and (after D-Day) against German forces in southern France. Carrier-based French SBDs saw action over Indochina in the early 1950s. Mexico used a few A-24Bs for anti-submarine patrol and as trainers from 1944–59.

Carrier-based Dauntlesses hit the Japanese hard. The SBD's performance led to the nickname 'Slow But Deadly'. (Via Robert F Dorr)

Specification: SBD-5 Dauntless
Type: single-engined naval dive-bomber
Crew: two
Powerplant: one 1,200-hp (895-kW) R-1820-60 Wright Cyclone radial piston
Dimensions: span 41 ft 6.5 in (12.66 m); length 33 ft 1.5 in (10.09 m); height 13 ft 7 in (4.14 m); wing area 325.0 sq ft (30.19 m²)
Weights: empty 6,533 lb (2963 kg); max. take-off 10,700-lb (4854 kg)
Performance: max. speed 252 mph (406 km/h); service ceiling 26,100 ft (7955 m); range 1,115 miles (1794 km)
Armament: two 0.50-in (12.7-mm) and two 0.30-in (7.62-mm) machine-guns; bomb load up to 2,250 lb (1021 kg)

Consolidated B-24 Liberator

United States
March 1939

With 18,188 built, the Liberator was the most numerous American warplane ever. This B-24D served with the 8th Air Force. (TRH Pictures)

Asked in 1938 to set up a secondary production line for the B-17 at San Diego, 'Mac' Laddon, chief engineer of Consolidated, instead proposed a new bomber based around the high-speed wing originally designed for a flying boat by David R Davis. A prototype contract was awarded and Laddon's team created an aircraft with a deep fuselage with a glazed nose and a high-mounted slender wing, ova-section tail fins and a two-part bomb bay with 'roller' doors.

The **XB-24 Liberator** flew on 30 March 1939, followed by seven **YB-24s**. The first deliveries went to the RAF, who took 139 **LB-30 Liberator IIs** and (later) 175 **LB-30MF Liberator Is**, which were used as bombers, transports, trainers and for anti-submarine patrol. The first US Liberator combat missions were also flown by LB-30s, over Java in February 1942. The **B-24A** and **B-24C** were minor USAAF variants, followed by the much-improved mass-produced **B-24D** with powered dorsal and tail turrets. This model saw service in all theatres, some as **PB4Y-1s** with the US Navy. A freighter version appeared as the **C-87 (Liberator C VII)**, the **C-87C** version having a single tail fin. There were 2,738 B-24Ds and variants. The **B-24G** was the first to have a powered nose turret and more armour, and was followed by 2,500 similar **B-24Hs (Liberator VIs)**. The

The PB4Y-2 Privateer was the last of the Liberator family, and was flown by the US Navy, Taiwan and France, as seen here. (Author's collection)

major variant was **the B-24J** (Navy **PB4Y-1** and RAF **Liberator VI**), followed by the **B-24L** and **B-24M**, all varying in detail and turret model. The **B-24N** had ball-type nose and tail turrets.

Among many hundreds of missions in Europe and the Pacific, the low-level raids against the Romanian oil fields around Ploesti in 1944 stand out as among the most spectacular flown by B-24s. Six of the nine Medals of Honor awarded to B-24 crewmen were won over Ploesti. Generally speaking, the B-24 had greater range, and could carry more bombs for a given distance than the B-17, but was more vulnerable to battle damage and harder to fly. RAF Coastal Command's use of the **B-24L (Liberator GR VI)** was instrumental in the defeat of the U-boats, by closing the 'mid-Atlantic gap' in patrol coverage.

The US Navy developed the **PB4Y-2 Privateer** with a large single fin, longer fuselage and waist blisters. They were used for long-range patrol in the Pacific in World War II and as electronic 'ferrets' in the Korean War and the Cold War. The Coast Guard, France, Nationalist China and Honduras also operated some of the 736 PB4Y-2s. A few Privateers still serve as fire bombers. The RAF supplied B-24Js to India and a few remained in service until about 1968.

Martin Maryland and Baltimore

The USAAC's 1937 requirement for a three-seat attack bomber called for an aircraft armed with a fixed battery of machine-guns, a maximum speed of over 200 mph (322 km/h) and a range of over 1,200 miles (1931 km). Unknown to the US, Japanese bombers were already in production with higher performance, but at the time these figures seemed impressive. The construction of prototypes for the competition led to two classic aircraft, the Douglas A-20 and the North American B-25, but also to the Martin **Model 167**, tested as the **XA-22**. Martin's design was rejected by the USAAC, but 115 had already been ordered by France as the **Model 167W** in January 1939. This became the **Model 167F** or the **167A-3** in French service with local equipment including six 0.295-in (7.5-mm) machine-guns. The 167 was a slender aircraft powered by two Pratt & Whitney Twin Wasps rated at 1,050 hp (783 kW). The crew were concentrated in the forward fuselage. A long nose-section protruded ahead of the cockpit. The bomb load was 1,874 lb (850 kg).

In September 1939 the French order was increased to 215. Most French Martins were delivered to North Africa, but others in Metropolitan France flew over 400 sorties before the French capitulation. Surviving aircraft mostly joined the Vichy French air force. Some saw action against the Allies in Syria and Morocco in 1941 and 1942. The RAF took 50 undelivered aircraft plus 75 of their own order as the **Maryland I**. A

The RAF acquired Marylands from French orders as well as purchasing their own. This Maryland I is one of the latter. (The Aviation Picture Library)

further 150 **Maryland II**s were built with a different subvariant of the Wasp engine. RAF Marylands were used by Coastal Command in Malta and issued to South African squadrons in North Africa.

The French had ordered an improved version as the **Model 187B** (US designation **A-30**) in 1940 but all were delivered to Britain, initially as the **Baltimore I** and similar **Baltimore II**. These had a deeper fuselage, more armour, a four-man crew and a larger bomb load. The engines were Wright R-2600-A5Bs of 1,600 hp (1193 kW). Twelve 0.303-in (7.7-mm) machine-guns were fitted, four in an aft-facing fixed mount angled downwards. The **Baltimore III** and **IIIA** had a Boulton-Paul four-gun upper turret and the **Baltimore IV** had a Martin turret with twin 0.50-in (12.7-mm) guns. The **Baltimore V** (**A-30A**) had fewer guns but a larger bomb load. The **GR VI** was a Coastal Command version. Baltimore production totalled 1,575. All went the RAF for use mainly in the Mediterranean by South African, Greek and Free French units. Some also went to the Italian Co-Belligerent Air Force in late 1944.

The Baltimore was derived from the Maryland but with a deeper fuselage and more powerful engines. (The Aviation Picture Library)

Specification: Martin Baltimore IV
Type: twin-engined light bomber
Crew: four
Powerplant: two 1,660-hp (1238-kW) Wright R-2600-19 Cyclone radial pistons
Dimensions: span 61 ft 4 in (18.69 m); length 48 ft 5.5 in (14.77 m); height 17 ft 9 in (5.41 m); wing area 538.5 sq ft (50 m²)
Weights: empty 15,875 lb (7201 kg); max. take-off 27,850 lb (12633 kg)
Performance: max. speed 305 mph (490 km/h); service ceiling 23,300 ft (7100 m); range 1,082 miles (1741 km)
Armament: six 0.303-in (7.7-mm) and two 0.50-in (12.7-mm) machine-guns in turret; bomb load up to 4,000 lb (1814 kg)

Short Stirling

United Kingdom
May 1939

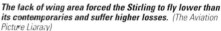

Of the RAF's four-engined 'heavies', the Short Stirling was the only one designed from the outset to take a quartet of powerplants, the Lancaster and Halifax starting off as twins. The 1936 specification called for long range, a large bomb load and multi-gun turrets. Prototypes were ordered from Short Brothers and Supermarine, but the latter company's prototype was destroyed in an air raid before completion. Although Short wanted a 112 ft (34.1 m) wing based on that of the Sunderland flying boat, the Air Ministry insisted on a 99 ft (30.2 m) wing to fit inside standard hangars. To test the new design, Short flew the half-scale S.31, powered by four 90-hp (67.1-kW) Pobjoy Niagara radials in September 1938.

The Stirling's tall undercarriage gave a high wing incidence for a short take-off run. The Air Ministry demanded a shallow incidence for the best cruise performance. A tall single fin was fitted at the end of a long slab-sided fuselage and there were twin tailwheels. Powered turrets were fitted in the nose (two 0.303-in/7.7-mm Browning machine-guns), tail (four 0.303s) and in the upper fuselage (two 0.303s). The first Short **S.29** prototype was wrecked on landing after its first flight on 14 May 1939, but the second flew in December and the first production **Stirling B I** in May 1940. Early aircraft had a power-operated retractable

The first Stirling looked much like those that followed. The tall undercarriage gave the best wing incidence for take-off. (The Aviation Picture Library)

The lack of wing area forced the Stirling to fly lower than its contemporaries and suffer higher losses. (The Aviation Picture Library)

ventral turret, but this was often removed, and pairs of Brownings fitted in beam windows.

The **Stirling B I Series 1** with 1,375-hp (1,025-kW) Hercules IIs was followed by the **Stirling B I Series 2** with 1,590-hp (1,185-kW) Hercules XIs driving constant-speed propellers. The **Stirling B I Series 3** had Bristol-designed nacelles and some had a new low-drag Boulton-Paul dorsal turret. The **Stirling B II** was intended for production in Canada with Wright R-2600 Cyclones, but only two prototypes were produced. The **Stirling B III** had the new dorsal turret, more fuel and 1,650-hp (1230-kW) Hercules XVIs.

Owing in part to its short wings, the Stirling flew lower than its contemporaries and was more vulnerable to flak and fighters. Loaded Stirlings sometimes found it hard to climb above 13,000 ft (3962 m). Despite this, it was manoeuvrable and well armed. Of the 2,370 Stirlings, 891 were lost in Bomber Command service. Australian Rawdon Middleton was posthumously awarded the VC for a raid on 29 November 1942. During 1943 the Stirling was retired from front-line bombing, but new versions were developed for the airborne forces role, including the **Stirling A Mk IV**, which could tow the heaviest gliders. Based on the Mk I, 579 were built.

Specification: Stirling B I Series 3
Type: four-engined heavy bomber
Crew: seven
Powerplant: four 1,595-hp (1190-kW) Bristol Hercules XI 14-cylinder radials
Dimensions: span 99 ft 1 in (30.2 m); length 87 ft 3 in (26.6 m); height 22 ft 9 in (6.94 m); wing area 1,460 sq ft (135.63 m²)
Weights: empty 44,000 lb (19600 kg); max. take-off 59,400 lb (26943 kg)
Performance: max. speed 270 mph (435 km/h); service ceiling 17,000 ft (5182 m); range 590 miles (949 km) fully loaded
Armament: eight 0.303-in (7.7-mm) Browning machine-guns; bomb load up to 18,000 lb (8165 kg)

Mitsubishi G4M 'Betty'

In September 1937 the Imperial Japanese Navy issued a specification to replace the Mitsubishi G3M 'Nell' in naval service. The 'Nell' had only been in service for a year, but the Navy called for a higher-performance aircraft powered by two 1,000-hp (746-kW) engines. Mitsubishi designers led by Kiro Honjo found this an impossible requirement and offered a design with two 1,500-hp (1118-kW) Mitsubishi Kasei radials. Even then, to meet the specifications a clean airframe without superfluous equipment such as armour or self-sealing fuel tanks was needed. The circular-section fuselage allowed the free movement of crew around the aircraft and permitted a large bomb bay. The defensive armament was limited initially to four 0.303-in (7.7-mm) Type 92 machine-guns, in nose, dorsal and beam positions. A low-set tapered wing mounted the large engine nacelles, into which the main undercarriage retracted. The first prototype Mitsubishi **G4M** flew on 23 October 1939. After completion of trials, the type was ordered as the **G4M1** or **Navy Type 1 Attack Bomber Model 11**, the first of which entered service in the summer of 1941. Named Isshikirikko or Rikko in Japanese, the Allies knew the bomber as the 'Betty'. In December 1941 G4M1s led the attack on the Philippines and, equipped with torpedoes, helped sink the British cruisers *Prince of Wales* and *Repulse*. In February 1942, they attacked Darwin, Australia.

The Japanese crews nicknamed the G4M the 'Flying Cigar' but American pilots called it the 'one-

The 'Betty' was one of the best medium bombers of the war. This G4M2 has no defensive armament fitted. (Philip Jarrett collection)

shot lighter' due to its propensity to catch fire when hit. The **G4M1 Model 12** had limited fuel tank protection. Admiral Isoroku Yamamoto was flying in a Model 12 when shot down by P-38s in April 1943. The **G4M2 Model 22** had boosted Kasei 21 engines, a 20-mm cannon in a dorsal turret and a new (unprotected) fuselage fuel tank. The **G4M2 Model 22b** had cannon in beam positions. The **Model 24** had more efficient Kasei 25 engines and the **24b** also had beam cannon.

One of the most interesting uses of the 'Betty' was as a carrier for the Yokosuka Ohka (Cherry Blossom) rocket-powered suicide plane. Ohka carriers were designated **G4M2 Model 24e**. Most of these were shot down before reaching their launch points. Major improvements to the 'Betty' came in late 1944 with deliveries of the **G4M3 Model 34**, which finally had armour, effective self-sealing, more tailplane dihedral and a redesigned tail turret. This was too late to make much difference, with only 60 G4M3s built from a total of 2,416 'Bettys' built. Many G4Ms were used as transports towards the end of the war.

This G4M2 'Betty 24' was captured by American forces and evaluated by the US Navy. (The Aviation Picture Library)

Specification: G4M3 Model 34
Type: twin-engined heavy naval bomber
Crew: seven
Powerplant: two 1,825-hp (1361-kW) Mitsubishi Kasei 25 14-cylinder radials
Dimensions: span 82 ft 0.25 in (25.0 m); length 63 ft 11.75 in (19.5 m); height 19 ft 8.25 in (6.0 m); wing area 841 sq ft (78.13 m²)
Weights: empty 18,409 lb (8350 kg); max. take-off 27,558 lb (12500 kg)
Performance: max. speed 292 mph (470 km/h); service ceiling 30,250 ft (9220 m); range 2,694 miles (4335 km)
Armament: four 0.303-in (7.7-mm) Type 89 machine-guns and two 20-mm Type 99 cannon; bomb load up to 2,205 lb (1000 kg)

Handley Page Halifax

United Kingdom
October 1939

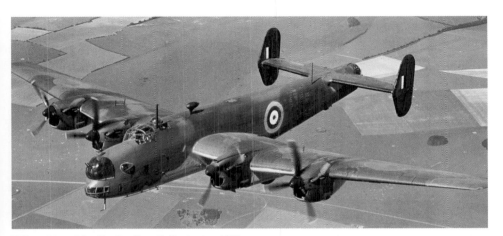

Early model Halifaxes had Boulton-Paul nose turrets and Merlin engines. This is the second prototype Halifax. (The Aviation Picture Library)

The origins of the Handley Page Halifax lay in a 1935 specification for a '100-foot span bomber' (in order to fit in standard hangars) and it was originally conceived (but not built) as a twin-engined design. After the RAF ordered a prototype, they issued a new requirement for a faster bomber. The designers shortened the wingspan and then decided to fit four Merlin engines rather than two Hercules or Vultures. The first **H.P.57** prototype flew on 25 October 1939, initially without armament. The H.P.57 featured a deep fuselage, long wings with square tips and twin tails.

The initial **Halifax B I Series 1** with Merlin Xs had a Boulton-Paul nose turret with two Browning 0.303-in (7.7-mm) machine-guns, four more in a tail turret and two Vickers guns in beam hatches. Some early models had three-bladed propellers on the inboard engines and four-bladed outboard props. There were 84 B Is produced, entering combat as night bombers from March 1941. They initially suffered heavy losses.

The **B I Series 3** adopted more powerful Merlin XX engines and a Boulton-Paul dorsal turret with twin guns. Only nine were made, but they led to the **Halifax B II**, notable mainly for being built in subassemblies by six plants, supplied by many subcontractors. Some were converted to **B II (Special)** standard for agent dropping with most

The Mk III introduced the Hercules radial engine. The glazed nose without turret had first appeared on the Mk II. (The Aviation Picture Library)

armament deleted and a parachute door. The **B II Series IA** had a low-profile top turret and a new glazed nose. The main Coastal Command version was the **GR II Series IA** with a 0.50-in (12.7-mm) nose gun. Mark II production totalled 1,977.

The **B III** switched to 1,615-hp (1204-kW) Bristol Hercules engines. The Mk III had capacity for 4,000-lb (1814-kg) and 8,000-lb (3629-kg) bombs. Later Mk IIIs had rounded wingtips and there were many variants for jamming, agent dropping and glider towing. The **B V** reintroduced the nose turret and Merlins with a revised undercarriage. There were 904 Mk Vs used in bomber, airborne and meteorological survey roles.

The **B VI** was intended for the Far East and was equipped with 1,800-hp (1342-kW) Hercules 100s and the glazed nose. Many were converted to C VI transport versions and others became the **GR VI** for maritime reconnaissance. The **B VII** and subvariants reverted to the lower-powered Hercules XVI engine. The **C VIII** was built as a transport and a number saw post-war service as airliners and civil freighters. The last RAF 'Halibags' (GR VIs) left service in 1952. Pakistan and Egypt had small numbers, the last of Egypt's being destroyed in the 1956 Suez campaign.

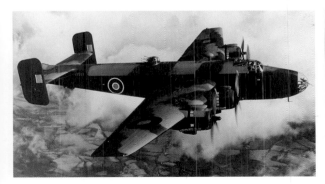

Specification: Halifax B III
Type: four-engined heavy bomber
Crew: seven
Powerplant: four 1,615-hp (1204-kW) Bristol Hercules XVI radial pistons
Dimensions: span 98 ft 10 in (30.12 m); length 71 ft 7 in (21.82 m); height 20 ft 9 in (6.32 m); wing area 1,250 sq ft (116.12 m²)
Weights: empty 38,240 lb (17346 kg); max. take-off 65,000 lb (29484 kg)
Performance: max. speed 282 mph (346 km/h); service ceiling 24,000 ft (7315 m); range 1,985 miles (3194 km)
Armament: one 0.303-in (7.7-mm) Vickers K and four 0.303-in Browning machine-guns; bomb load up to 14,500 lb (6577 kg)

Petlyakov Pe-2

The Petlyakov **Pe-2** light bomber, dive-bomber and reconnaissance aircraft began as the **V-100** fighter prototype of 1939. Vladimir Petlyakov was an assistant to Andrei Tupolev and had a large part in designing many Tupolev aircraft. In 1937 he was given the task of designing a heavy fighter. The V-100, which first flew in late 1939 and had such innovations as a pressurised cockpit, was such a fine aircraft that Petlyakov was given his own design bureau.

Despite its qualities, in May 1940 Petlyakov was ordered to abandon the fighter and develop a bomber version. The V-100 was converted to the **PB-100** and this first flew in June. It was immediately ordered into production as the Pe-2. The Pe-2 was a modern aircraft with a clean aerodynamic shape. The engine cowls were streamlined and the radiators were mounted in wing ducts rather than slung underneath. The cockpit was unpressurised and sat two crew in tandem, with the bomb-aimer lying prone in the nose. The tailplane had noticeable dihedral and oval fins. The engines were supercharged Klimov M-105s of 1,050 hp (783 kW) output. The Pe-2 was well armed with fixed and trainable guns in the nose and a ventral tray. An internal bay could carry 2,205 lb (1000 kg) of bombs and there were dive brakes and an automatic pull-out system to allow dive-bombing. Petlyakov himself was killed in February 1941 in the crash of the second production aircraft, being used as a company transport, and development carried on under several other chief designers, including

A Pe-2 taxies on an airfield near Voroshilovgrad in 1943. The versitile Pe-2 was well suited to Russia's harsh conditions. (The Aviation Picture Library)

Vladimir Myasishchev, later to have his own bureau.

Myasishchev's developments included the four-man **Pe-2FT**, which had a new gun mount for the navigator/bomb-aimer to allow rearward firing, and no dive brakes. The **Pe-2A** had a new canopy, revised tailplane, larger radiators and relocated bomb racks. The **Pe-2B** had an enlarged, wooden wing, VK-105PF engines of 1,180 hp (880 kW) and a reorganised cockpit. The **Pe-2MV** was an attack fighter variant with a ventral gondola containing two cannon and two machine-guns, and a remotely controlled dorsal turret. The **Pe-2UT** was an unusual-looking conversion trainer with a second cockpit behind the first. The **Pe-3** was a pure fighter development, appearing in 1941.

Only small numbers of Pe-2s were available in mid-1941. A notable mission was a 1941 attack on the Romanian oil industry around Ploesti, destroying millions of gallons of petroleum products. Production ended in 1945 with 11,427 delivered. Some went to Czechoslovakia, Yugoslavia and Poland.

A number of Pe-2s were captured by the Finns in the 1939–40 Winter War and entered service against their former owners. (The Aviation Picture Library)

Specification: Petlyakov Pe-2FT
Type: twin-engined light bomber
Crew: four
Powerplant: two 1,260-hp (939-kW) Klimov VK-105PF V-12 pistons
Dimensions: span 56 ft 2 in (17.11 m); length 41 ft 11 in (12.78 m); height 11 ft 3 in (3.42 m); wing area 436 sq ft (40.5 m²)
Weights: empty 13,119 lb (5951 kg); max. take-off 18,783 lb (8520 kg)
Performance: max. speed 360 mph (579 km/h); service ceiling 28,870 ft (8800 m); range 1,100 miles (1770 km)
Armament: four or five 0.30-in (7.62-mm) and one or three 0.50-in (12.7-mm) machine-guns; bomb load up to 3,527 lb (1600 kg)

Heinkel He 177 Greif

German bomber development in the 1930s mainly concentrated on medium bombers able to support Blitzkrieg attacks over relatively short distances. Only in 1938 was a specification for a long-range heavy bomber issued, and this included the stipulation that the aircraft be capable of dive-bombing. Heinkel responded with the **He 177**, powered by two Daimler-Benz DB 606 engines. The DB 606 was essentially two DB 601s coupled together to give a 24-cylinder powerplant with an output of 2,600 hp (1939 kW). Engine cooling problems were to be the Achilles' heel of the He 177. The **He 177V1** flew on 19 November 1939. Just slightly smaller than a B-17E, the V1 had a cylindrical fuselage and a domed front transparency. The double-wheel main undercarriage split to retract inwards and outwards of the engine nacelles.

Three of the eight prototypes were lost in crashes due to fires and structural failure. Thirty-five **He 177A-0** pre-production aircraft were built, armed with two MG FF 20-mm cannon and one 13-mm MG 131 machine-gun in the nose as well as defensive machine-guns. The initial production **He 177A-1** began combat trials in July 1942 but showed structural weaknesses and was replaced by the

The coupled engine layout of the He 177 gave poor cooling to the rear cylinders, resulting in many catastrophic fires.
(Philip Jarrett collection)

Captured in mid-1944, this He 177A-5 was evaluated by the RAF and wore 'D-Day' stripes to identify it as friendly. (TRH Pictures)

He 177A-3, most of which had DB 610 engines. The **He 177A-3/R-3** was employed as a launcher for the Hs 293 anti-shipping missile from October 1943. Daylight missile attacks had limited success, and night raids suffered fewer losses but found few targets. The **He 177A-5** was the final significant production version with a stronger wing, shorter gear legs and no Fowler flaps. Subvariants had armament variations, pressurised cockpits and armour protection. The **He 177A-7** with coupled DB 613s and longer-span wings was involved in two abortive long-range missions, the delivery of a pattern aircraft to Japan and an attack on US cities. One began modification for the German atomic bomb programme. Only six were completed.

Named Greif (Griffon) in service, He 177s suffered heavy losses on the Eastern Front, particularly around Stalingrad where some were employed as transports. He 177s were concentrated with other bombers for the 'Little Blitz' against London in January 1944, using dive attacks to outpace interceptors. Accuracy was poor. In almost all He 177 raids several aircraft were lost to engine fires or other mechanical problems.

The handful of **He 177Bs** were almost completely new with four separate DB 603s and a twin tail.

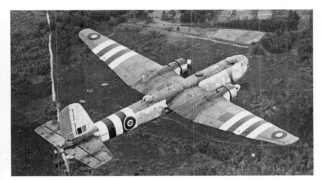

Specification: He 177A-1
Type: twin-engined heavy bomber
Crew: five
Powerplant: two 2,700-hp (2014-kW) Daimler-Benz DB 606 24-cylinder pistons
Dimensions: span 103 ft 2 in (31.42 m); length 66 ft 11 in (20.39 m); height 21 ft (6.4 m); wing area 1,098 sq ft (102 m²)
Weights: empty 35,494 lb (16100 kg); max. take-off 66,139 lb (30000 kg)
Performance: max. speed 317 mph (510 km/h); service ceiling 22,966 ft (7000 m); range 3,840 miles (6180 km)
Armament: three 0.295-in (7.9-mm) and two 13-mm (0.51-in) machine-guns, one 20-mm cannon; bomb load up to 13,200 lb (6000 kg)

North American B-25 Mitchell

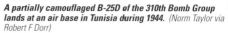

North American's entry in the USAAC's 1938 light bomber competition, the NA-40, was a failure, but many of its features, such as the twin tails and twin R-1830 engines were used in the **NA-62**, which was ordered as the **B-25** in September 1939. The prototype flew on 19 August 1940 and was followed by 25 more. Armour and self-sealing tanks were fitted on the 40 **B-25A**s, as was a wing with dihedral inboard of the engines.

The 120 **B-25B**s had a dorsal turret and a retractable belly turret but no tail gun. The RAF knew it as the **Mitchell Mk I**. In April 1942, in the famous 'Doolittle raid', 16 B-25s flew from the USS *Hornet* to bomb Tokyo and Yokohama in the first major US retaliatory attack of the war. The 1,620 **B-25C**s (**Mitchell II**) and 2,090 **B-25D**s were identical, but were built in Los Angeles and Kansas City, respectively. The USMC had 50 **PBJ-1D**s, equivalent to the B-25D. but with torpedo capability. Many had APS-2 or -3 search radar in the nose or under the fuselage.

A total of 463 'big gun' **B-25G**s were built or converted. Based on the B-25C, they were armed with four 0.50-in (12.7-mm) guns in the nose and a 75-mm M4 cannon in an offset position below them. This weapon had its origins as a World War I French

The Mitchell had a long post-war career with many nations. This B-25J served with a RCAF reserve unit in the 1950s. (Author's collection)

A partially camouflaged B-25D of the 310th Bomb Group lands at an air base in Tunisia during 1944. (Norm Taylor via Robert F Dorr)

infantry weapon and was used in low-level attacks against ships and airfields. The **B-25H** (1,000 built) had four machine-guns in the nose as well as the 75-mm cannon. The dorsal turret was moved forward. Waist guns, forward-firing 'package' guns and a new tail turret gave a total of 15 guns. The USMC version was the **PBJ-1H**. Many of the H features were incorporated in the **B-25J** (**Mitchell III**), although it had a traditional glazed nose without cannon or a solid eight gun 'strafer' nose, giving up to 18 guns. The J was the most important version, with 4,390 built. The **F-10** was an unarmed photo-reconnaissance version.

During World War II, B-25s were flown by RAF, RCAF, Soviet, Free French, Brazilian, Netherlands East Indies and Australian air forces. US B-25s saw action in all theatres of war except North-West Europe, although RAF Mitchells were widely used in this theatre with No. 2 Tactical Air Force.

After the war, most US B-25s were retired from front-line service but many became VB-25 transports or TB-25 bombardier and navigator trainers. A few TB-25Ks were used in Korea to ferret out enemy radars. A number of bombers were supplied to Latin American. Some served as late as 1979 as transports.

Specification: North American B-25J
Type: twin-engined medium bomber
Crew: five
Powerplant: two 1,700-hp (1268-kW) Wright R-2600-29 Cyclone 14-cylinder radial pistons
Dimensions: span 67 ft 7 in (20.59 m); length 51 ft (15.55 m); height 16 ft 4 in (4.98 m); wing area 610 sq ft (57.67 m²)
Weights: empty 19,530 lb (8858 kg); max. take-off 35,000 lb (15876 kg)
Performance: max. speed 285 mph (458 km/h); service ceiling 24,200 ft (7376 m); max. range 2,200 miles (3540 km)
Armament: up to 18 0.50-in (12.7-mm) machine-guns bomb load up to 3,200 lb (451 kg)

Ilyushin Il-2/Il-10 Shturmovik

USSR
October 1940

In 1935 the Soviet defence establishment called for the aircraft design bureaux to draw up a *Bronirovannii Shturmovik* (BSh), or armoured assaulter with heavy armour and armament, principally fixed cannon. Yakovlev's twin-engined design was rejected due to its lack of rough-field capability. Sergei Ilyushin and Pavel Sukhoi submitted single-engined designs. Ilyushin's **TsKB-55** prototype flew on 12 October 1940 but had poor longitudinal stability and was revised from twin to single-seat configuration as the **TsKB-57**. This entered service as the **BSh-2** (soon renamed **Il-2**) in March 1941. The Il-2 was a low-winged all-metal monoplane, notable mainly for its use of armour to protect all the vital components. The armour was part of the structure, not an additional fixture. The engine was a Mikulin AM-38 rated at 1,700 hp (1268 kW).

The Shturmovik was used more as 'flying artillery' in support of the Red Army than as a combat aircraft in the traditional sense. Cheaply made and sparsely equipped, it was fielded in enormous numbers against German armour and troop formations.

Combat experience showed the need for tail defence and the **Il-2M** again had two-seats. The gunner had a 0.50-in (12.7-mm) UB machine-gun, but his position was unarmoured and gunners suffered appalling casualties. To save light alloys, the outer

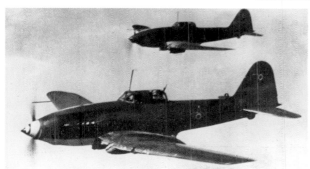

A view of post-war Hungarian Il-10s shows the cleaner lines and new wing planform. The gunner had better protection. (Philip Jarrett collection)

The Il-2M3 had heavy armour plating around the pilot's cockpit but a lack of it around the gunner. (Philip Jarrett collection)

wings and rear fuselage were wood on most Il-2Ms.

The all-metal **Il-2M3** had 15 degrees sweepback on the outer wings to reduce instability caused by the second cockpit. Later examples had the 20-mm ShVAK cannon replaced by the harder-hitting VYa 23-mm or even 37-mm NS-11-P-37s cannon. This latter gun could penetrate the upper armour of a Tiger tank.

The **Il-2T** was a torpedo-bomber version and the **Il-2U** a lightly armed conversion trainer. In total, 36,163 Il-2s were produced (942 before June 1941), making it the most numerous warplane of all time.

The completely redesigned **Il-10** with a 2,000-hp (1492-kW) AM-42 engine replaced the Il-2 in production from 1944. It was slightly smaller and aerodynamically cleaner. The undercarriage rotated to lie flush when retracted. On the post-war **Il-10M**, the wing design was new with square tips.

At the outbreak of the Korean War, the North Korean Air Force had about 65 Il-2s and Il-10s. Although active in early fighting, they were no match for F-80s and other fighters. The Il-10 was named 'Beast' by NATO (the Il-2 was the 'Bark'). Factories in the USSR built 4,966 Il-10s and 1,200 more were built under licence as the **B-33** by Avia in Czechoslovakia.

Specification: Ilyushin Il-2M3
Type: single-engined close support aircraft
Crew: two
Powerplant: one 1,770-hp (1320-kW) Mikulin AM-38F V-12 piston
Dimensions: span 47 ft 11 in (14.6 m); length 39 ft 4 in (12 m); height 11 ft 2 in (3.4 m); wing area 414.42 sq ft (38.5 m²)
Weights: empty 9,976 lb (4525 kg); max. take-off 14,021 lb (6360 kg)
Performance: max. speed 258 mph (415 km/h); service ceiling 19,685 ft (6000 m); range 497 miles (800 km)
Armament: two 0.30-in (7.62-mm) and one 0.50-in (12.7-mm) machine-guns, two 23-mm cannon; bomb load up to 2,205 lb (1000 kg)

De Havilland Mosquito Bombers

United Kingdom
November 1940

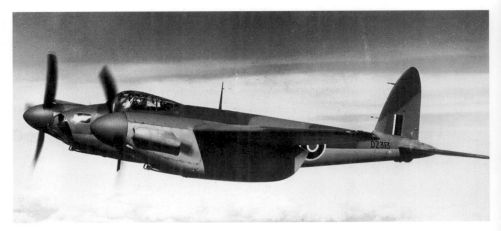

DZ313 was one of the first Mk IV bombers. The early Mk IVs also carried cameras for target reconnaissance. (The Aviation Picture Library)

In 1938 the de Havilland Aircraft Company offered the Air Ministry its privately funded proposal for an unarmed fast light bomber made primarily of wood to save on strategic materials. Despite official indifference, the company proceeded with construction of a prototype, designed by Ronald E Bishop and influenced by the Albatross and Flamingo airliner designs. In May 1940, the RAF ordered 50 (later 21) aircraft in photo-reconnaissance, fighter and bomber forms. The prototype **DH 98 Mosquito** flew on 25 November 1940 and soon demonstrated its speed, handling and load-carrying ability. The DH 98 was an exceptionally clean design, built primarily of laminated plywood and powered by two 1,250-hp (933-kW) Merlin 22 engines. The pilot and navigator sat side by side under a heavily framed canopy with a Perspex nose transparency used for bomb aiming.

The first reconnaissance sorties were flown in September 1941 by **Mosquito PR I**s. They flew many significant missions against German naval targets in particular, as did the **PR IV** and **PR VIII**.

The first production bomber was the **B IV Series 1**, able to carry four 250-lb (113-kg) bombs. The **B IV Series 2** was modified to carry four 500-lb (206-kg) bombs. Some had a bulged bomb bay and could carry one 4,000-lb (1814-kg) 'cookie' demolition bomb. Mosquito bombers made their first high-altitude raids in July 1942 and soon were making low-level precision attacks. Notable missions included the attack on the Oslo Gestapo HQ in September 1942. A few were converted to carry the 'Highball' bouncing bomb, although they were not used in action. Others became fast passenger and mail carriers on the 'ball-bearing' run between Scotland and Stockholm.

De Havilland of Canada built many hundreds of the **B VII**, **B XX** and **B 25** models, mainly differing in the engine used. The **B IX** had Merlin 72s with two-stage superchargers and could carry two extra bombs or fuel tanks under the wings. From early 1943 Mosquitoes had the important target-marking role using 'oboe' beam navigation.

The USAAF used a number of **PR XVI**s and other marks (including the **F-8** based on the B 25) for weather recon., chaff dropping, radar photography and recording transmissions from agents.

The **B 35** entered service in 1948. The last RAF (**PR 34**) Mosquitoes left service in Malaya in 1955. The **TT 35** was a target-towing variant with a heavily framed glazed nose and a winch. The **TT 39** was more conventional. PR 'Mossies' served with Canada, France, Israel, Australia the USSR and South Africa.

The last Mosquitoes in RAF service were the PR 34As of No. 81 Squadron in Singapore, flying the last sorties in December 1955. (Author's collection)

Specification: Mosquito B IV Series 2
Type: twin-engined light bomber
Crew: two
Powerplant: two 1,480-hp (1103-kW) Rolls-Royce Merlin 21 V-12 pistons
Dimensions: span 54 ft 2 in (16.49 m); length 40 ft 9.5 in (12.43 m); height 15 ft 3 in (4.65 m); wing area 454 sq ft (42.18 m²)
Weights: empty 14,900 lb (6759 kg); max. take-off 22,500 lb (10215 kg)
Performance: max. speed 380 mph (612 km/h); service ceiling 34,000 ft (10263 m); range 2,040 miles (3283 km)
Armament: bomb load up to 4,000 lb (1814 kg)

Martin B-26 Marauder

United States
November 1940

Built to the same US Air Corps specification as the B-25 Mitchell, the **B-26 Marauder** first flew on 26 November 1940. Designed by Peyton S Magruder of Martin Aircraft in Baltimore, the B-26 featured a sleek circular cross-section fuselage, a tall single fin and a high-mounted wing mounting two 1,850-hp (1380-kW) Pratt & Whitney R-2800-5 Double Wasp radials and four-bladed propellers. The Martin-designed dorsal turret was the first powered turret on a US bomber. Thirty-six B-26As were built, plus 49 equivalent **Marauder Is** and 19 **Marauder IAs** for the RAF.

Early versions were able to carry a torpedo slung externally, and this warload was used on the Marauder's combat debut in the Battle of Midway in June 1942, although rarely afterwards. Half the Marauders were lost and no hits scored. The B-26's high wing loading and high landing speed led to nicknames such as 'Baltimore Whore' (no visible means of support) and "Widowmaker" There were many training accidents in Florida, or 'one a day in Tampa Bay' as the cynics had it. The Truman defence committee twice recommended production be stopped, but improved training and aircraft modifications eventually lowered the crash rate.

Marauders served initially in the Pacific (two groups) and North Africa (three groups). The first

Marauders were particularly effective against transportation targets. This B-26B is seen in June 1944 attacking a road/rail junction. (TRH Pictures)

B-26Bs of the 387th Bomb Group fly over England in early 1944. They saw much combat in the Normandy campaign. (Jim Sullivan via Robert F Dorr)

European missions were flown by 8th Air Force B-26s in May 1943, initially on low-level precision raids, but after one disastrous mission in which all aircraft were lost, tactics switched to medium-level formation bombing. The B-26s transferred to the 9th Air Force in October 1943 and were heavily used to interdict German supply routes in France and V-1 flying bomb sites up to and after the D-day invasion. Despite its poor initial performance, the Marauder went on to have the lowest loss rate of any US bomber, and at least one flew over 200 missions.

Extra guns were added during **B-26B** production – two 0.50-in (12.7-mm) 'package' guns alongside the fuselage and two extra 0.30-in (7.62-mm) guns in the nose. To cure some of the Marauder's problems, a larger wing and taller fin was introduced on late B-26Bs and on the Omaha-built **B-26C**, 123 of which went to the RAF as the **Marauder II**. The **AT-23B**, was a stripped-down target-towing version and 225 of these went to the US Navy as the **JM-1**. The **B-26F** and the similar **B-26G** had a higher-incidence wing and heavier weights. About 350 Fs and Gs became **Marauder IIIs** with the RAF and SAAF squadrons serving in North Africa and Italy.

Specification: Martin B-26B
Type: twin-engined medium bomber
Crew: seven
Powerplant: two 1,920-hp (1432-kW) Pratt & Whitney R-2800-43 Double Wasp 18-cylinder radial engines
Dimensions: span 71 ft 0 in (21.64 m); length 58 ft 3 in (17.75 m); height 21 ft 6 in (6.55 m); wing area 658 sq ft (61.13 m²)
Weights: empty 24,000 lb (10886 kg); max. take-off 38,000 lb (17237 kg)
Performance: max. speed 280 mph (451 km/h); service ceiling 21,000 ft (6400 m); range 1,150 miles (1850 km)
Armament: up to 11 0.50-in (12.7-mm) and two 0.30-in (7.62-mm) machine-guns; bomb load up to 4,000 lb (1814 kg)

Curtiss SB2C Helldiver

In 1938 a rigid specification was issued by the US Navy for a scout/dive-bomber, to replace the SBD Dauntless. A team at Curtiss Aircraft led by Raymond Blaylock designed a much larger aircraft to broadly the same configuration with split flaps and a Wright R-2600 engine. A new feature was a large internal weapons bay which could carry two 1,000-lb (454-kg) bombs or, with modification, a Mk 13 torpedo. The wings had hydraulic folding. Curtiss named the new aircraft the Helldiver, even though the Curtiss SCB Helldiver biplane was still in production when the new design was ordered in May 1939.

The prototype **XSB2C-1** first flew on 18 December 1940. Badly damaged in February 1941, it was rebuilt and lengthened with a larger tail. Armed with two 0.50-in (12.7-mm) cowling guns and with an even larger tail, the first **SB2C-1** flew in June 1942. The weight had increased by a third due to the addition of armour and more fuel in self-sealing tanks. The cowl guns were removed in favour of four 0.50-in (12.7-mm) guns in the wings. After 200 aircraft, the armament changed again, to two 20-mm cannon in the wings on the 778 **SB2C-1C**s.

The building of a new factory at Columbus Ohio delayed production. Deliveries began to VS-9 on USS *Yorktown* in December 1942, but the Helldiver's first combat action did not occur until November 1943. The Truman defence committee heavily criticised the SB2C and its production programme and brought about the cancellation of most **A-25A Shrike**s

The Helldiver was built in large numbers but was never particularly popular with its crews. This aircraft is from the USS **Shangri-La**. *(Via Robert F Dorr)*

intended for the USAAF. Most were diverted to the Marines as **SB2C-1A**s. Nonetheless, the Army took over 500 A-25As, without wing-folding.

The large wing and relatively short fuselage contributed to poor low-speed handling and the Helldiver was nicknamed 'Beast' and 'Son of a bitch second class'. Maintenance was also problematic. The SB2C suffered badly at the Battle of the Philippine Sea in 1944, but became the premier US carrier strike aircraft by 1945, destroying many Japanese warships and supporting many invasions.

The **SB2C-3** introduced a four-bladed propeller and the R-2600-20 engine – 1,125 were produced. The **SB2C-4**, of which there were 2,450, had perforated flaps, as on the Dauntless, to reduce buffet. Some 970 **SB2C-5**s were completed. Two Canadian plants built Helldivers, 300 by Fairchild as the **SBF-1**, **SBF-3** and **SBF-4E**, and 832 by Canadian Car and Foundry (CCF) as the **SBW-1**, **SBW-3**, **SBW-4E** and **SBW-5**.

One Fleet Air Arm squadron (No. 1820) flew most of 26 **Helldiver I**s, although they never saw combat.

A grand total of 7,155 Helldivers were built, the highest number of any dive-bomber design. This is an SB2C-4. (The Aviation Picture Library)

Specification: Curtiss SB2C-3

Type: single-engined naval dive-bomber
Crew: two
Powerplant: one 1,900-hp (1417-kW) Wright R-2600-20 Cyclone 14-cyl radial
Dimensions: span 49 ft 8.75 in (15.14 m); length 36 ft 8 in (11.18 m); height 14 ft 9 in (4.49 m); wing area 422 sq ft (39.2 m²)
Weights: empty 10,493 lb (4760 kg); max. take-off 16,750 lb (7598 kg)
Performance: max. speed 293 mph (472 km/h); service ceiling 26,700 ft (8140 m); range 1,200 miles (1930 km)
Armament: two 20-mm cannon and two 0.30-in (7.62-mm) machine-guns; bomb load up to 3,000 lb (1362 kg)

Avro Lancaster

United Kingdom
January 1941

The most famous and successful British heavy bomber of the war, the Avro **Lancaster** was developed from the twin-engined Manchester, which was a failure owing to its unreliable Vulture engines. Even before the Manchester entered service, Roy Chadwick at Avro was designing a four-engined successor, which emerged as the **Manchester III**. This first flew on 9 January 1941 with Merlin XX engines. Immediately ordered as the **Lancaster B I**, early examples were converted from Manchesters on the production line. The Lancaster had a large mid-mounted wing, twin vertical fins and a fuselage of a more circular cross-section than the Halifax or Stirling. Powered turrets in the nose, upper fuselage and tail contained two, two and four 0.303-in (7.7-mm) machine-guns, respectively.

The Lancaster made its debut on the Augsburg daylight raid of 17 April 1942. Seven out of the 12 aircraft sent were lost and the Lancaster was mostly assigned night missions from then on. Thirty-three aircraft were converted to **Lancaster B I (Special)** configuration in order to carry the 22,000-lb (10000-kg) Grand Slam bomb. This was the heaviest weapon used in World War II. The conversion entailed removing the bomb bay doors and fitting an aerodynamic fairing.

The **Lancaster B II** was developed to reduce the

Lancaster VIIs were used by the Aéronavale well into the 1960s for maritime patrol around France's Pacific territories. (TRH Pictures)

A well-worn Lancaster I of No. 50 Squadron typifies the many thousands that served with Bomber Command from 1942–5. (The Aviation Picture Library)

demand on Merlin engines and was produced with the Bristol Hercules VI of 1,725 hp (1286 kW). Some of the 300 built were later re-engined with the Hercules XVI, but in general the Mk II 'Lanc' had lower performance than the Merlin versions. The **Lancaster B III** had American-built Packard Merlin 28s, 38s or 224s. With 3,030 built it was the most numerous model. B Xs were built by Canada's Victory Aircraft, most with the low-profile Martin dorsal turret.

The famous No. 617 Squadron was formed with 23 modified Lancaster B IIIs (code-named the **Type 464 (Provisioning) Lancaster**) to carry out raids on the Ruhr dams with the Barnes Wallis-designed 'bouncing' bomb. Guy Gibson was awarded a VC for leading this raid in which two dams were breached.

Versions for the Far East, the **B I (FE)** and **B III (FE)**, had increased range and no dorsal turret, but the war ended before Lancasters were sent to the theatre. The RAF's 100 Group specialised in jamming and spoofing German radars and gathering electronic intelligence. The **B VI** was developed for the jamming role, but only seven (with Merlin 85s) were built. The B VII was a post-war model with the dorsal turret (with 0.50-in/ 12.7-mm guns) moved forward. Some of the 180 built went to France's Aéronavale and served in the maritime patrol role up to 1967.

Specification: Avro Lancaster B III
Type: four-engined heavy bomber
Crew: seven
Powerplant: four 1,460-hp (1089-kW) Packard-built Merlin XX V-12 pistons
Dimensions: span 102 ft 0 in (31.1 m); length 69 ft 4 in (21.1 m); height 19 ft 7 in (5.97 m); wing area 1,300 sq ft (120.8 m²)
Weights: empty 36,900 lb (16705 kg); max. take-off 70,000 lb (31750 kg)
Performance: max. speed 287 mph (462 km/h); service ceiling 24,500 ft (7467 m); range (loaded) 1,660 miles (2675 km)
Armament: eight 0.303-in (7.7-mm) machine-guns; bomb load up to 14,000 lb (6350 kg) or one 22,000-lb (10000-kg) bomb

Tupolev Tu-2

Tupolev Tu-2 attack bomber. (D I Windle)

In 1940 the Soviet authorities issued a farsighted specification for a tactical bomber that called for a speed close to that of contemporary fighters, a large-capacity internal bomb bay, dive-bombing capability, long range and good defensive armament. The aircraft was to be twin-engined and suitable for all-weather operation. Andrei Tupolev was then out of favour with the Soviet hierarchy, but redeemed himself and his design bureau with the **ANT-58** or **Type 103**, an attractive machine with a tapered nose (the lower half of which was glazed for the bomb-aimer). The slender rear fuselage ended in twin dihedralled tailplanes.

The prototype flew on 29 January 1941 and although it passed all its official tests with distinction, deliveries of the production **ANT-60** (Air Force designation **Tu-2**) did not begin until November 1942 owing to the disruption caused by the German invasion. The original Mikulin AM-37 engines were underpowered, and the modified **ANT-59** and production aircraft had Shvetsov M-82FN (later ASh-82FN) radials of 1,850 hp (1380 kW). Tu-2s could nominally carry 2,204 lb (1000 kg) of bombs internally and the same amount on external racks. In action they were often flown in an overload condition with twice this amount. In early versions up to 10 RS-132 rocket launchers were fitted under the wing.

The **Tu-2S** had more powerful variants of the ASh-82FN and single 0.50-in (12.7-mm) machine-guns in place of the twin 0.30-in (7.62-mm) guns in the dorsal and ventral positions. The long-range version was the **Tu-2D** with longer wings and tailplanes and a crew of up to five. The propellers were changed to four-bladed units. The **Tu-2R** was built for reconnaissance and the **Tu-2Sh** for ground attack with a bizarre set-up of 48 PPSh sub-machine-guns in the nose as an anti-personnel weapon. Several other shturmovik models with 20-mm, 75-mm or 57-mm cannon were tested, as was a torpedo-bomber variant.

Although slightly later than and built in fewer numbers than the similar Petlyakov Pe-2, the Tu-2 handled better and was more popular with its crews. It was also 62 mph (100 km/h) faster and could carry a wider range of weapons. The Tu-2's loss rate was very low because of its high speed and good single-engine performance. One notable mission was the destruction of Vyborg railway station in June 1944.

A total of 2,527 Tu-2s were built, 1,514 of them from 1945 to 1948. Poland and China were users, and China supplied many to North Korea where they saw action against the United Nations forces.

The Tu-2 was an effective modern bomber that entered service in 1941 and served for many years post war. (Author's collection)

Specification: Tu-2S
Type: twin-engined medium bomber
Crew: four
Powerplant: two 1,850-hp (1380-kW) Shvetsov ASh-82FN radial pistons
Dimensions: span 61 ft 8 in (18.86 m); length 45 ft 2 in (13.80 m); height 14 ft 10 in (4.55 m); wing area 525 sq ft (48.80 m²)
Weights: empty 16,477 lb (7474 kg); max. take-off 25,044 lb (11360 kg)
Performance: max. speed 342 mph (550 km/h); service ceiling 35,990 ft (10790 m); range 1,553 miles (2500 km)
Armament: two 20-mm cannon, one 7.72-mm (0.304-in) and two 0.50-in (12.7-mm) machine-guns; 8,818 lb (4000 kg) bomb load

Lockheed Ventura

United States
July 1941

Not long after deliveries of the Hudson began, the British Air Ministry proposed a successor based on the Model 18 Lodestar airliner. With engines in the 1,600-hp (1194-kW) class, one of Lockheed's studies offered promise as a Blenheim replacement, and was duly ordered in February 1940. The powerplant was changed to the Pratt & Whitney R-2800 of 1,850-hp (1380-kW) and 300 were ordered in May 1940 as the **Ventura I**. Venturas were built by Lockheed's subsidiary Vega (which fully merged in December 1941). Similar in appearance to the Hudson, the larger heavier Ventura had a low-profile Martin turret relocated further forward. This contained two (later four) 0.303-in (7.7-mm) machine-guns and there were paired 0.303-in guns in the glazed nose and in a ventral position. On 31 July 1941 the first Ventura flew at Burbank. Deliveries to the UK began in September.

Initially used by RAF and Commonwealth squadrons for low-level raids against industrial targets in the Low Countries, Venturas suffered badly against German fighters and were switched to medium-altitude attacks. Squadron Leader Leonard Trent of 487(NZ) Squadron was awarded the VC during a raid on Eindhoven in May 1943 in which eight of nine aircraft were lost. Some **Ventura GR Is** were issued to Coastal Command. The **Ventura II** was fitted with the

The PV-1 was optimised for maritime patrol with a search radar in the nose. This USN example has auxiliary drop tanks. (The Aviation Picture Library)

AE748 was one of the first Venturas evaluated by the RAF. Ventura Is served with British, Australian and New Zealand squadrons. (Philip Jarrett collection)

R-2800-31 and 487 were built, 112 converted from Ventura Is before completion. The majority were retained by the USAAF as Model 37s. Twenty-seven went to the US Navy as the **PV-3**. The **Ventura IIA** was ordered under Lend-Lease and designated **B-34 Lexington** for US purposes. These had US-built 0.50-in (12.7-mm) weapons in the nose and dorsal turret. Most went to Canada or the USAAF, and were converted to **B-34A** trainers and target tugs.

In exchange for the use of a Navy-operated plant at Renton for B-29 production, the USAAF took over Ventura production in mid-1942 as the **PV-1**. The solid nose contained a search radar. The bomb-aimer was retained on early PV-1s and used a flat viewing window under the nose, but was later replaced with a gun pack containing three 0.50-in (12.7-mm) guns. The bomb bay was enlarged to carry a 3,000-lb (1361-kg) bomb load. The first of 1,600 PV-1s was delivered in December 1942 and the type first saw combat in the Aleutians. The RAF received 387 as **Ventura GR Vs** and South Africa 134, using some into the 1960s. New Zealand received 116 PV-1s to replace Hudsons. The PV-1 had tricky handling compared with the Hudson and a poor initial safety record. It was also harder to maintain, but became an effective patrol aircraft.

Specification: Lockheed PV-1 Ventura
Type: twin-engined medium patrol bomber
Crew: five
Powerplant: two 2,000-hp (1591-kW) R-2800-31 radial pistons
Dimensions: span 35 ft 6 in (19.96 m); length 51 ft 9 in (15.8 m); height 11 ft 11 in (3.66 m); wing area 551 sq ft (51.2 m²)
Weights: empty 20 197 lb (9161 kg); max. take-off 34,000 lb (15422 kg)
Performance: max speed 322 mph (518 km/h); service ceiling 26,300 ft (8016 m); range over 1,660 miles (2671 km)
Armament: seven 0.50-in (12.7-mm) and two 0.30-in (7.7-mm) machine-guns; bomb load up to 3,000 lb (1361 kg)

Grumman TBF/TBM Avenger

The Grumman Avenger came about from a 1939 US Navy request for a fast modern replacement for the Douglas TBD Devastator. Grumman came up with the **XTBF-1**, which first flew on 7 August 1941 and was not unlike an enlarged F4F Wildcat fighter. An elongated canopy enclosed the pilot and a radio operator, who also manned the spherical rotating turret. The bomb-aimer manned the ventral 'tunnel' gun in defensive combat. Below the mid-set wing was a large shallow bomb bay that could carry a Mk 13 torpedo or four 500-lb (227-kg) bombs. The wing itself folded back against the fuselage using Grumman's patented system. A basic sea-search radar set was fitted. A contract for 286 aircraft was issued in April 1940, before the prototype flew.

Deliveries of the **TBF-1**, named Avenger after Pearl Harbor, began in January 1942. The Avenger's combat debut was at the Battle of Midway when five of six TBFs flying from Midway Island were shot down without damaging the Japanese carriers. The **TBF-1C** added two 0.50-in (12.7-mm) guns in the wings. TBF production continued up to December 1943 with 2,921 built. Subvariants included the **TBF-1D** with a radar pod on the starboard wing.

The Fleet Air Arm took delivery of nearly 1,000 Avengers (initially named Tarpon) from mid-1943. They were particularly effective in the ASW role. The RNZAF had 48 TBF-1s and -1Cs, using the latter from Bougainville to attack Japanese island bases.

The Avenger served for many years after the war. The Royal Canadian Navy briefly flew the TBM-3S from HMCS Magnificent. (The Aviation Picture Library)

To meet demand, General Motors' Eastern Aircraft Division was contracted to build the Avenger, initially as the **TBM-1**. The vast majority of Avengers were TBMs, 2,882 of them TBM-1s and 4,664 **TBM-3s**, which had the more powerful R-2600-20 engine, revised cowl flaps and rocket and drop-tank capability. Most were reduced-weight **TBM-3Es**. After its inauspicious debut, the Avenger went on to participate in all major US naval actions of the war, from land and sea. Among the major warships sunk with the help of Avengers were the carriers *Ryujo* and *Zuikaku*, and the battleships *Musashi* and *Yamato*.

Variants included the utility transport **TBM-3U** and seven-seat **TBM-3R** and the **TBM-3S** and **TBM-3S2** with searchlight and data link. A major post-war version was the **TBM-3W2** with 'guppy' underfuselage APS-20 radar, exported to the UK, Canada, France and Japan. US Navy Avengers saw some use in Korea and Aéronavale machines participated in the Suez operation. Other post-war users included Brazil, Japan and Uruguay.

After a disastrous combat debut the Avenger went on to be an extremely effective bomber and torpedo-bomber. (The Aviation Picture Library)

Specification: Grumman TBF-1 Avenger
Type: single-engined naval torpedo-bomber
Powerplant: one 1,700-hp (1268-kW) R-2600-8 Wright Cyclone 14-cylinder radial piston
Crew: three
Dimensions: span 54 ft 2 in (16.51 m); length 40 ft (12.2 m); height 16 ft 5 in (5.0 m) wing area 490 sq ft (45.52 m²)
Weights: empty 10,555 lb (4788 kg); max. take-off 17,364 lb (7876 kg)
Performance: max. speed 271 mph (436 km/h); service ceiling 22,400 ft (6830 km); range 1,105 miles (1778 km)
Armament: two 0.30-in (7.62-mm) and one 0.50-in (12.7-mm) machine- guns; bomb load up to 2,000 lb (908 kg)

SAAB B 17

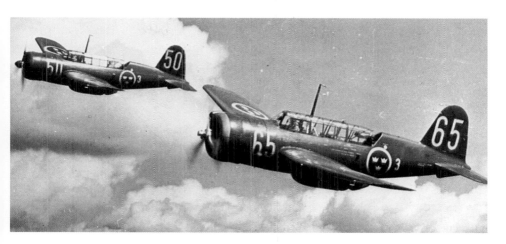

In 1938 the Swedish aero industry embarked on the design of an all-metal reconnaissance aircraft to replace elderly Fokker C.Vs. With little experience of metal fabrication, a large group of American technicians was hired. The resulting design had much in common with contemporary Curtiss designs, although it was a little smaller than the similar-looking SB2C Helldiver. The requirement evolved to include dive-bombing as well as reconnaissance and the SAAB **B 17** appeared in several variants. The prototype flew on 18 May 1942 and was powered by an 880-hp (656-6W) Bristol Mercury XII radial. It featured an elongated framed cockpit enclosure and a mid-mounted wing. The undercarriage doors were curved fairings, and by lowering the gear in flight, they acted as effective airbrakes for dive-bombing. The first production model was the **B 17B I**, of which 54 were made for the Swedish Air Force (Flygvapnet). The B 17B could carry a 1,102-lb (500-kg) bomb under the fuselage, which swung down on a cradle to clear the propeller, and could also carry bombs under the wings. The **B 17B II** was equipped for level bombing with an internal bomb bay.

In 1945 44 B 17Bs were converted to reconnaissance **S 17BLs** and a further 21 were built to this standard. The **S 17BS** was a floatplane version

Ethiopia was the only military customer for the B 17. One of the first batch delivered in 1947 is seen in Sweden before delivery. (Philip Jarrett collection)

The B 17 was SAAB's first aircraft. It was built in reasonable quantities with three different engines. (Philip Jarrett collection)

of which 56 were built new and 18 were converted from S 17BLs. The B 17 had been intended to use Pratt & Whitney Twin Wasp engines, but the outbreak of war had made these unavailable. The B 17Bs had licence-built Bristol Mercuries, whereas the 77 **B 17C** level bombers used 1,040-hp (776-kW) Piaggio P XI bis RC 40D engines.

In late 1942, the **B 17A** appeared, fitted with reverse-engineered 1,065-hp (794-kW) Twin Wasps. Sweden paid Pratt & Whitney a licence fee for these engines after the war. There were 132 of this model, equivalent to the B 17B II, although faster, with a longer range and with a higher altitude capability. The B 17 could be operated on skis in the winter. A retractable ski installation was designed that imparted less drag than the wheeled version and improved performance slightly.

Swedish B 17s saw no combat in World War II. A Swedish-based Danish volunteer unit was armed and ready to enforce the German surrender in May 1945 but was not called into action. Swedish B 17s were retired in 1949, but some served as target tugs and jamming aircraft with private companies until the 1960s. Ethiopia was sold batches of B 17As in 1947 and 1953, a total of 46. Some of these reliable aircraft were still in service as late as the mid-1970s.

Specification: SAAB B 17B I
Type: single-engined dive-bomber
Crew: two
Powerplant: one 980-hp (731-kW) Nohab (Bristol) Mercury XXIV radial piston
Dimensions: span 44 ft 10 in (13.7 m); length 32 ft 3 in (9.8 m); height 13 ft 2 in (4.0 m); wing area 307 sq ft (28.5 m²)
Weights: empty 5,809 lb (2635 kg); max. take-off 8,520 lb (3865 kg)
Performance: max. speed 245 mph (395 km/h); service ceiling 26,247 ft (8000 m); range 870 miles (1400 km)
Armament: bomb load up to 1,543 lb (700 kg)

Douglas A-26/B-26 Invader

Douglas created the **A-26 Invader** as a private venture replacement for its own A-20 and the B-25 and B-26 medium bombers. Preliminary work began in 1940, before these aircraft had even entered service. Generally speaking, the A-26 was an improved A-20 with more power, better streamlining and heavier armament. Two separate versions were designed by Ed Heinemann and his team, a three-man light bomber with a glass nose and a solid-nose night-fighter. After government-induced delays, these appeared as the **A-26C** bomber and the **A-26B** ground attack fighter, with the first flight of the **XA-26** on 10 July 1942. Production totalled 1,355 Bs and 1,091 Cs.

The Invader was a well-proportioned twin-engined aircraft with shoulder-mounted wings and a single tail fin. It was equipped with a pair of powerful Pratt & Whitney R-2800 18-cylinder radials. The pilots of the A-26C had a clamshell cockpit cover and on the B and C a centrally located gunner controlled low-profile dorsal and ventral gun turrets. Up to eight guns could be carried in the nose of the A-26B, supplemented by four 'package' guns mounted on the fuselage sides.

The USAAF 9th and 12th Air Forces received Invaders in September 1944. They flew over 11,500 sorties in Europe before war's end. In the Pacific, one bomb group on Okinawa was equipped from early 1945. Redesignated as the **B-26** (B and C), Invaders of the 8th Bomb Squadron dropped the first and last US bombs of the Korean War. In between they flew over 50,000 sorties, 80 per cent of them at night.

The Invader was an extremely well armed light bomber. This is a Long Beach-built A-26B with a six-gun nose. (The Aviation Picture Library)

US Navy utility squadrons used 33 **JD-1**s, built for the RAF as **Invader I**s in 1945 but not delivered. Surplus Invaders were widely exported, particularly to Latin America. Users included Brazil, Chile, Colombia, Dominican Republic, Guatemala, Nicaragua, Peru and Cuba. Cuban (FAR) B-26Cs fought B-26Bs flown by CIA-backed Cuban exiles during the Bay of Pigs débâcle in April 1961. Eight exile B-26s were lost, mainly to T-33s. The loss of the bombers caused the invasion to fail. French Invaders were heavily used in Algeria and Indo-China. B-26s were also supplied to Portugal, Saudi Arabia, Turkey and Indonesia.

The USAF Air Commandos flew Invaders in an 'advisory' role with the South Vietnamese Air Force (VNAF) from 1961. Some were **B-26K Counter Invaders** modified by the On Mark Corporation with tip tanks and rocket stubs for counter insurgency (COIN) work. In one form or another the Invader served with the USAF until 1972. It was the only combat aircraft to serve in World War II, Korea and Vietnam. The B-26 saw combat in numerous other conflicts including Biafra, Angola and the Congo.

French Invaders like this B-26C were heavily used in the colonial wars in Algeria and Indo-China. (Author's collection)

Specification: A-26C Invader
Type: twin-engined medium bomber
Crew: four
Powerplant: two 4,000-hp (2982-kW) Pratt & Whitney R-2800-79 Double Wasp radial pistons
Dimensions: span 70 ft 0 in (21.34 m); length 51 ft 3 in (15.62 m); height 18 ft 3 in (5.56 m); wing area 540 sq ft (50.17 m²)
Weights: empty 22,850 lb (10365 kg); max. take-off 35,000 lb (15876 kg)
Performance: max. speed 373 mph (600 km/h); service ceiling 22,100 ft (6735 m); range 1,400 miles (2253 km)
Armament: six 0.50-in (12.7-mm) machine-guns; up to 4,000 lb (1814 kg) bombs

Boeing B-29 Superfortress

The Superfortress was the largest and most sophisticated bomber of the war. This B-29A has a 20-mm tail cannon. (TRH Pictures)

Work on a long-range pressurised high-altitude bomber began at Boeing before World War II. When the Air Corps issued a specification in January 1940, Boeing quickly responded with its Model 345 design, which was soon ordered as the **XB-29** prototype. By March 1942, before the XB-29's first flight, over 1,500 **B-29**s had been ordered for production in three factories. Eventually, 2,513 of this initial model were built.

The B-29 had a large tubular fuselage with a glazed nose and a large single fin. Only the crew compartments were pressurised, connected by a long tunnel over the bomb bay. The wing was equipped with Fowler flaps to reduce landing speed. The armament consisted of two ventral and two dorsal 0.50-in (12.7-mm) turrets controlled from a central position and a manned tail turret with two machine-guns and a 20-mm cannon. Later B-29s had a four-gun upper forward turret and deleted the 20-mm tail gun. Two bomb bays carried up to 20,000 lb (9072 kg).

Engine and other problems delayed the B-29's combat debut from Indian bases until May 1944.

When Pacific island bases were captured by the Marines, B-29s struck Japanese cities and industry day and night. The modified 'Silverplate' B-29s *Enola Gay* and *Bock's Car* dropped the atomic bombs on

Hiroshima and Nagasaki, bringing the Pacific War to an end. The B-29 provided America's only nuclear delivery capability for several years.

There were 1,119 **B-29A**s built at Renton, Seattle with a different wing structure, and 311 **B-29B**s from Atlanta. Four plants eventually built 3,965 Superfortresses. In Korea, B-29s dropped over 167,000 tons of bombs, including large TARZON and RAZON-guided weapons against bridges. Some 34 were lost in combat, 16 to MiG fighters. **KB-29M** and **KB-29P**s became some of Strategic Air Command's first airborne tankers.

Interned B-29s were copied by the Soviet Union as the **Tu-4 'Bull'**, which became the USSR's first nuclear-capable bomber. China was given a number of these, some of which were later converted to turboprop power. At least one served into the 1990s as an AWACS test-bed. The RAF operated 87 B-29s on loan as the **Washington I** from 1950–55 while they waited for the Canberra to become available. The B-29 was later developed into the post-war **B-50** with many improvements, including a much taller fin and, on later models, auxiliary jet engines. Variants included the **B-50A** and several **KB-50** tankers.

The B-29 had a notable post-war career. This one sports the post-1947 national insignia and 'buzz number'. (The Aviation Picture Library)

Specification: B-29 Superfortress
Type: four-engined strategic bomber
Crew: 11
Powerplant: four 2,200-hp (1641-kW) Wright R-3350-23 Duplex Cyclone 18-cylinder radial pistons
Dimensions: span 141 ft 3 in (43.05 m); length 99 ft 0 in (30.18 m); height 29 ft 7 in (9.02 m); wing area 1,736 sq ft (161.27 m²)
Weights: empty 70,140 lb (31815 kg); max. take-off 124,000 lb (56245 kg)
Performance: max. speed 358 mph (576 km/h); service ceiling 31,850 ft (9710 m); range 3,250 miles (5230 km)
Armament: 10–12 0.50-in (12.7-mm) machine-guns; bomb load 20,000 lb (9072 kg)

Mitsubishi Ki-67 Hiryu 'Peggy'

Mitsubishi Ki-67 Hiryu. (D I Windle)

Anticipating a possible future war with the USSR, in 1940 the Imperial Japanese Army issued a specification for a heavy bomber, and in early 1941 Mitsubishi was directed to build three prototypes of the **Ki-67 Hiryu** (Flying Dragon), of which the first flew on 27 December 1942. The engines were a pair of Mitsubishi Ha-104 18-cylinder radials, which were used on all but a few later test aircraft.

In December 1943, the new design was ordered after successful testing but prolonged indecisiveness by the Army general staff as the **Army Type 4 Heavy Bomber Model 1** or **Ki-67-I**. The Hiryu was only a heavy bomber by Japanese standards, being similar in size and weight to Allied medium bombers. In general, the Ki-67 looked like a slimmer version of the G4M 'Betty', with a very similar tail fin and an elongated glazed nose-section. At the rear of the deeper centre fuselage was a turret with limited traverse.

Even the first prototypes were well armed in Japanese bomber terms, with single 0.312-in (7.92-mm) machine-guns in the nose and beam positions and single 0.50-in (12.7-mm) guns in the dorsal and tail turrets. Early production aircraft had 12.7-mm guns in the nose and tail and a 20-mm cannon in the tail turret. From the 20th Ki-67, all guns except the tail cannon were 12.7-mm calibre. After 450 aircraft, firepower was increased again, slightly, with twin 12.7mm guns in the tail and a 20-mm in the dorsal position.

Other than these armament variations, there were only two designated variants completed, the **Ki-67-KAI** and the **Ki-109**. The former were aircraft converted for kamikaze attacks with a three-man crew. Turrets were faired over and the fuselage packed with 6,393 lb (2900 <g) of explosives. A long detonating rod projected out from the nose. The effectiveness of this conversion is unknown. There were several projected escort fighter versions, but only the Ki-109 heavy fighter actually entered production. Twenty-two were built with a 75-mm Type 88 anti-aircraft cannon projecting from a solid nose. The only other weapon was the tail gun.

The first combat use of the 'Peggy', as it was known to the Allies, occurred in the torpedo-carrying role off Taiwan in 1944, damaging two US cruisers. In the bomber role, Ki-67s carried out many attacks on US B-29 bases on Iwo Jima and other Marianas airfields. The Hiryu was designed for modular construction and was built at three Mitsubishi plants and by two subcontractors. In all, only 698 were built, production being hampered by Allied bombing and an earthquake in December 1944.

The 'Peggy' was the most modern Japanese bomber. This one served with the 7th Sentai at Obihiro on Hokkaido. (Philip Jarrett collection)

Specification: Mitsubishi Ki-67-I
Type: twin-engined heavy bomber
Crew: six
Powerplant: two 1,900-hp (1417-kW) Mitsubishi Ha-104 18-cylinder radial pistons
Dimensions: span 73 ft 10 in (22.50 m); length 61 ft 4.25 in (18.70 m); height 25 ft 3 in (7.70 m); wing area 709 sq ft (65.9 m²)
Weights: empty 19,070 lb (8650 kg); max. take-off 30,347 lb (13765 kg)
Performance: max. speed 334 mph (537 km/h); service ceiling 31,070 ft (9470 m); range 2,361 miles (3800 km)
Armament: five 0.50-in (12.7-mm) machine-guns and one 20-mm cannon; bomb load up to 1,764 lb (800 kg) or one torpedo

Arado Ar 234 'Blitz'

The Arado 234 was the first jet bomber to see action, although it was designed as a reconnaissance platform and saw its most useful service in that role. Arado's designers Walter Blume and Hans Rebeski began work on a fast reconnaissance aircraft as early as 1940 and the **Arado 234 V1** first flew on 15 June 1943. The Ar 234, 'Blitz' (Lightning) had a narrow fuselage, high-mounted wings and underslung Jumo 004B-0 turbojets.

The prototypes and the early production **Ar 234A** aircraft had no undercarriage in order to save weight. They took off on a wheeled trolley, which was left behind on the ground, and landed on a retractable skid. The pilot sat on an ejector seat (the first fitted in a bomber) in a pressurised cockpit. He had a good forward view from the glazed nose. A prominent periscope fitting gave the only aft view.

Following the D-Day landings, the Ar 234 V5 and V7 were dispatched to France to give the Germans a much-needed view of Normandy. After many delays, the Ar 234 made its first operational flight on 2 August 1944, undetected by Allied forces.

The **Ar 234B** was the main production version, and had a traditional retracting undercarriage in a slightly wider fuselage. Approximately 230 were built, although far fewer reached the front line because of

The Ar 234C was a four-engined development with redesigned glazing and a bomb sight window fitted under the nose. (TRH Pictures)

The Arado 234B (a captured example is shown) was the world's first jet bomber in service, although initially used for reconnaissance. (TRH Pictures)

Allied bombing. The 20 pre-production **Ar 234B-0**s were mainly used for test purposes. Next was the **Ar 234B-1** reconnaissance platform. The **Ar 234B-2** was optimised for bombing and path-finding, with a secondary reconnaissance role.

The first bombing missions took place on Christmas Eve 1944 when small groups from KG 76 flew twice against rail and industrial targets in Liege. After that they mainly flew nuisance raids until they took part in Operation *Baseplate* against Allied airfields. In early March 1945, the Arados of KG 76 flew numerous sorties against the Remargen bridge, making both low- and high-level attacks with bombs of up to 3,036 lb (1800 kg). Several were lost to Allied fighters, but the bridge was not destroyed (although it collapsed later). Some 37 sorties were flown against British forces dug in near Cleve on 21 February 1945 in the heaviest attacks mounted by the Arados during the war. Disruption to fuel supplies prevented much operation after this date.

The **Ar 234C** was a four-engined version, powered by BMW 109-003A-1 turbojets giving 1,764 lb (7.845 kN) thrust each in paired nacelles. Only about 14 **Ar 234C-1**s and C2s were produced.

Specification: Arado 234B-1
Type: twin-engined jet bomber/recon. aircraft
Crew: one
Powerplant: two 1,962-lb (9.1-kN) thrust Junkers Jumo 004B turbojets
Dimensions: span 46 ft 3.5 in (14.10 m); length 41 ft 5.5 in (12.64 m); height 14 ft 1.5 in (4.30 m); wing area 284.18 sq ft (26.40 m²)
Weights: empty 11,464 lb (5200 kg); max. take-off 21,715 lb (9850 kg)
Performance: max. speed 460 mph (740 km/h); service ceiling 32,810 ft (10000 m); range 1,013 miles (1630 km)
Armament: bomb load up to 4,409 lb (2000 kg)

Avro Lincoln

United Kingdom
June 1944

The **Avro Lincoln B I** was originally known as the **Lancaster B IV,** and that appellation describes how it came into being. In fact, the prototype was a conversion of a standard Lancaster III, first flying on 9 June 1944. Despite this, the production Lincoln was a mostly new aircraft and boasted a new nose-section, a stretched rear fuselage, slightly enlarged rudders with larger trim tabs, a new and larger outer wing and the more powerful Merlin 68 engines in new cylindrical-section nacelles. The armament was increased to twin 0.50-in (12.7-mm) machine-guns in three turrets. A new angular bomb-aimer's position somewhat spoiled the handsome looks inherited from the Lancaster.

The **Lincoln B II** (designed as the Lancaster V) had Packard-built Merlins and a new ventral gun turret housing two 0.50-in (12.7-mm) guns. The dorsal turret had a pair of 20-mm cannon. Subvariants were the **B II (IIIG)** and **B II (IVA)** with different versions of H2S ground-mapping radar. The **B IV** had Merlin 85s.

Several squadrons used Lincolns for electronic intelligence gathering (ELINT) missions and (briefly) for monitoring Soviet nuclear test emissions. One Lincoln was shot down over the Berlin corridor by Soviet MiG-15s in 1957. Lincolns were widely based in the Middle and Far East, with detachments sent to hot spots as needed, such as South Arabia (Yemen) in 1947 and Oman in 1955. During the Mau Mau uprising in Kenya of 1952–6, five squadrons of Lincolns were rotated through Eastleigh (Nairobi). Between November 1953 and April 1955 they used 500-lb (227-kg) and 1,000-lb

This view of a Lincoln Mk I clearly shows its Lancaster heritage, but also its increased length, longer nose and new nacelles. (TRH Pictures)

(454-kg) bombs and 350-lb (159-kg) cluster bombs on rebel concentrations and mountain hideouts.

The Lincoln's main period of action was in Malaya from 1948 to 1958 against communist terrorist (CT) groups. Initially rotating detachments of RAF Lincolns were sent to Singapore, but from 1950 No. 1 Squadron RAAF was permanently based at Tengah. The bombers expended many tons of bombs on jungle areas, often in combined strikes with fighter-bombers and ground forces.

Australia's Government Aircraft Factory (GAF) built 73 Lincolns, most as **Mk 30** bombers and 12 (plus eight conversions) as **GR.Mk 31** anti-submarine variants from 1946 to 1953. The fleet was grounded in 1961 when extensive corrosion was discovered. The Mk 31 had an elongated nose. Argentina used Lincolns from 1947 to 1967. One unusual use was for polar survey flights from 1951. In 1955 Argentine Lincolns were flown as a show of force during the Navy-led coup that ousted Juan Péron, although they are not thought to have dropped bombs. The last RAF Lincolns were retired in 1963.

A small number of Lincoln B IIs were converted to the unarmed R.I electronic intelligence model, which gathered Soviet radar and radio signals. (TRH Pictures)

Specification: Avro Lincoln B II
Type: four-engined heavy bomber
Crew: seven
Powerplant: four 1,750-hp (1306-kW) Packard Merlin 85 V-12 pistons
Dimensions: span 120 ft (36.57 m); length 78 ft 3.5 in (23.90 m); height 17 ft 3.5 in (5.27 m); wing area 1,421 sq ft (132.0 m²)
Weights: empty 43,400 lb (19686 kg); max. take-off 75,000 lb (34019 kg)
Performance: max. speed 295 mph (475 km/h); service ceiling 30,500 ft (9295 m); range 3,555 miles (5760 km)
Armament: six 0.50 in (12.7 mm) machine-guns and two 20-mm cannon; bomb load up to 14,000 lb (6350 kg)

Douglas AD/A-1 Skyraider

Designed as a replacement for the Avenger and the Dauntless in the torpedo and dive-bomber roles, the Skyraider began its life as the Douglas XBT2D-1 Destroyer II, which first flew on 18 March 1945. The first order, for 548 aircraft (now called the **AD-1 Skyraider**), was made in April. Unlike many of its contemporaries, the orders were not cut back when World War II ended. Ed Heinemann and his design team emphasised simplicity, weight reduction and carrying ability. Fifteen wing pylons could carry 8,000 lb (3629 kg) of bombs, torpedoes, mines or rockets. The AD (or 'Able Dog') was even given a 'one-way' nuclear delivery role. Up to 3,000 lb (1361 kg) of fuel in external tanks increased the AD's already long endurance. The engine was the powerful R-3350.

Carrier suitability trials were completed in 1946 and the AD entered service with VA-19A at Alameda in December 1946. Like the Avenger, the Skyraider was adaptable to many roles such as AEW and electronic countermeasures (ECM). Variants for these tasks such as the **AD-3W** and **AD-1Q** were quickly tested and interspersed into production. Structurally strengthened **AD-2** and **AD-3** variants were soon being turned out and later the adaptable **AD-5** with side-by-side seating, which could quickly be converted to different tasks. The Marine Corps received the AD

The Skyraider remained an effective attack aircraft until the late 1960s. This A-1J served on the USS Oriskany.
(TRH Pictures)

In 1947 the equipment of US carriers was still piston-powered. This AD-1 and F8F-1 were in the USS Boxer air group. (The Aviation Picture Library)

in 1951 and operated 15 regular squadrons of Skyraiders until 1958. The **AD-4** was an AD-3 with radar and a new autopilot. Many were 'winterised' as the **AD-4L** and others became AEW **AD-4W**s, some supplied to the Royal Navy. The **AD-6** and strengthened **AD-7** were optimised for low-level use.

During the Korean War the AD was used for close air support (CAS), minelaying and as a torpedo-bomber during the epic attack on the Hwachon Dam. Dropping bombs in the mouths of North Korean railway tunnels was another speciality.

By 1964, when US naval air power was first used in Vietnam, 200 **A-1**s (as they were known after 1962) were still in Navy service. Flying mainly from smaller 'Midway'-class carriers, they flew attack, CAS and rescue combat air patrols. Two MiG-17s even fell to the 20-mm guns of Skyraiders. Retired by the USN in 1968, many **A-1E**s and **A-1J**s were then transferred to the USAF, and later to the VNAF. Under the 1962 system, the AD-4 became the **A-1D**, the AD-5 the **A-1E**, the AD-6 the **A-1H**, and the AD-7, the A-1J.

A total of 3,180 Skyraiders were built. In addition to the USN and USMC, they served with the UK and France, South Vietnam, Cambodia, Chad and Gabon.

Specification: Douglas AD-2 Skyraider
Type: single-engined naval attack aircraft
Crew: one
Powerplant: one 2,700-hp (2013-kW) Wright R-3350-26WA 18-cylinder radial piston
Dimensions: span 50 ft (15.24 m); length 38 ft 2 in (11.58 m); height 15 ft 5 in (4.69 m); wing area 400.33 sq ft (37.2 m²)
Weights: empty 10,546 lb (4743 kg); max. take-off 18,263 lb (8284 kg)
Performance: max. speed 321 mph (516 km/h); service ceiling 32,700 ft (9967 m); range 915 miles (1473 km/h)
Armament: two 20-mm cannon; bomb load up to 8,000 lb (3629 kg)

Convair B-36 Peacemaker

Plans for an intercontinental bomber able to strike European targets from the USA were studied as early as the beginning of 1941 when it was thought possible that the UK might be invaded with the loss of potential US bases. A contract for two **XB-36** prototypes was issued to Consolidated Aircraft in November 1941. Consolidated became Consolidated-Vultee in 1943 and (officially) Convair in 1954. A hundred **B-36 Peacemakers** were ordered, but engine and labour difficulties and priority given to other projects delayed the first flight to 8 September 1945.

The XB-36 was the largest and heaviest landplane built up to that time. Its moderately swept wing mounted six Pratt & Whitney R-4360 engines facing backwards in pusher configuration. The undercarriage featured massive 110-in (2.8-m) diameter mainwheels. These were later replaced by four-wheel bogies. With other changes, the prototype became the **YB-36A**. Twenty-two initial production **B-36A**s were completed, mostly without armament, in 1948/9. Later they were armed and fitted with cameras as the **RB-36E**. The B-36 was very controversial at the time because of its performance shortfalls and the Navy's desire to take on the strategic attack role with a new class of supercarriers. The **B-36B** was the first fully capable production version, with a full complement of no fewer than 14 20-mm cannon in six remotely operated retractable turrets and nose and tail turrets.

The **B-36D** introduced paired J-47 jet pods on each

The B-36D was the first Peacemaker to have auxiliary jets. The sight and sound of these 10-engined monsters will never be forgotten by those who saw them. (TRH Pictures)

wing, for a total of 'six turning and four burning'. This increased speed and reduced take-off length. The bomb load was up to 86,000 lb (39010 kg), sometimes consisting of two 42,000-lb (19051-kg) Grand Slam bombs. Eighty were built or converted from B-36Bs. The **RB-36D** could carry up to 23 cameras. The 34 **B-36F**s had better radar and higher-output R-4360s. The major production version was the **B-36H** (83 built), with a revised interior and new gunnery radar. The reconnaissance equivalent was the **RB-36H** (73 built). The **B-36J** had more fuel and higher gross weight. The last 14 of 33 Js were called 'featherweights' with reduced armament and crew.

A single **XC-99** transport with an entirely new fuselage was built. The **NB-36H** carried an operating nuclear reactor although the reactor did not run any systems. Several experimental programmes tested the 'parasite fighter' concept, including Project 'Tom Tom' with an RB-36H and wingtip RF-84Fs, the XF-85 Goblin project and the FICON (FIghter CONveyer), which married **GRB-36D**s with an RF-84K on a bomb-bay trapeze. This actually saw service during 1955.

The last B-36Js were retired in February 1959.

The XB-36 looked somewhat different to production aircraft, having no armament and a different nose. (The Aviation Picture Library)

Specification: Convair B-36H
Type: 10-engined strategic bomber
Crew: 15
Powerplant: six 3,800-hp (2834-kW) Pratt & Whitney R-4360-53 radials and four 5,200-lb (24.1-kN) thrust GE J47-GE-19 turbojets
Dimensions: span 230 ft 0 in (70.1 m); length 162 ft 1 in (49.4 m); height 46 ft 8 in (14.2 m); wing area 4,772 sq ft (443 m²)
Weights: empty 168,487 lb (76425 kg); max. take-off 370,000 lb (16832 kg)
Performance: max. speed 439 mph (706.5 km); service ceiling 44,000 ft (13411 m); range 6,226 miles (10020 km)
Armament: 12 20-mm M24A1 cannon; bomb load up to 86,000 lb (39010 kg)

Republic F-84 Thunderjet/streak

The F-84E Thunderjet served initially as a fighter, but in Korea was mainly used for ground attack because of its toughness. (The Aviation Picture Library)

Republic Aircraft began studies for a jet replacement for the P-47 Thunderbolt in 1944. After rejecting a simple conversion to jet power they began again with an all-new design featuring a low-set laminar flow wing with tip tanks and an axial flow engine fed from a nose intake.

The USAF ordered three prototypes and 400 production aircraft in March 1945, but suspended them at the end of World War II. In January 1946 they were partly reinstated with orders for 15 test and 85 production models. The prototype **XP-84 Thunderjet** flew on 28 February 1946 with a 4,000-lb (18.6-kN) thrust Allison J35, followed by the 15 **YP-84As**. The production model **P-84B** (redesignated **F-84B** in June 1948) had an ejector seat and six improved M3 0.50-in (12.7-mm) machine-guns. A further 141 P-84Bs were ordered with retractable rocket racks. The **P-84C** (**F-84C**) had revised fuel and electrical systems and the Allison J35-A-13C engine. Deliveries totalled 191.

The **F-48D** had a higher thrust J35-A-17D engine and numerous minor improvements. The **F-84E** (543 built) had a slightly longer fuselage, a radar gunsight and JATO (jet-assisted take-off) rockets. The F-84E was the main version in use at the outbreak of the Korean War, and was used initially as an escort fighter. After losing 18 to MiGs (for nine kills) the Thunderjets were assigned ground-attack duties. They were later

The swept-wing F-84F Thunderstreak led to the long-serving RF-84F Thunderflash reconnaissance aircraft seen here. (The Aviation Picture Library)

joined by some of the 3,025 **F-84Gs**, a version usually assigned the nuclear strike role. The F-84G had a refuelling receptacle and a heavily framed canopy. Over 1,900 went to Nato nations as well as Taiwan, Yugoslavia, Iran and Thailand.

A major revision of the series came with the **F-84F Thunderstreak**, which had wings set at 38.5 degrees sweep with slight anhedral and swept tail surfaces. First flying on 3 June 1950, the **XF-84F** was a converted F-84E. Production models had the Curtiss-Wright J65, a licence-built Armstrong-Siddeley Sapphire rated at 7,200 lb (33.4 kN) thrust, requiring a deeper fuselage and an elliptical intake. Production F-84Fs had a canopy that raised on a pivoting arm, a raised spine and side-mounted speed-brakes. Over 2,700 F-84Fs were produced and they served with both Tactical and Strategic Air Commands.

F-84Fs served until 1971 with the Air National Guard, but longer with some Nato nations. Non-Nato member France used F-84Fs in action at Suez in 1956. The **RF-84F Thunderflash** was an important reconnaissance version with a camera nose and wingroot-mounted intakes. There were 715 RF-84Fs, serving with the USAF from 1954. Over half went to the Nato F-84F users and France, and also to Denmark. The last were retired in the 1970s.

Specification: F-84F Thunderstreak
Type: single-engined fighter-bomber
Crew: one
Powerplant: one 7,220-lb (33.5-kN) thrust Curtiss Wright J65-W-3 turbojet
Dimensions: span 33 ft 7 in (10.3 m); length 43 ft 5 in (13.29 m); height 14 ft 3 in (4.42 m); wing area 325 sq ft (30.2 m²)
Weights: empty 14,014 lb (6357 kg); max. take-off 28,000 lb (12,701 kg)
Performance: max. speed 695 mph (1118 km/h); service ceiling 46,000 ft (14021 m); range 2,140 miles (3444 km)
Armament: six 0.50-in (12.7-mm) Browning M2 machine-guns; ordnance load up to 6,000 lb (2722 kg)

Boeing B-47 Stratojet

In 1944 the USAF asked major airframe manufacturers to submit concepts for a multi-engined bomber. Boeing initially responded with a design akin to a jet B-29, but the analysis of German wartime research led to the abandonment of the straight wing in September 1945 and the adoption of a 35-degree swept wing. This was mounted high on the fuselage and the main undercarriage was installed in a bicycle arrangement in the fuselage. Outrigger wheels were fitted on the inboard engine pods, which contained two engines. The outer pods contained a single engine each. Locating the engines correctly along the span to prevent wing twisting was a major task for the designers. After inspection of Boeing's mock-up, a contract was awarded in April 1946.

The prototype **XB-47 Stratojet** flew on 17 December 1947 with six Allison J35-2 turbojets, soon replaced by more powerful J47-GE-3s. In early models a battery of 18 JATO rockets was installed in the rear fuselage to boost take-off performance, which was marginal under some conditions. It was only used for alerts and for training. All defensive armament except two 0.50-in (12.7-mm) tail machine-guns was dispensed with, as the B-47 was expected to outpace most fighters and would only face rear attacks.

The initial order of 10 **B-47A**s was followed by one for 398 **B-47B**s with more engine power but without ejection seats. Only two **B-47C**s (or **XB-56**s) were produced – and these were modified to **XB-47D**s with two jets and two Wright YT49 turboprops.

The B-47E was the main production Stratojet. This example was later converted to WB-47E weather reconnaissance standard. (TRH Pictures)

The **B-47E** of 1953 had 6,000-lb (26.6-kN) thrust J47-GE-25A engines (which gave 7,200 lb (33.4 kN) thrust on take-off with the use of water injection). Crew ejection seats were returned and the machine-guns were replaced with twin 20-mm cannon. During the production of 1,341 B-47Es there were many improvements and later aircraft had larger bomb loads, but smaller bomb bays owing to the decreasing size of nuclear weapons.

The B-47 formed the backbone of SAC until 1959 when the B-52 began to take over. With relatively short range, the B-47 was heavily dependent on aerial refuelling and in order to meet its needs, Boeing developed the KC-135, which led to the 707 airliner.

Numerous reconnaissance and electronic warfare variants were created, including the **RB-47B**, **RB-47E**, **RB-47K**, **RB-47H** and **EB-47E**. The B-47 never saw action as a bomber, but several **RB-47**s were shot down by communist fighters in encounters near the Soviet Union and North Korea. Between 1947 and 1956, a total of 2,032 B-47s were built, 1,373 by Boeing, 274 by Douglas and 385 by Lockheed.

The RB-47E reconnaissance version had a longer nose containing large cameras. 51-5259 seen here was the second production RB-47. (Boeing)

Specification: B-47E Stratojet
Type: six-engined strategic bomber
Crew: three
Powerplant: six 7,200-lb (33.4-kN) thrust General Electric J47-GE-25A turbojets with water injection
Dimensions: span 116 ft 0 in (35.35 m); length 109 ft 10 in (33.49 m); height 17 ft 11 in (8.50 m); wing area 1,428 sq ft (435 m²)
Weights: empty 80,000 lb (36287 kg); max. take-off 175,000 lb (79378 kg)
Performance: max. speed 630 mph (1013 km/h); service ceiling 40,500 ft (12344 m); range 1,600 miles (2574 km)
Armament: two 20-mm cannon; maximum bomb load of 20,000 lb (9071 kg)

Ilyushin Il-28 'Beagle'

USSR
July 1948

Design work on a jet bomber for the Soviet Air Force began as a private venture at the Ilyushin design bureau in 1947. The Il-24 design was hampered by the lack of a suitable engine, but when Rolls-Royce Nenes were supplied by the UK, the design was revised to accommodate them. The prototype **Il-28** first flew on 8 July 1948 with Nenes. Series aircraft used the local copy, the Klimov VK-1.

The Il-28 had a conventional layout with high wings featuring straight leading edges and a slightly tapered trailing edge. The swept tailplane ensured pitch control in high-speed dives. At the rear of the circular-section fuselage was a tail-gunner's position with two NR-23 cannon. The 'glasshouse' nose compartment contained the navigator/bomb-aimer and a visual bomb-sight. A fixed pair of NR-23s were fitted in the nose and the bomb load was carried internally.

The Il-28 entered Soviet service in 1950 as a low/medium-altitude day bomber and was given the Nato code-name 'Beagle'. It soon formed the backbone of the USSR's bomber forces. Export customers included Afghanistan, China, Czechoslovakia, Egypt, Hungary, Indonesia, North Korea, North Vietnam and Poland.

The threat of Il-28 attacks was enough to justify the deployment of many USAF interceptors to Vietnam,

The H-5 still serves in significant numbers (over 600) in China. A few may remain in use in Romania. (Via Robert Hewson)

The Il-28 was the Eastern Bloc's equivalent of the Canberra. It was one of the most numerous jet aircraft ever produced. (Philip Jarrett collection)

although – as in Korea – no attacks were ever recorded by them. Similar situations where the threat from a handful of 'Beagles' was overstated occurred in Korea, Indonesia, Cuba and Africa.

Export Il-28s fought in the 1956, 1967 and 1973 Arab–Israeli wars and in Yemen in 1962 and Nigeria/Biafra. Generally speaking, they suffered minimal losses in action. In Afghanistan the tailguns were used to suppress Mujahideen fire as the bomber left the target. The Il-28 had the lowest loss rate of any tactical type used in the war. Soviet Il-28s were retired in the 1980s, the last serving as target tugs and ECM platforms. Target-towing versions were also flown by East Germany and Finland. Finnish aircraft also carried reconnaissance cameras.

The **Il-28T** torpedo-bomber for the Navy could carry two 21-in (533-mm) torpedoes. The **Il-28R** introduced wingtip fuel tanks, which were not fitted if a full bomb load was carried. The trainer version with a raised instructor's cockpit was the **Il-28U 'Mascot'**.

Large-scale production in China as the **Harbin H-5** (or **Hong-5**) contributed to the impressive total of about 6,000 Il-28 derivatives built. H-5s were used by a number of nations including North Korea and Albania.

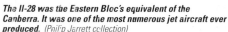

Specification: Il-28 'Beagle'
Type: twin-engined light bomber
Crew: three
Powerplant: two 5,952-lb (24.5-kN) thrust VK-1A turbojets
Dimensions: span 70 ft 4.5 in (21.45 m); length 57 ft 11 in (17.65 m); height 22 ft (6.70 m); wing area 654.5 sq ft (60.8 m²)
Weights: empty 28,417 lb (12890 kg); max. take-off 46,737 lb (21200 kg)
Performance: max. speed 560 mph (902 km/h); service ceiling 40,350 ft (13000 m); range 1,335 miles (2180 km)
Armament: four NR-23 23-mm cannon; bomb load up to 6,614 lb (3000 kg)

English Electric Canberra

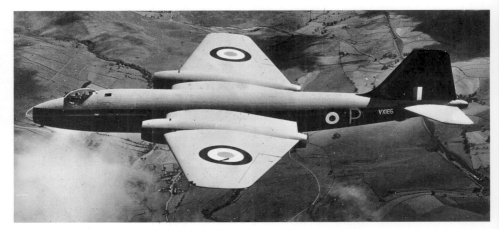

The Canberra was the most successful British jet bomber and was widely exported, seeing action in many conflicts. In 1945 the first specification was issued for a British jet bomber. English Electric, a company then only known as a subcontractor with little design experience, was chosen to produce four prototypes by the end of 1949. 'Teddy' Petter and his team produced a quite conventional design with mid-mounted wings and mid-span Avon engines. Defensive armament was omitted in favour of speed and altitude capability. The prototype flew on 13 May 1949, followed by three more **Canberra B.1**s. The production **B.2** model entered service in May 1951, initially in the strategic bombing role pending the arrival of the Valiant. The **B.6** was an improved variant with three ejection seats. Some were converted to an interim interdictor (or intruder) version as the **B(I)6** with a gun pack and rockets. This led to the **B(I)8** with an offset teardrop canopy, to be used in the low-level nuclear strike role. Reconnaissance versions included the **PR.3** and **PR.7**, based on the B.2, and the **PR.9**, based on the B(I)8, with longer span wings. The main trainer model was the **T.4**.

RAF Canberras were based in Britain, Germany, and the Middle East. Cyprus-based B.2s dropped the first bombs (on Egyptian airfields) during the Suez Crisis in 1956 and were joined by B.6s from Malta. One PR.7 was shot down by an Egyptian MiG-17 during the conflict. Export versions were based on either the B.6 or the B(I)8. Customers included Argentina, Chile,

The prototype Canberra differed little in appearance from the bomber and trainer versions that followed. (Author's collection)

New Zealand, Peru, South Africa, Sweden, West Germany, Venezuela, India, the USA, France, Ethiopia and Rhodesia.

Australia's Commonwealth Aircraft Corporation built 48 **B.20**s and **T.21** trainers. They saw action alongside RNZAF **B(I)12**s in Malaya and one RAAF squadron was used in Vietnam. Indian **B(I)58**s were used against Pakistan in 1965 and 1971, with a number lost in action. South African Air Force (SAAF) B(I)12s saw action in the bush wars and conducted South Africa's nuclear weapon test in 1979. Argentine **B.62**s were used against British forces in the Falklands. Two were shot down, one by a Sea Harrier and another by a Sea Dart SAM. India, Chile and Argentina retired their last Canberras in 1999–2001.

Peru still operates some of 35 Canberras and used them against Ecuador in 1995. In all, 1,376 Canberras were built up to 1963, excluding **B-57**s licence-built by Martin in the USA. A small number of **PR.9**s and one T.4 are still in use by the RAF. The PR.9s have been used in many recent conflicts, from the Gulf War to Afghanistan.

The PR.9 reconnaissance model was based on the interdictor versions of the Canberra. A handful are still in RAF service with No. 39 Squadron. (Author)

Specification: Canberra B.2
Type: twin-engined medium bomber
Crew: three
Powerplant: two 6,500-lb (30.1-kN) thrust Rolls-Royce Avon 101 turbojets
Dimensions: span 64 ft 0 in (19.51 m); length 65 ft 6 in (19.96 m); height 15 ft 6 in (4.72 m); wing area 960 sq ft (89.19 m²)
Weights: empty 22,205 lb (10072 kg); max. take-off 46,000 lb (20866 kg)
Performance: max. speed 570 mph (917 km/h); service ceiling 48,000 ft (14630 m); mission radius 1,220 miles (1965 km)
Armament: one nuclear weapon; up to six 1,000-lb (454-kg) bombs

Vickers Valiant

United Kingdom
May 1951

In 1947 the Air Ministry issued a specification for a bomber able to carry a 10,000-lb (4536-kg) bomb at 500 kt (926 km/h) at 50,000 ft (15240 m). This led to the famous V-bombers, the Avro Vulcan, Hardley Page Victor and the Vickers Valiant, which was the first to fly, the first to see action and the first to retire. The Vickers **Type 660** prototype was flown for the first time on 18 May 1951 and was very conventional compared with the Vulcan and Victor, but included the same arrangement of engines buried in the wing roots. The **B.1**, of which there were 35, entered service from June 1954.

To meet the specified secondary reconnaissance role, the **B(PR).1** version (11 built) was developed with eight cameras in the bomb bay. The 14 similar **B(PR)K.1**s could also carry a hose-and-drogue refuelling package. This was also fitted to the definitive bomber/tanker **BK.1**, of which 44 were made. The **B.2** was a strengthened model with a new undercarriage and would have had Conway engines. Built for the low-level target-marking role, only one B.2 was built before cancellation in 1955. A total of 107 Valiants were built including the two prototypes.

The aircraft's weapons capability included a range of nuclear and thermonuclear bombs. There was room in the bomb bay for one 'Blue Danube' or two 'Red

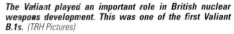

The Valiant played an important role in British nuclear weapons development. This was one of the first Valiant B.1s. (TRH Pictures)

Beard' nuclear weapons, or four US-made B28 or B43 tactical nuclear bombs. The conventional ordnance comprised up to 21 1,000-lb (454-kg) bombs. The Valiant played an important role in the British atomic weapons programme, dropping a live nuclear weapon at Maralinga, Australia, in October 1956, and the UK's first H-bomb at Malden Island on 15 May 1957, followed by others in 1958. The Valiant saw action in Suez in October/November 1956, with aircraft from four squadrons attacking Egyptian airfields for no loss.

It was realised in the early 1960s that the Valiant would be no match for Soviet fighters and SAMs at medium altitudes. The Valiant's role was switched to low-level tactical operations in 1962/3 and the aircraft received tactical camouflage. Training at low level put excess strain on the airframe, and in 1964 several wing spar failures occurred. Inspections showed that the problem was widespread and all Valiants were grounded in December. Too expensive to fix, the Valiant was retired in January 1965, except for a few on test duties. This left the RAF without a tanker aircraft and Victors were hastily modified to fulfil this role. The last Valiant was retired from trials duties with BAC (successor to Vickers) in early 1968.

The bomber/tanker BK.1 was the most numerous version of the Valiant. XD863 is seen in the markings of No. 90 Squadron. (TRH Pictures)

Specification: Valiant B.1
Type: four-engined strategic bomber
Crew: five
Powerplant: four 10,050-lb (46.6-kN) thrust Rolls-Royce Avon Mk 204 turbojets
Dimensions: span 114 ft 4 in (34.85 m); length 108 ft 3 in (33.0 m); height 32 ft 2 in (9.80 m); wing area 2,362 sq ft (219.43 m²)
Weights: empty 75,880 lb (23419 kg); max. take-off 175,000 lb (79330 kg)
Performance: max. speed 567 mph (912 km/h); service ceiling 54,000 ft (16460 m); range 4,500 miles (7240 km)
Armament: up to four thermonuclear weapons or up to 21 1,000-lb (454-kg) bombs

Boeing B-52 Stratofortress

Boeing designed the eight-engined B-52 Stratofortress in 1948 to replace the B-47 in SAC service with a true intercontinental bomber. The **YB-52** flew on 15 April 1952, before the outwardly identical **XB-52**, and incorporated many B-47 features, such as the high-mounted wing and podded engines (in four units of two). The undercarriage was a more complex version of the bicycle layout on the B-47, with outriggers near the wingtips. The maingear could swivel to allow 'crab' landings in high crosswinds. The wings incorporated ailerons, flaps and spoilers, giving better low-speed handling.

The first prototypes had a tandem cockpit arrangement like the B-47, but all later models had a conventional airliner-type cabin. Defensive systems operators sat behind the two pilots and offensive systems operators sat in a lower compartment. The defensive armament was four remotely controlled 0.50-in (12.7-mm) machine-guns. Three **B-52A** test aircraft were followed by 50 production **B-52B**s, 35 **B-52C**s and 170 **B-52D**s with relatively minor changes. The 100 **B-52E**s had upgraded weapons systems and more powerful engines. The **B-52G** (193 built) had a lighter airframe, no ailerons and could carry the AGM-28 Hound Dog missile. The **B-52H** has a cruise missile capability as well as conventional and nuclear bomb capability. The tail armament was a 20-mm cannon, which was removed in the 1990s. New TF-33 turbofans were fitted. The 'BUFF' (Big

Re-engined B-52Hs may still be serving in 2037, when the airframes will be nearing 80 years of age. (Author)

Ugly Fat Fellow) force spent much of the 1960s on 24-hour airborne alert, ready to counter-attack the USSR. The 744th and last was delivered in October 1962.

The first 'Arc Light' combat missions were flown by **B-52F**s against Viet Cong forces in June 1965. During the Linebacker II campaign in December 1972, B-52Ds and Gs were used against strategic North Vietnamese targets. In all, 33 B-52s were lost in the war, 17 of them to SAMs. Over 2.5 million tons of bombs were dropped in the theatre by B-52s.

During the Gulf War, B-52s were used to destroy Iraqi armour concentrations and dropped 29 per cent of all US bombs on Iraq and Kuwait. In Operation *Allied Force* B-52Hs attacked targets in Kosovo.

Most recently, B-52Hs were involved in Afghanistan. Use of new precision weapons allowed the B-52 to be used in the close air support role, a mission unimagined when the bomber was first flown 50 years before. The B-52H is the last version in service, with 94 still operational with Air Combat Command and Air Force Reserve Command.

The B-52 was one of the icons of the Vietnam War. This B-52D was later preserved at Andersen AFB, Guam. (Author's collection)

Specification: B-52H Stratofortress
Type: eight-engined strategic bomber
Crew: usually five
Powerplant: eight 17,000-lb (75.62-kN) thrust Pratt & Whitney TF-33-P-3 turbofans
Dimensions: span 185 ft (56.39 m); length 160 ft 10.9 in (49.05 m); height 40 ft 8 in (12.40 m); wing area 4,000 sq ft (371.6m²)
Weights: empty 184,250 lb (83575 kg); max. take-off 505,000 lb (229088 kg)
Performance: max. speed 509 mph (819 km/h); service ceiling 55,000 ft (16765 m); unrefuelled range 10,130 miles (16302 km)
Armament: one M61A1 20-mm cannon; up to 50,000 lb (22680 kg) of nuclear or conventional ordnance

Tupolev Tu-16 'Badger'

USSR
April 1952

In 1948 the Soviet Government ordered a prototype of a high-speed but relatively short-ranged bomber from Tupolev to replace the Tu-4 'Bull' (an unlicensed B-29 copy). The range and payload specification was similar to the Tu-4. The TU-85 prototype, the USSR's first swept-wing aircraft, first flew in March 1949, but with the success of the Il-28, the design was abandoned in favour of the larger Tu-88 or **'Aircraft N'**, which first flew on 27 April 1952. Later named the **Tu-16** (Nato name **'Badger A'**), this aircraft had a long tubular fuselage, 40-degree wing sweep and two of the new Mikulin AM-3A engines buried in the wingroots. At the tail was a manned two-gun turret with 23-mm AM-23 cannon. Remotely operated dorsal and ventral blister turrets each contained two more cannon. A fixed cannon was fitted in the nose.

Series production began in 1953, and by May 1954 nine of the initial series Tu-16s were available for the May Day flypast. Fifty-five were displayed in August 1955, and 2,000 of all models were eventually completed in Soviet factories. The **Tu-16A** (also **'Badger A'**) could carry a nuclear bomb in its capacious bomb bay. The Tu-16Es were As converted to tanker/bomber configuration with a wingtip-to-wingtip hose refuelling system. The Tu-16M was the

The majority of surviving 'Badgers' are in fact Xian H-6s, many of which remain in use in China as bombers, missile carriers and tankers. (Via Robert Hewson)

The Tu-16K-10 'Badger C' had a duckbill nose containing 'Puff Ball' radar for search and mapping and for missile targeting. (TRH Pictures)

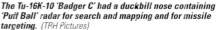

naval maritime strike version. The **Tu-16N** was a probe-and-drogue tanker, mainly used to refuel Tu-22s and Tu-22Ms. The **Tu-16T** could carry anti-shipping missiles, depth-charges or torpedoes. From 1965 these were converted into **Tu-16S** lifeboat carriers.

The **Tu-16K**s were the first strategic missile carriers. The Naval **Tu-16KS 'Badger B'** with a solid nose carried the short-range KS-1 Kometa missile and the **Tu-16K-10 'Badger C'** carried the K-10S (AS-2 'Kipper') anti-ship cruise missile and had a large radome containing 'Puff Ball' radar. The **Tu-16R 'Badger E'** family were reconnaissance variants and the **'Badger G'** or **Tu-16K-11-16** could carry AS-5 'Kelt' or AS-6 'Kingfish' long-range air-to-surface missiles (ASMs) under the wings. The **Tu-16PP 'Badger H'** was an ECM support variant and the **Tu-16P 'Badger J'** a jamming platform.

'Badgers' were supplied to Egypt and Iraq, and saw combat in most of the Middle-East wars. Many were destroyed on the ground by Israel during the Six Day War in 1967 and one was shot down by a Mirage III.

China acquired a licence to build the Tu-16 in 1957, although the first Harbin (later X'ian) H-6 (or B-6) did not fly until December 1968. Variants included the H-6A and H-6A-I bombers and the H-6D missile carrier.

Specification: Xian H-6D

Type: twin-engined heavy bomber
Crew: seven
Powerplant: two 20,944-lb (93.16-kN) thrust Xi'an WP-8 turbojets.
Dimensions: span 112 ft 2 in (34.19 m); length 114 ft 2 in (34.8 m); height 32 ft 4 in (9.85 m); wing area 1,772 sq ft (164.65 m²)
Weights: empty 84,944 lb (38530 kg); max. take-off 167,108 lb (75800 kg)
Performance: max. speed 630 mph (1014 km/h); service ceiling 39,370 ft (12000 m); range 4,475 miles (7200 km)
Armament: seven AM-23 23-mm cannon; bomb load up to 19,841 lb (9000 kg)

Avro Vulcan

United Kingdom
August 1952

To meet the Air Ministry's requirement for a bomber able to carry a 10,000-lb (4536-kg) bomb at 500 kt (926 km/h) at 50,000 ft (15240 m) issued in 1947, Avro drew up a large tailless delta-winged aircraft with engines buried deep in the wingroots. More radical flying-wing designs were considered but rejected. With little data on the low-speed handling of delta wings, two one-third scale models were ordered and the first of these Avro 707s was flown in September 1949, but crashed soon after. The second aircraft, however, contributed greatly to knowledge of deltas and to the design of the **Avro 698** or **Vulcan**.

The Vulcan featured a massive delta wing without flaps, forward of which was the pressure cabin for five crew on three decks. Only the two pilots had ejection seats, the navigator, radar operator and air electronics operator had to escape via a chute and hatch in an emergency. The lower nose contained the large scanner for an H2S radar installation.

On 30 August 1952, the prototype Vulcan flew for the first time. To cure buffeting, a kink was added in the wing leading edge from the sixth aircraft onwards. Deliveries of the **Vulcan B.1** began in September 1956, although the crash of the first aircraft delayed equipment of the first training unit until May 1957.

The much-improved **Vulcan B.2** flew in 1958 with longer-span wings, giving greater maximum take-off weight. The control system was revised to consist of eight elevons, rather than elevators and ailerons, and the intakes were enlarged. Later, ECM equipment was

The last Vulcan squadron was disbanded in March 1984, but one B.2/K.2 was retained as a historic flight aircraft until 1993. (TRH Pictures)

installed in an extended tailcone. Avro also built the Blue Steel missile, first tested in 1960 and intended to be launched over 100 miles (160 km) from the target, climbing to 70,000 ft (21336 m) and accelerating to Mach 2.5. In October 1962 this weapon entered service ard soon equipped five squadrons. Much work was done on its successor, the Anglo-American Mach 9 Skybolt, before it was cancelled in 1962.

The **B.2A** designation marked those aircraft with the Olympus 201 engine. The **B.2MRR** was a version for the maritime radar reconnaissance role. Total production of Vulcans equalled 134 and at least two static-test airframes.

On the brink of retirement in 1982, the Vulcan was called into action during the Falklands conflict. Five 'Black Buck' raids were carried out against Argentine forces by Vulcans flying from Ascension Island. At up to 16 hours' duration, these were at the time the longest bombing raids in history. Six Vulcans were also hastily converted to **K.2** single-point tankers, freeing VC-10s to support the Falkands air bridge.

The first production Vulcan B.1 was the first to be fitted with the 'kinked' wing leading edge. Vulcans were initially in silver finish. (TRH Pictures)

Specification: Avro Vulcan B.2A
Type: four-engined strategic bomber
Crew: five
Powerplant: four 17,000-lb (78.8-kN) thrust Bristol (Rolls-Royce) Olympus 201 turbojets
Dimensions: span 111 ft (33.83 m); length (over probe) 105 ft 6 in (32.15 m); height 26 ft 1 in (7.94 m); wing area 3965 sq ft (368.3 m²)
Weights: empty not released; max. take-off 204,000 lb (92534 kg)
Performance: max. speed 645 mph (1038 km/h); service ceiling 65,000 ft (19812 m); range 4,600 miles (7400 m)
Armament: Blue Danube or Yellow Sun nuclear weapons, Blue Steel stand-off missile, or 21 1,000-lb (454-kg) bombs

Sud-Ouest Vautour

France
October 1952

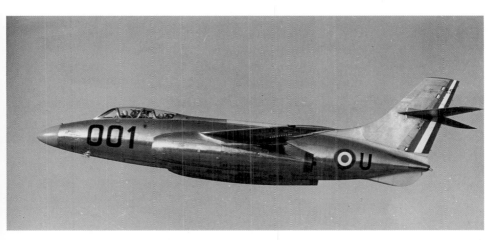

At the end of World War II, the French aviation industry lagged behind the UK, US and USSR, and in particular had no experience with jets. In an effort to develop a modern bomber, Société Nationale de Sud-Ouest (SNCASO) built the abortive SO.4000 and flew it once in 1951. The same year a requirement was issued for a twin jet in three versions, a bomber, a close-support aircraft and a night interceptor. Learning from their mistakes, SNCASO came up with an unusual configuration, although one that owed much to the B-47. The Vautour (Vulture) had a mid-set swept wing and a bicycle undercarriage mounted at each end of the bomb bay. Retractable outrigger wheels were fitted to the engine nacelles. The first of three prototypes flew on 16 October 1952 and soon proved supersonic in a shallow dive. British (Nene and Sapphire) engines were replaced by Atar 101E-3s (and later E-5s) on all production versions.

The **Vautour IIA** (Attaque) was a single-seat attack fighter with four 30-mm DEFA cannon and the **Vautour IIN** (Nuit) night-fighter had tandem cockpits and radar. Seventy of this version were built. The **Vautour IIB** (Bombardement) two-seat bomber had a glazed nose for the bomb-aimer and no cannon. Forty of this model were produced and served with the Armée de l'Air from 1958. Although capable of carrying a nuclear weapon, the Vautour IIB's range

The Vautour IIN.

All versions of the Vautour retained an internal bomb bay. This is a Vautour IIN night-fighter. These models had cannon armament. (TRH Pictures)

was inadequate for more than a one-way trip to the USSR, and it was designated a 'pre-strategic' bomber and mostly used to develop strike tactics until a supersonic successor (the Mirage IV) was available. All versions had the internal bomb bay, which featured retractable doors and a roof which lowered the bombs closer to the outside, preventing a vacuum that would stop them from falling. Wing hardpoints could be used for fuel tanks or for AS.30 ASMs or AA.20 air-to-air missiles (AAMs).

The Israeli Defence Force/Air Force received 28 Vautours including 17 IIAs, seven IINs and four IIBs from 1957 until the early 1970s when they were replaced by A-4 Skyhawks and F-4 Phantoms. Vautours were first used in the attack role in 1962 against positions on the Golan Heights. Some were converted to reconnaissance aircraft with day and night photo capability. Vautours were later used as electronic warfare (EW) aircraft, jamming Egyptian defences at the start of the Six Day War in 1967. Eight Vautours were lost on attack missions during the war and one MiG-21 was credited to a Vautour's cannon. The last French Vautour IIBs were retired in 1978, although one served later as a trials aircraft.

Specification: SO.4050 Vautour IIB
Type: twin-engined, two-seat bomber
Crew: two
Powerplant: two 7,716-lb (35.8-kN) thrust SNECMA Atar 101E-3 turbojets
Dimensions: span 49 ft 6.5 in (15.1 m); length 51 ft 10 in (15.80 m); height 15 ft 5 in (4.77 m); wing area 484.4 sq ft (45 m²)
Weights: empty 23,325 lb (10580 kg); max. take-off 45,635 lb (20730 kg)
Performance: max. speed 684 mph (1100 km/h); service ceiling 49,000 ft (14935 m); combat radius 820 miles (1320 km)
Armament: one nuclear weapon or conventional bombs up to 5,291 lb (2400 kg)

Douglas A3D/A-3 Skywarrior

United States
October 1952

The Bureau of Aeronautics (BuAer) requested proposals in 1947 for a bomber to fly from the new class of 'supercarriers'. Douglas's response was the **A3D**, a heavy (60,000-lb/27,200-kg) swept-wing bomber powered by two Westinghouse J40 engines. This would meet the requirement of carrying a 10,000-lb (4,536-kg) nuclear bomb a distance of 2,000 nautical miles (3700 km) and then returning to its carrier.

The design leader was Harry Nichols supervised by Ed Heinemann and Leo Devlin. They designed the fuselage around a large bomb bay that could be accessed in flight for arming the nuclear weapons. Otherwise, the crew was in the nose and the only defensive armament was a remotely operated turret with a pair of 20-mm cannon. The swept, shoulder-mounted wing necessitated that the undercarriage retracted into the fuselage. Pod-mounted engines were a fortunate choice, as this allowed alternative powerplants to be used. Although the specification allowed for a weight of up to 100,000 lb, (45360 kg), Heinemann kept the weight as low as possible as he forecast (correctly) that the 'United States'-class supercarriers would be cancelled. With its A3D pared down to 68,000 lb (30644 kg), Douglas was awarded the prototype contract in March 1949, and on 28 October 1952 the first **XA3D-1 Skywarrior** flew from Edwards AFB. The engines were XJ40-WE-3s, which provided only 7,000 lb (32.5 kN) thrust. The A3D was quickly re-engined with water-injected Pratt & Whitney J57s that gave up to 11,600 lb (53.8 kN) thrust and

Built as an A3D-2 (later A-3B), this Skywarrior landing on USS America in the Gulf of Tonkin was converted to a KA-3B and then to an EKA-3B. (TRH Pictures)

this transformed it into a viable combat aircraft.

The first **A3D-1** (**A-3A** after September 1962) squadron, VAH-1 was formed in 1956. The definitive **A3D-2** (**A-3B**) joined VAH-2 in 1957. In August 1959 an A3D was launched from USS *Independence* at a record weight of 84,000 lb (38102 kg).

The basic bomber was joined by specialist electronic reconnaissance/ECM, photo and tanker variants. These all proved useful in Vietnam where the bomber itself saw little combat. Broken into detachments, the bombers and specialist aircraft flew on combat or support missions from the 'Essex'-class carriers from 1965 to 1973. The **KA-3B** tanker and the **EKA-3B** electronic warfare/tanker variants were the largest refuelling aircraft available to the Navy. **RA-3B** photo platforms were used to detect vehicles through the jungle canopy with infra-red cameras. Twenty 'Whales' were lost in Vietnam, one to Chinese MiGs.

The tail guns were soon replaced by electronic jammers. A-3s served with VQ-2 in the 1991 Gulf War and were finally retired from US Navy service in 1993. A few still fly with private contractors.

The Skywarrior was mainly used as a tanker and jammer aircraft. This is a EKA-3B 'Queer Whale' in service with VQ-2 'Ironmen' (Austin J Brown/The Aviation Picture Library)

Specification: Douglas A-3B Skywarrior
Type: twin-engined carrier-based bomber
Crew: three
Powerplant: two 12,400-lb (57.5-kN) thrust (with water injection) Pratt & Whitney J57-10 turbojets
Dimensions: span 72 ft 6 in (22.1 m); length 76 ft 4 in (23.27 m); height 22 ft 9.5 in (6.95 m); wing area 812 sq ft (7 5.43 m²)
Weights: empty 39,409 lb (17876 kg); max. take-off 84,000 lb (38102 kg)
Performance: max. speed 618 mph (995 km/h); range 2,900 miles (4667 km)
Armament: twin 20-mm cannon in tail barbette; up to 8,560 lb (3892 kg) of conventional or nuclear ordnance

Tupolev Tu-95/Tu-142 'Bear'

USSR
November 1952

The Tupolev design bureau was given the job of designing a new intercontinental bomber in July 1951. Using elements of the abandoned Tu-85, itself based on the Tu-4 'Bull' (B-29), and four immensely powerful 14,795-ehp (11033-ekW) Kuznetsov NK-12M turboprops, Tupolev created the only swept-wing propeller-driven combat aircraft, the **Tu-95**. This flew for the first time on 12 November 1952 and entered Soviet Air Force service as the **Tu-20** (Nato **'Bear A'**). The 'Bear's high-speed and high-altitude capability and its five twin-gun turrets were its defence until improvements in SAMs and AAMs saw the role-change to stand-off missile launchers. The **Tu-95K-20 'Bear B'** was armed with the Kh-20 (AS-3 'Kangaroo') with an 800-kT warhead and 400-mile (643-km) range. The **Tu-95KM 'Bear C'** was an interim version, supplanted by the **Tu-95K-22 'Bear G'** with two smaller Kh-22 (AS-4 'Kitchen') attack missiles.

The **Tu-95MS 'Bear H'** was a late-production model with many Tu-142 features, developed to carry six Kh-55 (AS-15 'Kent') nuclear cruise missiles. Tu-95 product on finally ended in 1992, with about 263 Tu-95s built in two periods (173 in 1959–69 and 90 in 1982–92). Twenty-five were based in the Ukraine when the Soviet Union broke up. Three were sold back to Russia in 1999 but most will be scrapped. The

Since the early 1990s, several 'Bears' such as this Tu-142M 'Bear F Mod 2' have visited Western airshows.
(Austin J Brown/The Aviation Picture Library)

The 'Bear' is unique in being a swept-wing turboprop. The Tu-95 'Bear H' remains the backbone of the Russian bomber arm. (Austin J Brown/The Aviation Picture Library)

40 Tu-95MSs based in Kazakhstan were handed back to Russia in 1994. Since 1995 Russian 'Bears' have been slowly undergoing upgrade.

Development of the **Tu-142 'Bear F'** long-range ASW aircraft based on the Tu-95 began in 1963 and the type was in service by December 1972. The Tu-142 had new double-slotted flaps, a stronger undercarriage (with longer trailing-edge fairings), major internal changes and all-new systems. The bomb bays were completely revised to carry depth-charges and sonobuoys, eliminating the ventral turret. Two new ventral radomes appeared. A subvariant is the **Tu-142 'Bear F Mod 1'** with the original wing fairings. **The Tu-142M 'Bear F Mod 2'** is slightly longer with no chin radome, a revised cockpit enclosure and a drooped IFR probe. The **Tu-142M2 'Bear F Mod 3'** has a MAD boom protruding rearwards from the fin top. Eight of this type were sold to the Indian Navy in 1988. The **Tu-142MR 'Bear J'** is a communications relay variant. The **Tu-142MZ 'Bear F Mod 4'** reintroduced the chin radome and had a new sonobuoy system. Production of the Tu-142 family ceased in 1994 with approximately 100 built, again in two periods (1968–72 and 1974–94).

Specification: Tu-95MS 'Bear H'
Type: long-range strategic bomber
Crew: seven
Powerplant: four 14,795-ehp (11033-ekW) Kuznetsov NK-12M turboprops.
Dimensions: span 164 ft 2 in (50.04 m); length 161 ft 2 in (49.13 m); height 43 ft 8 in (13.30 m); wing area 3,120 sq ft ((269.9 m²)
Weights: empty 208,116 lb (94400 kg); max. take-off 407,885 lb (135000 kg)
Performance: max. speed 516 mph (830 km/h); service ceiling 34,450 ft (10500 m); range 5,670 miles (10500 km)
Armament: two NR-23 23-mm cannon, six Kh-55 (AS-15) or Kh-555 'Kent' air-launched cruise missiles (ALCMs)

Handley Page Victor

The third and last of the V-bombers, the Handley Page Victor saw operations in two wars, but not in the role for which it was designed. Handley Page's approach to the Air Ministry's bomber requirement was less radical than the Vulcan, but still futuristic in appearance with a T-tail and a swept 'crescent' wing. This wing was considerably thicker at the root than at the tip and contained the four engines (initially Sapphires, later Conways). The HP.80 (later, Victor) had a larger pressurised compartment than the other V-bombers, including a bomb-aimer's window under the nose. Again, ejection seats were only provided for the pilots. Handley Page tested the crescent wing on the Supermarine type 510 (a modified Attacker), which became the HP.88 before its loss in August 1951. The **HP.80** prototype flew on Christmas Eve 1952, and in February 1956 the first **Victor B.1** was flown. Bomber Command declared the Victor operational in April 1958. The initial strategic weapon was the Yellow Sun H-bomb, and later the Blue Steel stand-off missile.

The Victor flew no operational bombing missions, but when Indonesia threatened Malaysia in 1963 Victor B.1s were deployed to Singapore as a show of force, helping to discourage further incursions.

The improved **B.1A** had tail warning radar in an enlarged tailcone and revised engines. Although improved defences were pointing the way to low-level under-the-radar tactics, the **Victor B.2** was designed to fly higher and faster with longer-span wings and

For the majority of its career, the Victor served as a tanker. This is one of No. 57 Squadron's K.2s, seen in the 1980s. (Author's collection)

Conway engines, requiring extensive revision to the intakes. First flying in 1959, the B.2 was soon switched to the low-level tactical role like the Valiant and Vulcan. As B.2s entered service, B.1s were phased out and converted to **K.1** and **K.1A** three-point refuelling tankers to make up the shortfall caused by the withdrawal of the Valiant. As a stopgap, six B.1s were quickly converted to **BK.1A** two-point tankers, retaining bombing gear. Nine B.2s were delivered for the strategic reconnaissance role as the **SR.2**. Overall Victor production totalled 86 aircraft.

Handley Page folded in 1970 and Hawker Siddeley was contracted to convert the B.2s to tankers as **K.2**s, which entered service in 1974. Only 24 conversions were carried out due to budget cuts, and the K.2s were stretched by the Falklands war. Eleven Victors were needed to support one Vulcan raid, some refuelling the bomber and others refuelling each other. Victors were also used for radar reconnaissance. In the Gulf War of 1991, the RAF used eight Victors to refuel RAF, Nato and USN types.

One of the first Victor B.1s shows off its finish of anti-flash white, designed to reflect the initial heat of an atomic detonation. (TRH Pictures)

Specification: Handley Page Victor B.2
Type: four-engined strategic bomber
Crew: five
Powerplant: four 17,250-lb (80-kN) thrust Rolls-Royce Conway 103 turbojets
Weights: span 120 ft 0 in (36.58 m); length 114 ft 11 in (35.30 m); height 28 ft 11 in (8.80 m); wing area 2,597 sq ft (241.3 m²)
Weights: empty 91,430 lb (41473 kg); max. take-off 233,000 lb (101150 kg)
Performance: max. speed 645 mph (1038 km/h); service ceiling 61,000 ft (18590 m); range 4,600 miles (7400 km)
Armament: one Blue Steel Mk 1 cruise missile; up to 35 1,000-lb (454-kg) bombs

McDonnell Douglas A-4 Skyhawk

United States
July 1954

The Douglas A-4 Skyhawk was designed by Ed Heinemann in an effort to reverse the trend of increasing weight and complexity of carrier-based combat aircraft. The **X4AD-1** that first flew on 22 June 1954 came in significantly under the target weight and cost. The **A4D-1** (**A-4A** after 1962) entered service in September 1956 with the Wright J65 engine. The **A4D-2** (**A-4B**) introduced a refuelling probe, the **A4D-2N** (**A-4C**) had improved 'all-weather' avionics and greater weapons capacity. The **A4D-5** (**A-4E**) introduced the 8,500-lb (39.4-kN) thrust Pratt & Whitney J52 engine. Late A-4Es and most A-4Fs had an avionics 'hump' on the spine. The **A-4M** for the USMC had self-start capability, a larger canopy and better avionics. The **OA-4M** was a dedicated Forward Air Control (FAC) variant for the Marines. The **TA-4F** and **TA-4J** were combat-capable two-seaters. A-4 production ended in 1979 with 2,960 built.

In Vietnam 196 Navy Skyhawks were lost in combat and a further 77 in operational accidents. The Marines lost a further 101. Israel made much combat use of its **A-4H** and **TA-4H** models in 1967 and 1973 and later received the **A-4N**, similar to the A-4M. Over 330 A-4s **A-4KUs** and **TA-4KUs** saw action in 1991. In 1997 they were sold to Brazil and became **AF-1s** and **AF-1As**.

The last US Navy squadron to use Skyhawks is VC-8 'Redtails', which flies TA-4Js on various fleet support missions. (Author)

The Skyhawk could carry more than its own weight in weapons and fuel. This A-4F from VA-155 is loaded with bombs and Bullpup AGMs. (Author's collection)

Argentina operated early Skyhawks (all single-seaters) as the **A-4P** (Air Force) and **A-4Q** (Navy). In the 1982 Falklands War they sunk four British ships and seriously damaged four, but lost 21 of their number to SAMs, AAA and Sea Harriers. In 1994, Argentina purchased 36 surplus A-4Ms and OA-4Ms, all for Air Force service as the **A-4AR** and **TA-4AR Fightinghawk**, upgraded with APG-65 (ARG-1) radar and other modern avionics.

Australia's **A-4Gs** and **TA-4Gs** were operated from HMAS *Melbourne* from 1967 to 1982 before the surviving examples were sold to New Zealand. New Zealand's **A-4Ks** and **TA-4Ks** served from 1970 until 2001 when they were retired but not replaced for political reasons. In the mid-1980s they were updated with APG-66(NZ) radar, modernised cockpits and precision-guided munitions under Project *Kahu*.

About 70 of Singapore's Skyhawks are still in service, 18 with a training detachment in France. The **A-4S** and **TA-4S** were refurbished A-4Bs and Cs, later modernised to **S-1** standard and then to **A-4SUs** and **TA-4SUs** with non-afterburning F404 turbofan engines and improved avionics. Malaysia converted 40 A-4Cs into the **A-4PTM** and **TA-4PTM** in the mid-1980s but no longer operates them.

Specification: A-4M Skyhawk
Type: single-engined naval attack aircraft
Crew: one
Powerplant: 11,280-lb (50-kN) thrust Pratt & Whitney J52-P-408 turbojet
Dimensions: span 27 ft 6 in (8.38 m); length 41 ft 8.5 in (12.72 m); height 14 ft 11.75 in (4.57 m); wing area 260 sq ft (24.2 m²)
Weights: empty 10,250 lb (4747 kg); max. take-off 24,000 lb (10206 kg)
Performance: max. speed 685 mph (1102 km/h); service ceiling 40,000 ft (12190 m); range 2,000 miles (3219 km)
Armament: two Mk 12 20-mm cannon; maximum ordnance 9,155 lb (4153 kg)

Republic F-105 Thunderchief

As early as 1950 the USAF was looking towards a supersonic successor to the Republic F-84 Thunderjet and new F-84F Thunderstreak. The legendary Alexander Kartveli of Republic designed a tactical fighter able to carry a nuclear weapon as well as perform air-to-air combat. The airframe was designed to handle the stresses of high-speed low-level attack runs. Approval came in September 1952 with an order for 199 **F-105 Thunderchiefs**, to be powered by the J71 engine. Many detail changes and reductions of orders came about before the Air Force settled on acquiring two Pratt & Whitney J57-powered **YF-105A**s and 10 J75-powered **F-105B**s for evaluation. Even more revisions preceded production. The wingroot intakes were changed to a unique forward-raked horizontal design on the F-105B and the so-called 'Area Rule' was applied to its fuselage, leading to a 'wasp-waist' effect.

The YF-105A flew on 22 October 1955, and the **YF-105B** on 26 May 1956, but it was wrecked on landing. Deliveries to the USAF finally began in May 1958. In 1964, the 'Thunderbirds' demonstration team was briefly equipped with F-105Bs. The same year the **F-105D** entered service with all-weather capability provided by the AN/ASG-19 'Thunderstick' radar and weapons system in a larger nose. The D also had a higher-thrust J75-P-19W engine with water injection. A refuelling boom receptacle was fitted during production. A total of 610 F-105Ds were built.

To carry the large nuclear weapons of the day, the

An F-105D thunders down a Thai runway en route for a target in Vietnam armed with 750-lb bombs and a jamming pod. (Author's collection)

F-105 had an internal bay almost 16 ft (4.88 m) long as well as four underwing hardpoints. With modification, up to 16 750-lb (340-kg) bombs could be carried.

The F-105 entered combat in South-east Asia from August 1964 and flew most of the missions against North Vietnam up to 1968. In all, 397 'Thuds' were lost to enemy action in Vietnam and to operational accidents. Twenty-three were lost to MiGs and 31 to SAMs. In return F-105s managed to shoot down 27 North Vietnamese MiGs, many with the cannon.

The two-seat **F-105F** systems trainer was longer with a taller fin and retained full weapons capability. The 143 F-105Fs were converted from Ds during production. Eighty-six were converted for the 'Wild Weasel' SAM suppression role with jammers and AGM-45 Shrike missiles. With improved avionics and the addition of AGM-78 standard anti-radar missiles, many were modified to **F-105G** standard. The use of 'Wild Weasels' to destroy air defence radars or force them to shut down saved many aircrews in Vietnam. The F-105D left Vietnam in 1970, but the G served until the war's end and with the ANG until 1983.

The 'Thud' could carry a heavy bomb load – here eight 500-lb bombs. This F-105D is from the 44th TFS based at Korat. (The Aviation Picture Library)

Specification: Republic F-105D Thunderchief
Type: single-engined fighter-bomber
Crew: one
Powerplant: one 17,200-lb (80-kN) thrust Pratt & Whitney J75-P-19-W afterburning turbojet
Dimensions: span 34 ft 11.25 m (10.65 m); length 64 ft 3 in (19.58 m); height 19 ft 8 in (5.99 m); wing area 385 sq ft (35.76 m²)
Weights: empty 27,500-lb (12474 kg); max. take-off 38,034 lb (17252 kg)
Performance: max. speed 1,390 mph (2237 km/h); service ceiling 52,000 ft (15850 m); range 1,850 miles (2975 km)
Armament: one 20-mm Vulcan cannon; bomb load over 12,000 lb (5443 kg)

Dassault Etendard/Super Etendard

France
July 1956

The long-serving Etendard and Super Etendard series of strike aircraft stemmed from the Nato requirement for a lightweight tactical assault fighter that could operate away from large airbases. France's contender, the Dassault Etendard, flew on 24 July 1956. It was a simple design, similar to the later Mirage III with the same (if non-afterburning) Atar engine, but with a swept wing and tailplane. The Fiat G.91 won the Nato competition, but the French Navy (Aéronavale) took on the Etendard design to provide a strike aircraft for its carriers, *Clemenceau* and *Foch*. The Naval **Etendard IVM** had folding wings and other carrier features, a retractable refuelling probe and twin 30-mm cannon. Under the slim nose was a long blade antenna, which looked like a stabilising fin. This was part of the guidance system for the Nord 5103 AAM and AS.30 anti-ship missile (ASM).

Delivered from 1961, 68 IVMs served until 1980 aboard the carriers and up to 1991 with land-based units. There were 21 **Etendard IVP** reconnaissance aircraft/tankers, upgraded in 1995 to **IVPM** standard, which served until 2000.

When the superior navalised Jaguar M was cancelled owing to political pressure from Dassault the Aéronavale ordered 71 of the **Super Etendard**

The upgraded Etendard IVPM reconnaissance aircraft/tanker saw action over Bosnia, this aircraft being damaged by a SAM. (Author)

Best known as an Exocet launcher, the fairly unsophisticated 'Sue' can also carry bombs and rockets. (CEV)

This featured improved aerodynamics, AM39 Exocet anti-ship missile capability and a Thomson/Dassault Agave radar in a new nose. The usual weapons carriage was an Exocet on one wing pylon balanced by a fuel tank on the other. The first 'Super' (actually a modified IVM) flew on 28 October 1974 and entered service in 1978.

France leased five Super Etendards to Iraq in late 1982, where they were used to attack tankers carrying Iranian oil. About 50 attacks were made and numerous tankers were hit by Exocets fired by Super Etendards but none were sunk. It is thought that the four survivors were returned to France in 1985.

Fourteen Super Etendards were supplied to the Argentine Navy from 1981. Five were in service, along with five Exocets, by the time of the Falklands War. Flown from land bases, Super Etendards destroyed HMS *Sheffield* and the merchant ship *Atlantic Conveyor*. The success of these missions was to give both the Super Etendard and Exocet a reputation as a deadly anti-ship combination that they probably didn't deserve. France's 'Sue's were used over Lebanon, over Bosnia in 1995 and most recently, flew from the *Charles de Gaulle* during operations over Afghanistan.

Specification: Dassault Super Etendard
Type: single-engined maritime strike aircraft
Crew: one
Powerplant: one 11,025-lb (49-kN) thrust SNECMA Atar 8 non-afterburning turbojet
Dimensions: span 31 ft 6 in (9.6 m); length 47 ft 3 in (14.4 m); height 14 ft (4.3 m); wing area 306 sq ft (28.43 m²)
Weights: empty 14,330 lb (6500 kg); max. take-off 26,455 lb (12000 kg)
Performance: max. speed 733 mph (1180 km/h); service ceiling 44,950 ft (13700 m); combat radius 447 miles (720 km)
Armament: two 30-mm DEFA cannon, one AM52 or ASMP nuclear weapon or various conventional weapons.

Convair B-58 Hustler

During the 1950s, the increasing sophistication of air defences threatened to make conventional bomber tactics obsolete. Radar tracking and SAMs meant that formations of relatively slow bombers would be too vulnerable over the Soviet Union. As early as 1946 Convair (formerly Consolidated) began studies on a bomber capable of high-altitude supersonic penetration of defended airspace. In 1952 their delta-winged MX-1965 proposal was given a development contract by the USAF and the resulting **B-58 Hustler** prototype flew on 11 November 1956.

The B-58 had a sophisticated navigation and bombing system and made much use of honeycomb sandwich skin panels. There was no room in the wasp-waisted fuselage for bombs, so they were carried in a large droppable pod slung under the fuselage. This unit was built in several versions, containing fuel and either a nuclear weapon or a reconnaissance package. Alternatively, four nuclear or conventional weapons could be carried on underwing hard points. The three crew consisted of a pilot, navigator-bombardier and a defensive systems operator, who controlled ECM equipment as well as the tail-mounted 20-mm Vulcan cannon. The crew did not have ejection seats but were enclosed in Escapac ejection capsules with individual canopies.

The mid-set delta wing had leading edge sweepback of 60 degrees and was extremely thin. The only control surfaces were two elevons and a rudder. There were no flaps or high-lift devices. The

The Hustler was the first Western supersonic bomber. It was expensive to operate and only served for 10 years. (TRH Pictures)

B-58 broke many speed records, notably on 5 March 1952 when a regular service aircraft flew from New York to Los Angeles and back at an average speed of 1,214.71 mph (1954.83 km/h).

Because of the high technological and performance advances embodied in the B-58, 30 prototype and pre-production aircraft were needed in addition to the 86 production aircraft delivered to Strategic Air Command. Ten of the pre-production **YB-58**s were brought up to **B-58A** production standard and issued to SAC. A number were built as **TB-58A** trainers.

The high cost of the Hustler at $12.4 million each meant that far fewer were ordered than of SAC's less-advanced bombers such as the B-47 and B-52. The B-58 was also seen as an interim bomber until the eventual arrival of the B-70 Valkyrie. Although it had longer range than the B-47, the B-58 had a greater requirement for tankers as it was not based outside the USA. The high operating cost was the main reason that the B-58 was retired after only 10 years' service, although the restricted internal space allowed little room for new avionics and ECM gear.

The huge pods under the B-58 contained fuel, weapons or cameras. The fuselage and wings were too slim for any internal stores. (TRH Pictures)

Specification: Convair B-58A Hustler
Type: four-engined, supersonic bomber
Crew: three
Powerplant: four 15,600-lb (63.5-kN) thrust J79-GE-5A turbojets
Dimensions: span 56 ft 10 in (17.32 m); length 96 ft 10 in (29.49 m); height 31 ft 5 in (9.58 m); wing area 1,542 sq ft (470 m²)
Weights: empty 55,560 lb (25501 kg); max. take-off 163,000 lb (73935 kg)
Performance: max. speed 1,321 mph (2125 km/h); service ceiling 63,150 ft (19248 m); combat radius 1,750 miles (2816 km)
Armament: up to 19,450 lb (8823 kg) of stores (nuclear, fuel, cameras) in pod; one 20-mm Vulcan cannon in tail

Blackburn Buccaneer

United Kingdom
April 1958

Blackburn Aviation, a company with a distinguished history of naval aircraft, won the contract to produce a prototype to meet a July 1953 Naval Staff Requirement. This called for a long-range strike aircraft able to carry a nuclear weapon at high speed below radar coverage. The **NA.39** was constructed in great secrecy and flew on 30 April 1958. A development batch of 20 was produced, followed by 50 **Buccaneer S.1**s. The company abbreviation BNA (Blackburn Naval Aircraft) led to the nickname 'banana jet' throughout the Buccaneer's career.

The Buccaneer S.1 incorporated all the military and naval features, such as radar, wing-folding and weapons capability. It was very advanced for its day, with new construction techniques and innovative features such as a rotating bomb bay and boundary layer control (BLC), a technique for blowing engine bleed air over the upper surface of the wing to produce extra lift, allowing for shorter take-offs and higher weapons loads. The fuselage had an area-ruled 'wasp-waist' and a long tail 'stinger', which opened to form airbrakes. The engines were de Havilland Gyron Junior turbojets rated at 7,100 lb (31.59 kN) thrust, which proved inadequate in many single-engined situations.

Only 40 S.1s were delivered before the improved

The Buccaneer was famous for its speed and stability at low level. This is a No. 208 Squadron S.2B seen just after take-off. (Robert Hewson)

The Buccaneer was one of the best naval strike aircraft ever built. Here a bomb-loaded Buccaneer S.2D launches from Ark Royal. *(Author's collection)*

S.2 came along in 1963. This had the 11,030-lb (49.08-kN) thrust Rolls-Royce Spey turbofan, which greatly improved safety. Royal Navy 'Buccs' entered Fleet Air Arm service from July 1962 and served on the carriers *Eagle*, *Hermes*, *Victorious* and *Ark Royal*. Some were later updated to **S.2C** and **S.2D** standard.

The RAF, which initially disdained the Buccaneer, received its first **S.2A** aircraft (transferred from the Navy) in 1969 following cancellation of the TSR.2 and the F-111K. New-build **S.2B**s arrived in 1970. This model had a bulged bomb bay door, which contained a fuel tank, and gained Martel TV-guided anti-ship missile capability. Buccaneers also carried the Red Beard and WE.177A nuclear bombs. Production of Buccaneers for the RAF ended in 1977 with the 49th S.2B. When *Ark Royal* was paid off in 1978, the remaining Navy Buccaneers joined the RAF.

South Africa received 15 **S.50**s, a version of the S.2 with additional booster rocket packs for 'hot and high' take-offs and 'slipper' wing tanks. They were used in action over Angola and were retired in 1991.

During the Gulf War 12 RAF Buccaneers were despatched to Bahrain, initially to provide laser designation for Tornadoes, but later dropped 48 LGBs themselves. The Buccaneer retired in early 1994.

Specification: Buccaneer S.2B
Type: twin-engined carrier/land-based strike aircraft
Crew: two
Powerplant: two 11,100-lb (51.5-kN) thrust Rolls-Royce Spey turbofans
Dimensions: span 44 ft (13.41 m); length 63 ft 5 in (19.32 m); height 16 ft 6 in (5.03 m); wing area 514/7 sq ft (47.82 m²)
Weights: empty 30,000 lb (13608 kg); max. take-off 62,000 lb (28123 kg)
Performance: max. speed 645 mph (1038 km/h) at sea level; service ceiling 40,000 ft (12192 km); range 2,300 miles (3702 km)
Armament: up to 12,000 lb (5443 kg) of conventional bombs and rockets or one WE.177A nuclear weapon

North American A-5 Vigilante

United States
August 1958

The Vigilante bomber/reconnaissance aircraft began as the privately funded NAGPAW (North American General-Purpose Attack Weapon) intended to replace the less-than-successful piston-engined AJ Savage. The US Navy imposed strict performance requirements, including a Mach 2 top speed and the ability to launch at maximum weight from a carrier in no-wind conditions. Frank Compton's team revised the NAGPAW to meet these demands and produced a sleek aircraft with two General Electric J79 engines fed by variable hinged intakes, a large wing and a single tail. The tail surfaces were all single-piece 'slab' units, but the wing featured leading- and trailing-edge flaps and complex spoilers.

The first of two **YA3J-1 Vigilante** prototypes was flown on 31 August 1958 followed by 33 **A3J-1**s, (later **A-5A**s). Fleet service began in 1961.

The pilot had a hinged canopy and a large wraparound windscreen, whereas the weapons systems operator (WSO) sat behind in a separate cockpit with only small windows. Optimised for low-level attacks at high-speed, one unique feature of the A3J was its linear bomb bay. A 'train' of fuel tanks and the nuclear weapon (usually a B28) were fitted in a cavity between the engines.

The main bombing tactic was for the Vigilante to run towards the target before pulling up and releasing the bomb/fuel package, which would climb in a parabolic arc before falling on the target. The aircraft would complete a half-Cuban manoeuvre and exit the target

An RA-5C Vigilante of RVAH-12 'Speartips' prepares for launch from USS Forrestal *(CVA-59) in the Atlantic, June 1968. (TRH Pictures)*

area as quickly as possible. Level bombing was also possible, and all modes were controlled by the sophisticated ASB-12 bombing computer. This compared the radar and/or TV picture with target images stored on magnetic tape.

In December 1960, a standard A3J-1 demonstrated the ability to carry a 4,409-lb (2000-kg) load from a carrier to a height of 91,446 ft (27872 m). Only 18 of the improved **A3J-2** (**A-5B**) with a hump-backed fuselage containing extra fuel, larger flaps and fully-blown leading-edge flaps were built.

Shortly after the Vigilante entered service, the Navy finally admitted that strategic bombing was an Air Force role and converted the surviving aircraft to the tactical reconnaissance role. The **RA-5C** fleet consisted of 18 converted A-5Bs, 43 A-5A conversions and 79 new-builds. The total series production was 156 airframes. RA-5Cs were extensively used in Vietnam where they were able to both outpace MiGs and escort Phantoms. The last 'Vigi' was retired in September 1979.

The Vigilante lasted into the late 1970s. This RA-5C was seen with its wings and tail folded on the USS Nimitz. *(Austin J Brown/The Aviation Picture Library)*

Specification: RA-5C Vigilante
Type: twin-engined supersonic carrier-borne strike aircraft
Crew: two
Powerplant: two 17,000-lb (78.8-kN) thrust General Electric J79-8 afterburning turbojets
Dimensions: span 53 ft 0 in (16.15 m); length 73 ft 3 in (22.33 m); height 19 ft 5 in (5.9 m); wing area 754 sq ft (70.0 m²)
Weights: empty 34,350 lb (15581 kg); max. take-off 61,000 lb (27670 kg)
Performance: max. speed 1,388 mph (2234 km/h); service ceiling 52,100 ft (15900 m); range 2,050 miles (3300 km)
Armament (A-5A): one nuclear weapon carried internally

Dassault Mirage IV

In 1954 the French Government announced ambitious plans to build an independent nuclear deterrent, including its own air-cropped bombs and the platform to carry them. The bomber version of the Vautour was able to carry a nuclear weapon to a Soviet target, but only one way, and was used as an interim type while a truly strategic successor was built. The bomber specification was issued in 1956, calling for an aircraft with a 2000-km (1,242-mile) range capable of carrying a 3000-kg (6.614-lb) bomb at a speed of at least Mach 1.7. In competition with a stretched Vautour, Dassault drew up an enlarged version of its Mirage III fighter with two engines and double the wing area. The radar was fitted in the underside, allowing the nose to be finer than that of the Mirage III. Even before the prototype flew on 17 June 1959, the **Mirage IVA**'s range was considered inadequate and work concentrated for a time on an enlarged **Mirage IVB**. This was cancelled in favour of air refuelling from C-135F tankers and all 62 production aircraft were similar to the three IVA prototypes.

The Mirage VA entered service with the strategic bomber forces in 1964 and took up rapid alert duties armed with the AN52 bomb in a semi-recessed underbelly position. The Mirage IV had the same

A line-up of the original Mirage IVA prototypes reveals AN52 nuclear bomb shapes under their bellies. (TRH Pictures)

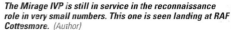

The Mirage IVP is still in service in the reconnaissance role in very small numbers. This one is seen landing at RAF Cottesmore. (Author)

60-degree wing sweep as the Mirage III, but two seats, two engines and four wheels on each main gear leg. Despite having every spare inch of space crammed with fuel, the Mirage IV's range was still marginal.

The Mirage IV served with France's strategic bomber force and stood alert duties armed with a semi-recessed AN52 (later AN22) free-fall nuclear weapon. In order to be airborne in the fastest possible time, inertial navigation was dispensed with (it took too long to align) and JATO rockets were fitted to allow operations from smaller dispersed airfields in a crisis.

In 1983, fifteen of the IVAs were gutted and rebuilt as the **Mirage IVP**, with capability for the ASMP nuclear cruise missile. A reconnaissance capability was also added with a CT52 camera and sensor pod under the fuselage. The Mirage IV bomber was retired in July 1996 and the ASMP mission passed to the Mirage 2000N.

Although slated for retirement many times, five Mirage IVPs remain in service. They flew reconnaissance missions over Bosnia and Kosovo in the 1990s, and were the first French contribution to the Afghan campaign in October 2001.

Specification: Dassault Mirage IVP
Type: delta-winged strategic bomber
Crew: two
Powerplant: two 15,432-lb (71.6-kN) thrust SNECMA Atar 9K afterburning turbojets
Dimensions: span 33 ft 10.5 in (11.85 m); length 77 ft 1 in (23.49 m); height 18 ft 6 in (5.65 m); wing area 839.6 sq ft (78 m²)
Weights: empty 31,966 lb (14500 kg); max. take-off 73,799 lb (33475 kg)
Performance: max. speed 1,454 mph (2340 km/h); tactical radius 770 miles (1240 km)
Armament: one ASMP nuclear cruise missile (Mirage IVA one AN22 nuclear bomb or 16,000 lb (7288 kg) of conventional bombs)

Tupolev Tu-22 and Tu-22M

USSR
September 1959

Revealed to shocked Western observers for the first time at the 1961 Aviation Day flypast at Tushino, the Tupolev **S-105A** appeared to have more in common with a fighter than a bomber design. In fact, the design, work on which began in 1955, owed a lot to the Tu-98 interceptor. The first flight was on 7 September 1959. Entering service in 1962, as the **Tu-22B** (Nato code-name 'Blinder'), this new bomber featured a pair of VD-7M turbojets at the base of the fin, wings swept at 70 degrees and a very long nose and forward fuselage. The crew of three sat one behind the other on downward-firing ejection seats. The Tu-22B was less than successful, and was supplanted by the **Tu-22K 'Blinder B'**. The majority had 24,250-lb (107.9-kN) thrust RD-7M2 engines. These gave a dash capability of Mach 1.5. Other variants were the **Tu-22R 'Blinder C'** reconnaissance aircraft and the **Tu-22UD** trainer with a raised instructor's cockpit.

The **Tu-22P** was the last model, equipped as an escort jammer. These and Tu-22Rs saw service over Afghanistan. Some Tu-22Rs rebuilt as bombers were supplied to Libya and used in combat over Chad. At least four were shot down. Iraq had at least 12 'Blinders', which saw much action in 1980–88. Tu-22 production ran from 1959 to 1969 with 313 produced.

Development of the completely new swing-wing **Tu-22M 'Backfire'** began in 1962, concurrently with the variable-geometry Su-17 programme. The first of

The main production version of the Tu-22 was the Tu-22K 'Blinder B' with a semi-retractable refuelling probe. (Philip Jarrett collection)

about nine **Tu-22M-0** prototypes made its maiden flight on 30 August 1969. Nine pre-production **Tu-22M-1**s were used for test and evaluation, and the first of 211 production **Tu-22M-2 'Backfire-B'** bombers made its first flight in 1975 with a longer-span wing, a redesigned forward fuselage for four crew and a revised undercarriage, retracting inwards. The tail armament was increased to two remotely controlled NR-23 23-mm cannon.

In the later **Tu-22M-3 'Backfire-C'**, the weapons bays can accommodate the rotary launchers for the RKV-500B (AS-16 'Kick-back') short-range attack missile with two more under each wing. The defensive armament is reduced to a single cannon. The new variant also introduced completely new wedge-type engine intakes, and a recontoured upturned nose. The 'Backfire-C' is believed to have entered service in 1985, and 268 were built. Nearly 70 Tu-22Ms continue to serve in the Russian air forces and with Russian naval aviation (82), and 54 to 70 more are in service in the Ukraine.

The definitive version of the very different Tu-22M 'Backfire B' is the Tu-22M-3 with MiG-25 type intakes. (Austin J. Brown/The Aviation Picture Library)

Specification: Tu-22M-3 'Backfire C'
Type: twin-engined supersonic bomber
Crew: four
Powerplant: two 55,115-lb (245-kN) thrust Kuznetsov NK-25 turbojets
Dimensions: span (spread) 112.47 ft (34.28 m); length 139.3 ft (42.46 m); height 36.25 ft (11.05 m); wing area 1,976 sq ft (183.58 m²)
Weights: empty 119,048 lb (54000 kg); max. take-off 286,596 lb (130000 kg)
Performance: max. speed 1,320 mph (2125 km/h); service ceiling 59,055 ft (18000 m); range 8,000 lb (3629 kg)
Armament: one GSh-23 23-mm cannon in tail turret; bomb load up to 26,455 lb (12000 kg)

Grumman A-6 Intruder

By the mid-1950s, the US Navy was studying an all-weather attack aircraft to fly missions at night and in bad weather that kept the current carrier aircraft on deck. In 1957 they issued their requirements and Grumman's design was selected in December. The prototype Grumman **YA2F-1** that first flew on 19 April 1960 featured a bulbous radar nose and Pratt & Whitney J52 engines located in the forward fuselage. The two-man crew sat side by side on Martin-Baker ejection seats. There was no internal bomb bay, all weaponry being carried on external pylons. The wing had long-span leading- and trailing-edge flaps.

The production **A-6A Intruder** dispensed with the prototype's pivoting exhausts and had a revised tail. Split wingtip airbrakes were added and perforations made in the fuselage side airbrakes as they were otherwise too effective. The original navigation and attack system had many teething troubles but when these were fixed the Intruder became an extremely effective all-weather attacker. Entering service in early 1963, the A-6 was involved in Vietnam from June 1965 until 1973. A total of 59 Navy and 25 Marine Intruders were lost in the war.

The **A-6B** was a SAM-suppression version able to launch the AGM-78 anti-radiation missile. The **A-6C** was another special version with electronics for

The Intruder was developed into the EA-6B Prowler for electronic attack. This Prowler is from VAQ-140 on the USS **John F Kennedy.** *(Author)*

The USMC retained the early A-6A into the 1980s. The Navy retired the Intruder in 1996 and gave up all-weather heavy attack. (Author's collection)

tracking vehicles on the Ho Chi Minh trail. From 1970 the **KA-6D** tanker appeared with some avionics replaced with a hose reel system. The KA-6D was the principal carrier-based tanker throughout the 1970s and 1980s. The **EA-6A** was developed for the USMC as a jamming aircraft. A large fin pod contained the bulk of the ECM equipment.

The **A-6E** was the longest-serving attack model, equipped with a new terrain-avoidance radar and other new avionics. Too late for service in Vietnam, A-6Es led the attack on Libya in 1986 and dropped many kinds of weapons in Operation *Desert Storm*. Three Intruders were lost in combat. Upgraded models with an undernose Target Recognition Attack Multisensor turret were designated **A-6E (TRAM)**.

The **A-6F** was to have F404 engines, new graphite/epoxy wing structure and all-new avionics. Five were built before the programme was cancelled, but 33 later production A-6Es had the new wing.

The **EA-6B Prowler** is a four-seat derivative for electronic warfare and suppression of enemy air defences (SEAD). Entering service in 1971, the EA-6B saw some Vietnam service and has fired HARMs in combat over Iraq and Kosovo.

Specification: A-6E Intruder
Type: twin-engined naval attack bomber
Crew: two
Powerplant: two 9,300-lb (43.1-kN) thrust Pratt & Whitney J52-P408 turbojets
Dimensions: span 53 ft 0 in (16.15 m); length 54 ft 9 in (16.69 m); height 15 ft 6 in (4.72 m); wing area 528.9 sq ft (49.1 m²)
Weights: empty 27,613 lb (12525 kg); max. take-off 60,400 lb (27397 kg)
Performance: max. speed 644 mph (1037 km/h); service ceiling 40,600 ft (12375 m); range 2,740 miles (4410 km)
Armament: bomb load up to 18,000 lb (8165 kg)

North American XB-70 Valkyrie

United States
September 1964

Even as the B-52 entered service, SAC was looking towards its successor. The NPB (nuclear-powered bomber) project was short-lived, but the CPB (chemically-powered bomber) project led to the extraordinary **XB-70 Valkyrie**. In 1955 a prototype contract was awarded to North American (and Boeing). Neither company's design looked like meeting the USAF's high-speed and range requirements until NAA studied the research by NACA scientist Alfred Eggers into 'compression lift', resulting in a complete redesign. The new design featured a huge delta wing over a box-shaped intake structure and engine housing. The wingtips drooped up to 65 degrees in high-speed flight to box in the airflow under the wing and made the best use of the shockwave, reducing drag and allowing high speed to be matched by long range. There was a complex intake ramp system that reduced the airflow from Mach 3 to subsonic speeds at the compressor face. Other (then) novel features were twin tail fins and large canard foreplanes.

In December 1959, well before the prototype was completed, the Secretary of Defense cancelled plans to put the **B-70A** into production and the Valkyrie was reduced to the status of a research programme. Intercontinental ballistic missiles (ICBMs) were then thought to soon make the manned bomber obsolete, and new air-launched ballistic missiles (ALBMs) such as Skybolt did not require a Mach 3 platform. The Valkyrie programme was briefly revived as the **RS-70**

The first XB-70 is seen at the time of its first flight in 1964. Although the Valkyrie last flew in 1969, it still looks futuristic. (TRH Pictures)

(for reconnaissance-strike), but reduced again in 1961 to three prototypes, two unequipped XB-70s and an **XB-70B** in bomber configuration.

With airframe temperatures expected to exceed 330°C (630°F), the Valkyrie was incredibly complex and difficult to build. Much new technology was developed for the programme. Nearly 70 per cent of the structure was made of a new type of stainless steel. The first XB-70 flew on 21 September 1964 and achieved Mach 3 on 14 October 1965.

On 17 July 1965, while taking part in a formation of General Electric-powered aircraft for publicity photos, the No. 2 aircraft was struck by an F-104 Starfighter and crashed. The crew ejected using the capsule escape system, but the back-seater was killed.

The No.1 aircraft continued to be used in tests relating to long-range, high-speed flight, which provided useful data for the US SST (supersonic transport aircraft) programme, until it was retired to the USAF Museum in February 1969. A side effect of the B-70 programme was that Mikoyan developed the MiG-25 to intercept it.

The surviving XB-70 was used for high-speed research. It is seen here with wingtips drooped for high-speed flight. (TRH Pictures)

Specification: XB-70 Valkyrie
Type: six-engined Mach 3 strategic bomber
Crew: two
Powerplant: six 27,200-lb (126.2-kN) thrust General Electric YJ93-3 turbojets
Dimensions: span (spread) 105 ft 0 in (32.0 m); length (with probe) 196 ft 6 in (59.89 m); height 30 ft 9 in (9.45 m); wing area 6,297 sq ft (585 m²)
Weights: empty 205,000 lb (92990 kg); max. take-off 550,000 lb (249476 kg)
Performance: max. speed 2,035 mph (3275 km/h); service ceiling 75,000 ft (22860 m); range (proposed) 7,600 miles (12230 km), actual 4,288 miles (6900 km)
Armament: (proposed) up to 14 nuclear weapons, or conventional weapons

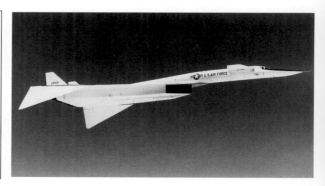

General Dynamics F-111 Aardvark

**United States
December 1964**

The General Dynamics F-111 originated from a 1958 USAF requirement for a tactical strike fighter. The Navy's FAD (Fleet Air Defence) fighter requirement was merged with this to create the TFX (Tactical Fighter Experimental) programme. Development was protracted and fraught with politics, notably US Defense Secretary McNamara's insistence on 'commonality' between the two versions, despite the two services' very different requirements.

The **F-111A** eventually emerged with a variable-geometry wing, a single fin, Pratt & Whitney TF30-P-1 turbofan engines and the two crew sitting side by side in a jettisonable escape capsule. The first test aircraft, which flew on 21 December 1964, had conventional ejector seats. A 20-mm Vulcan cannon could be fitted in the small bomb bay. Most weapons were carried on swivelling pylons. The long nose led to the nickname (eventually official) 'Aardvark'.

The first 'Combat Lancer' deployment of F-111s to Vietnam in 1968 began with the loss of three of the six aircraft in quick succession to mechanical failure. Once the cause had been established and rectified, the F-111 went on to be the best USAF all-weather strike aircraft of the war. Its terrain-following radar (TFR) allowed a steady hands-off ride at low level.

The **F-111B** for the Navy was intended to carry the

The F-111F was the definitive bomber version of the 'Aardvark'. Too late for Vietnam, it saw action in 1986 and 1991. (The Aviation Picture Library)

The F-111A had a troubled combat debut in Vietnam. This example is seen over Lake Mead, Nevada. (USAF via Robert F Dorr)

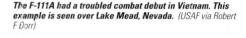

AIM-54 Phoenix AAM, but proved too heavy for carrier use and was abandoned after six were built.

After long delays, Australia received 20 **F-111C**s and four **RF-111C**s in 1973. The latter carries a camera pack as well as retaining full weapons capability. The C had longer wings with eight pylons and a beefed-up undercarriage.

The **FB-111A** was ordered in 1965 to replace the B-58 and early B-52s in SAC. The long wing and the stronger landing gear were fitted as was provision for four short-range attack missiles (SRAMs). The 76 FBs were redesignated **F-111G**s in 1988 as their strategic role was removed to meet treaty obligations.

The **F-111D** had advanced avionics and more air-to-air capability. Because of delays with the F-111D, the simpler **F-111E** with larger engine inlets preceded it into service in 1970. The **F-111F** that entered service in 1972 actually had the more powerful TF30-P100 engines. UK-based F-111Es and Fs attacked Libyan targets in 1986. The F-111Fs used in the Gulf War destroyed up to 1,000 Iraqi tanks and many other targets mostly by night. The **EF-111A Raven** was a dedicated unarmed jamming aircraft. Forty-two were converted from F-111As and they served until 1998.

Specification: General Dynamics F-111F
Type: twin-engined supersonic bomber
Crew: two
Powerplant: two 25,100-lb (116-kN) thrust Pratt & Whitney TF30-P100 afterburning turbofans
Dimensions: span (spread) 63 ft 0 in (19.20 m); length 73 ft 6 in (22.4 m); height 17 ft 0 in (5.18 m); wing area 525 sq ft (48.77 m²)
Weights: empty 46,172 lb (20944 kg); max. take-off 98,950 lb (44884 kg)
Performance: max. speed 1,453 mph (2338 km); service ceiling 56,650 ft (17267 m); range 3,634 miles (5848 km)
Armament: bomb load up to 25,000 lb (11600 kg)

Vought A-7 Corsair II

United States
September 1965

*eeking a supplement and eventual replacement for the A-4 Skyhawk, the US Navy drew up its VAL (light attack aircraft) requirement in 1963. By February 1964 Ling-Temco-Vought (LTV) had been awarded the contract to build its **A-7 Corsair II** design, which first flew on 27 September 1965. The first **A-7A** squadron entered service in October 1966. The design of the A-7 was based on that of the F-8 Crusader although there was no common structure. The A-7 had a larger wing with less sweep and six pylons, a shorter fuselage and a turbofan engine – a Pratt & Whitney TF30-6 rated at 11,350 lb (52.6 kN) thrust. A pair of Mk 12 cannon was fitted to the forward fuselage.

By December 1967, the A-7 was in action in Vietnam. A total of 99 were lost in the conflict up to 1973, 15 of them to SAMs. The **A-7B** followed with a refined engine giving 1,000 lb (4.64 kN) more thrust, although there were still numerous problems with the TF30 mainly relating to compressor stalls.

The USAF saw the utility of the Corsair and ordered its own version, the **A-7D**, which flew in April 1968 and was delivered from December that year. This version had the TF41-A-1 turbofan (based on the Rolls-Royce Spey) and an Air Force-type refuelling receptacle as well as a new navigation system and a 20-mm Vulcan cannon. One Thailand-based wing used A-7Ds in action over Vietnam to good effect from October 1972. Six were lost before the war's end.

When production ended in 1976, 459 had been supplied to the USAF, including 30 new-build **A-7K**s

The Corsair II was one of those rare US Navy aircraft adopted by the USAF. This is an A-7K of the Arizona ANG. (Author's collection)

with two-seats and no cannon. After 1973 most A-7Ds were transferred to the ANG. Some saw action in Panama in 1989.

Two lengthened **YA-7F** aircraft were converted with afterburning engines and new avionics in 1989, but no orders were forthcoming. The last ANG A-7s were retired in 1993.

The Navy bought 535 new-build **A-7E**s, a navalised version of the A-7D with a retractible refuelling probe. These followed 67 **A-7C**s with the TF30 engine and Mk 12 cannon. A-7Es were used in Vietnam, Grenada, over Libya and in the Gulf War. Navy A-7s were retired in late 1991. There were 60 two-seat Navy **TA-7C**s, and six **EA-7L**s used as land-based electronic adversaries.

The only new-build export sales went to Greece, 60 **A-7H**s and five **TA-7H** models based on the A-7E. The 44 **A-7P**s and six **TA-7P**s for Portugal were rebuilt from A-7As. Fourteen US-surplus A-7Es and four TA-7Cs were supplied to the Royal Thai Navy for land-based use in 1995. These and the Greek aircraft are still in service.

The A-7E was introduced during the Vietnam War and retired after the Gulf War. This A-7E was from VA-86 on the USS Nimitz. (Author's collection)

Specification: A-7E Corsair II
Type: single-engined naval attack aircraft
Crew: one
Powerplant: one 15,000-lb (69.7-kN) thrust Allison TF41-2 turbofan
Dimensions: span 38 ft 9 in (11.8 m); length 46 ft 1.5 in (14.06 m); height 16 ft 1 in (4.88 m); wing area 375 sq ft (34.83 m²)
Weights: empty 19,127 lb (8676 kg); max. take-off 42,000 lb (19050 kg)
Performance: max. speed 691 mph (1112 km/h); service ceiling 43,000 ft (13106 m); range 2861 miles (4604 km)
Armament: one 20-mm M61A1 Vulcan cannon; bomb load up to 20,000 lb (9072 kg)

Sukhoi Su-17/Su-22 'Fitter'

USSR
August 1966

First appearing in public in 1967, the Sukhoi Su-17 was a development of the Su-7 fighter, which had excellent speed and climb capability but poor range and low-speed handling. To overcome this, the same type of outboard-pivoting variable-sweep wing designed for the Tu-22M was trialled on the **S-22I** or **Su-7IG**, a converted Su-7BMK which first flew in this configuration on 2 August 1966. Nato designated this initial 'swing-wing' aircraft the 'Fitter-B'. The fixed inner wing allowed the same undercarriage to be used. An initial pre-production batch of **Su-17 'Fitter C'**s (with a longer forward fuselage and a dorsal spine) was delivered to the Soviet Air Force. The success of these led to the full-production **Su-17M** (also 'Fitter C') with a new navigation/attack system and the larger Lyul'ka AL-21F-3 engine giving 24,802 lb (110.32 kN) thrust in afterburner. Nine hardpoints were provided on the fuselage and inner wing.

Su-17 production continued until 1990. An export model with downgraded avionics was supplied to Afghanistan, Algeria, Angola, Egypt Iraq, North Korea, Syria, Poland and Vietnam as the Su-20.

In 1974 the **Su-17M-2D 'Fitter D'** entered service, this model having a slightly 'humped' profile and a fixed intake centrebody with a laser rangefinder (but without the Su-7's ranging radar). The 'Fitter D' was

The export Su-17s were designated Su-22. This Czech Su-22M-4K was seen in the UK in June 1993. A total of 2,820 'Fitters' were built. (Author)

The Russian forces in East Germany were equipped with many 'Fitters' like this Su-17M-4 in the strike role. (Robert Hewson)

nuclear capable, but a 'sanitised' version was supplied to Angola, Libya and Peru as the **Su-17M-2K 'Fitter F'**. This version had Atoll AAM capability.

The two-seat **Su-17UM-2D 'Fitter E'** was to lead to a new family of variants. A second cockpit for the instructor was added and the front cockpit was moved forward. Afghanistan, Algeria, Iraq, Libya, Peru, Vietnam and North and South Yemen received this model. The later 'Fitter G' had a taller fin and reduced combat capability and was designated **Su-17UM-3K**. For export (to Afghanistan, Czechoslovakia, East Germany, Hungary and Poland) it was renamed the **Su-22UM-3K**. The 'Fitter G's deeper airframe served as the basis for the single-seat **Su-17M-3** (export **Su-22M-3**) or 'Fitter H'. Angola, Hungary, Libya, Peru and the Yemens received Su-22M-3s.

The final production versions were the single-seat **Su-17M-4** and **Su-22M-4 'Fitter K'**, identifiable by the prominent inlet at the fin root. The long spine held extra fuel. M4s were widely exported and saw action with all factions in Afghanistan, including the Taliban. Angolan, Yemeni and Peruvian Fitters have also seen varying degrees of combat over the years.

Specification: Su-17M-4 'Fitter K'
Type: single-engined swing-wing fighter-bomber
Crew: one
Powerplant: one 24,802-lb (110.32-kN) thrust Lyul'ka AL-21F-3S afterburning turbojet
Dimensions: span (spread) 44 ft 7 in (13.6 m); length 63 ft 2 in (19.26 m); height 16 ft 10 in (5.129 m); wing area 432 sq ft (40.1 m²)
Weights: empty 23,523 lb (10670 kg); max. take-off 42,835 lb (19430 kg)
Performance: max. speed 870 mph (1400 km/h); service ceiling 49,870 ft (15200 m); range 1,430 miles (2300 km)
Armament: two 30-mm NR-30 cannon; bomb load up to 3,973 lb (4070 kg)

BAe/McDonnell Douglas Harrier

United Kingdom
December 1967

The Harrier 'Jump Jet' vertical take-off and landing (VTOL) fighter-bomber has seen many changes of name by its makers since it first flew as the Hawker **P.1127** on November 1960. Hawker became Hawker Siddeley, then British Aerospace and is now BAE Systems. The P.1127 led to the joint RAF/Luftwaffe/US **Kestrel** development aircraft and then to the **Harrier GR.1**, which first flew in 1967. The **T.2** was the two-seat equivalent. The first-generation Harriers were small aircraft with a shoulder-mounted wing that had pronounced anhedral. The undercarriage was of bicycle layout, balanced by outrigger wheels at the wingtips. The tapered nose contained no radar, and avionics were generally simple. The heart of the Harrier is the Rolls-Royce Pegasus turbofan, rated at 21,000 lb (95.64 kN) thrust on the GR.1. This exhausts through four swivelling nozzles under the wing to give vertical and forward thrust and also allows vectoring in forward flight ('VIFF'ing) to give extra combat manoeuvrability. The RAF Harriers were updated with a nose-mounted laser seeker as the **GR.3** and **T.4**. RAF GR 3s saw combat in the Falklands in the ground-attack role.

McDonnell, later McDonnell Douglas and now Boeing, was interested in the Harrier for many years and took up a manufacturing licence in mid-1969 to build 102 **AV-8A** and eight **TAV-8A** Harriers for the USMC. These were the same as GR.1s except for new radios and AIM-9 capability and were operated from amphibious support ships. The Spanish Navy

These Marine Corps AV-8Bs are the Night Attack variant. The later AV-8B+ introduced air-to-air radar. (McDonnell Douglas)

bought 11 **AV-8A(S)** and two **TAV-8A(S)** Matadors. These were later sold to Thailand. The **Sea Harrier** fighter was the last of the first-generation Harriers. The USMC sought an improved version of the Harrier, not least because of heavy attrition of AV-8As, and McDonnell Douglas led the development of the **Harrier II**. The **AV-8B** had an enlarged carbon-fibre supercritical wing, a new cockpit and larger canopy, a more powerful engine and greater load capability. The two-seater is the **TAV-8B**. Later USMC models incorporated night vision goggle (NVG) compatibility (**AV-8B Night Attack**) and then APG-65 radar and advanced medium-range air-to-air missile (AMRAAM) capability as the **Harrier II Plus**. Marine Harriers saw considerable combat in the Gulf War. Spain bought 12 **EAV-8B**s, one TAV-8B and 13 Harrier II Plus models.

The RAF developed its own Harrier II, initially as the **GR.Mk 5**, later modified to Night Attack standard as the **GR.7** (two-seat **T.10**). The **GR.9** is a further upgrade, which will replace all the RAF's single-seaters and the FAA's Sea Harriers from about 2006.

First-generation Harriers like this AV-8A were unsophisticated but ideally suited to close air support from forward locations. (Author's collection)

Specification: AV-8B Harrier II
Type: single-engined VTOL attack aircraft
Crew: one
Powerplant: one 23,800-lb (105.87-kN) thrust Rolls-Royce F402-RR-408 (Pegasus) turbofan
Dimensions: span 30 ft 4 in (9.25 m); length 46 ft 4 in (14.12 m); height 11 ft 8 in (3.55 m); wing area 230 sq ft (21.37 m²)
Weights: empty 13,968 lb (6336 kg); max. take-off 22,950 lb (10410 kg)
Performance: max. speed 662 mph (1065 km/h); service ceiling 50,000 ft (15240 m); range 1,500 miles (2410 km)
Armament: one GAU-12A 25-mm cannon; ordnance load up to 13,235 lb (6003 kg)

SEPECAT Jaguar

France/United Kingdom
September 1968

Designed to meet a 1965 joint Anglo-French specification for an advanced trainer, the SEPECAT (*Société Européenne de Production de l'Avion de l'Ecole de Combat et d'Appui Tactique* or European Production Company for the Combat Training and Tactical Support Aircraft) Jaguar was transformed into a potent low-level all-weather fighter-bomber. The first prototype flew on 8 September 1968 and the RAF received 200 Jaguars, comprising 165 single-seat **GR. 1**s (**Jaguar S**) with a Ferranti laser rangefinder and marked target seeker (LRMTS) in a 'chiselled' nose and a tail-mounted RWR, and 35 **T.2** trainers (**Jaguar B**), all fitted with a sophisticated nav/attack system.

The RAF's Jaguars received more powerful Adour Mk 104 engines from 1978–84, while the **GR. 1A/T.2A** upgrade added a new nav/attack system to 75 single-seaters and 14 trainers. The aircraft also received AIM-9G Sidewinders, AN/ALE-40 flare dispensers, Phimat chaff/flare dispensers and AN/ALQ-101 jamming pods. For Operation *Granby* (the Gulf War) in 1991, the RAF's Jaguars received defensive systems improvements, overwing AIM-9Ls, CRV-7 rockets and CBU-87 cluster bombs. During the war, 12 RAF Jaguars flew 618 sorties and destroyed both land and naval targets with bombs and rockets.

Upgraded RAF Jaguars use a variety of precision weapons as well as 'dumb' bombs as seen on this GR.1. (Author's collection)

The Jaguar E is the French advanced combat trainer version. It has seen little upgrading in service. (Author)

Since 1994, the surviving RAF Jaguars have been upgraded to **GR.3A** standards adding GPS, TERPROM (terrain prompting equipment), the TIALD laser designator, an advanced NVG-compatible cockpit, helmet-mounted sight and a sophisticated new mission planner. They are due to serve until 2008/9, and perhaps even longer.

The French Armée de l'Air received 160 single-seat **Jaguar A**s and 40 **Jaguar E** trainers with more austere avionics. Some had an undernose TAV-38 laser rangefinder, and all had an OMERA 40 vertical camera. The French Jaguars equipped two wings and one squadron in the attack, strike and defence suppression roles. The surviving French Jaguars, still powered by the original Adour 102, will be withdrawn by 2004. The aircraft now use ATLIS laser designator pods, AS30 missiles and various LGBs (laser-guided bombs). French Jaguars have seen action in Mauritania, Chad, the Gulf and the Balkans.

The **Jaguar International** (based on the RAF variants) was sold to Ecuador (12), India (40). Nigeria (18) and Oman (28). HAL in India also builds the type under licence (131 so far). India's 'Jags' include some **Jaguar IM** (local name **Samsheer**) maritime attack aircraft, with Agave radar and Sea Eagle missiles.

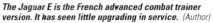

Specification: Jaguar GR.1
Type: twin-engined attack aircraft
Crew: one
Powerplant: two 8,074 lb (37.5-kN) thrust Rolls-Royce/Turboméca Adour Mk 104 turbofans
Dimensions: span 28 ft 6 in (8.69 m); length 55 ft 2 in (16.83 m); height 16 ft 1 in (4.89 m); wing area 260 sq ft (24.18 m²)
Weights: empty 15,432 lb (7000 kg); max. take-off 34,600 lb (15700 kg)
Performance: max. speed 1,056 mph (1699 km/h); service ceiling 46,000 ft (14020 m); range 1,060 miles (1704 km)
Armament: two 30-mm ADEN cannon; bomb load up to 10,000 lb (4536 kg)

Sukhoi Su-24 'Fencer'

USSR
May 1970

Sukhoi's Su-24 (Nato code-name 'Fencer') was intended to be an all-weather low-level supersonic bomber able to attack fixed and mobile targets with pinpoint accuracy and able to fulfil a secondary photographic reconnaissance role. It was developed from the unsuccessful T-6-1 delta-winged VTOL bomber prototype, which had separate cruise and lift engines. The heavy lift jets were removed and a variable-geometry wing was added to produce the **T-6-2IG** prototype, which made its maiden flight in May 1970. The resulting aircraft bore a passing resemblance to the F-111, although with a taller undercarriage and rear-hinged canopy halves.

The production **Su-24 'Fencer-A'** was powered by a pair of Perm/Soloviev AL-21F-3 turbofans. The **Su-24 'Fencer-B'** had an extended-chord 'kinked' tail fin, and introduced a heat exchanger above the fuselage. Late-model 'Fencer-Bs' had a refined rear fuselage (more closely following the jet pipes), and a brake chute fairing below the rudder. **The Su-24 'Fencer-C'** had triangular radar warning receiver (RWR) fairings on the sides of the fin-tip and on the engine intakes.

The improved **Su-24M 'Fencer-D'** attack variant entered service in 1986 and introduced a retractable inflight refuelling probe above the nose, an upgraded avionics suite and provision for a UPAZ-A buddy refuelling pod. Its shortened, reshaped radome houses Orion-A forward-looking attack radar and Relief terrain-following radar. The Kaira 24 laser and TV

The Su-24 has a formidable maritime attack capability. It was first seen while flying with naval units over the Baltic.
(Flygvapnet via Robert Hewson)

sighting system provides compatibility with the newest Soviet TV- and laser-guided ASMs. Russian 'Fencers' saw combat in Afghanistan and again in 1988 to cover the Soviet withdrawal.

Soviet Su-24 bombers could carry free-fall TN-1000 and TN-1200 nuclear bombs, and a variety of conventional free-fall bombs and guided ASMs. 'Fencer-Bs', '-Cs' and '-Ds' remain in widespread front-line use with Russia, and with a number of former Soviet states including Azerbaijan, Kazakhstan, Uzbekistan and Tajikistan. Downgraded, non-nuclear capable export **Su-24MK**s have been delivered to Algeria, Iran, Iraq, Libya and Syria. The 24 Iraqi aircraft fled to Iran during the Gulf War, and were absorbed by the IIAF, adding to the 14 already in service.

The **Su-24MR 'Fencer-E'** tactical reconnaissance aircraft uses internal and podded sensors of various types, and is able to transmit data from some sensors to a ground station in real time. The **Su-24MP 'Fencer-F'** is believed to have a primary ELINT-gathering role and is similar in appearance to the Su-24MR, but with a prominent undernose fairing.

This Russian 'Fencer C' was seen over the Baltic in 1985. Su-24s have since been exported to several Middle East countries. (TRH Pictures)

Specification: Sukhoi Su-24 'Fencer C'
Type: twin-engined strike aircraft
Crew: two
Powerplant: two 24,802-lb (110.32-kN) thrust NPO Saturn (Lyul'ka) AL-21F-3A turbofans
Dimensions: span (spread) 57 ft 10 in (17.63 m); length 80 ft 5.75 in (24.53 m); height 4.97 m (16 ft 3.75 in); wing area 594 sq ft (55.17 m²)
Weights: empty 41,887 lb (19000 kg); max. take-off 87,522 lb (39700 kg)
Performance: max. speed 1,441 mph (2320 km/h); service ceiling 57,415 ft (17500 m); range 1,300 miles (2100 km)
Armament: one GSh-6-23M 23-mm cannon; maximum ordnance 17,637 lb (8000 kg)

Fairchild A-10 Thunderbolt II

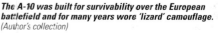

Conceived during the Vietnam War for use against Warsaw Pact and North Korean tanks, the Fairchild A-10A Thunderbolt II emerged in 1972 as a dedicated close air support aircraft, with a primary anti-armour role. The **YA-10A**'s first flight was on 10 May 1972 and it was selected in preference to the Northrop YA-9 in January 1973.

The **A-10A**'s operating environment dictated a highly survivable design incorporating a large-area wing for excellent low-altitude manceuvrability, rear-mounted engines shrouded from ground fire by either the wings or tailplane and redundant, armoured and duplicated flight controls and hydraulic systems. Titanium 'bathtubs' protect both the pilot and the ammunition tank for the enormous GAU-8/A Avenger 30-mm seven-barrelled rotary cannon. The unconventional appearance of the A-10 has led to the unofficial nickname 'Warthog'.

The principal weapon is the AGM-65 Maverick anti-armour missile, but nine weapons pylons allow for a wide variety of standard and precision ordnance. The A-10's avionics remained very basic for most of the aircraft's career, with no laser designator or rangefinder fitted. The pilot has a head-up display (HUD), and a screen for displaying images from Maverick or other electro-optical guided weapons.

This view shows the unique planform of the 'Warthog'. The newer grey colours include a false canopy on the underside. (Author)

The A-10 was built for survivability over the European battlefield and for many years wore 'lizard' camouflage. (Author's collection)

One example of a two-seat version, the **YA-10B** or **A-10 N/AW**, was built for evaluation as a trainer and later for night/adverse weather missions. It was not selected for production.

The A-10 entered USAF service in 1977. At its peak deployment, six A-10 squadrons were stationed in the UK, with more in Korea and the Continental USA. Debates raged as to the vulnerability of the A-10, and it was finally decided to gradually withdraw the type in favour of the F-16. At the same time, redundant A-10s became available to replace OV-10s in the forward air control role. Externally unchanged, these were redesignated **OA-10A** and issued to tactical air support squadrons.

For the forward air control (FAC) role the A-10s are armed with rocket pods for marking targets and AIM-9s for self-defence. Although said by some critics to be too slow for the modern battlefield, the A-10 proved its worth during the 1991 *Desert Storm* operations, destroying huge numbers of tanks, artillery pieces and vehicles. A-10s were based in Afghanistan in 2002 to provide close air support.

A total of 713 A-10s were built and the type is expected to remain in service until 2028. A modest upgrade programme is now underway.

Specification: Fairchild A-10A
Type: twin-engined ground-attack aircraft
Crew: one
Powerplant: two 9,065-lb (40.32-kN) thrust General Electric TF34-GE-100 turbofans
Dimensions: span 57 ft 6 in (17.53 m); length 53 ft 4 in (16.26 m); height 14 ft 8 in (4.47 m); wing area 506 sq ft (47.02 m²)
Weights: empty 21,541 lb (9771 kg); max. take-off 50,000 lb (22580 kg)
Performance: max. speed 439 mph (706 km/h); range (ferry) 2,454 miles (3949 km)
Armament: one GAU-8/A 30-mm cannon; maximum ordnance load of 16,000 lb (7258 kg)

Panavia Tornado IDS

Germany/Italy/United Kingdom
August 1974

The Panavia Tornado, initially known as the Multi-Role Combat Aircraft (MRCA), was designed to fulfil a tri-national requirement for a strike, interdiction, counter-air, close air support, reconnaissance, and maritime attack aircraft. The prototype flew on 14 August 1974. The **Tornado IDS** (interdictor/strike) variant was a compact variable-geometry (swing-wing) aircraft, optimised for low-level penetration in all weathers. The aircraft was designed around sophisticated attack and terrain-following radars.

Nine prototypes were followed by six pre-production aircraft, before production began. RAF orders totalled 228 production **GR.1**s, including 14 new **GR.1A** reconnaissance aircraft (and 14 conversions). Some 26 were converted to **GR.1B**s for the maritime attack role with BAe Sea Eagle ASMs, and 18 more were converted to carry the BAe ALARM anti-radar missile, without change of designation.

A mid-life update planned for the early 1990s was cut back to cover only the provision of a new HUD, a forward-looking infra-red (FLIR), a digital moving map, colour displays, and an updated weapon control system. A total of 142 aircraft are being converted to **GR.4** and **GR.4A** standard.

In Germany, the Luftwaffe received 212 aircraft and the Marineflieger received 112, while Italy's Aeronautica Militare Italiana (AMI) received 100. The German and Italian reconnaissance requirements were initially met using a simple multi-sensor pod on standard IDS aircraft. The Luftwaffe and AMI opted for

The GR.4 is the latest RAF version of the Tornado. This example is from No. 31 Squadron at Marham and carries a Sky Shadow ECM POD. (Author)

a more sophisticated variant for defence suppression. The **Tornado ECR** (Electronic Combat and Reconnaissance) variant incorporates an advanced emitter location system, and has provision for two AGM-88 HARM missiles under the fuselage. The last 35 German IDS aircraft were completed as ECRs, with an infra-red (IR) linescan and a FLIR. The linescan was subsequently removed and added to a new recce pod. Italy produced 16 ECRs (without FLIR or linescan) by converting existing aircraft.

A total of 96 IDS aircraft were delivered to the Royal Saudi Arabian Air Force under the Al Yamamah and Al-Yamamah II contracts, some with Sea Eagle and ALARM missiles, and some in **GR.1A – IDS(R)** – recce configuration. Saudi, Italian and RAF Tornadoes were used in the Gulf War. Six RAF and one Italian aircraft were shot down by surface defences, mainly while attacking airfields. In Yugoslavia in 1999, Italian and German ECRs attacked Serbian air defence radars. These were the first combat missions flown by the Luftwaffe since World War II.

Defence suppression is the role of the Tornado ECR. A Luftwaffe ECR armed with HARM missiles is seen during an exercise in the USA. (DASA)

Specification: Panavia Tornado GR.1
Type: twin-engined strike aircraft
Crew: two
Powerplant: two 16,075-lb (71.50-kN) thrust Turbo-Union RB.199 Mk 103 turbofans
Dimensions: span (spread) 45 ft 7.5 in (13.91 m); length 54 ft 10.25 in (16.72 m); height 19 ft 6.25 in (5.95 m); wing area 286.3 sq ft (26.6 m²)
Weights: empty 31,065 lb (14091 kg); max. take-off 61,620 lb (27951 kg)
Performance: max. speed 921 mph (1482 km/h); service ceiling over 50,000 ft (15240 m); range 3,797 miles (2050 km)
Armament: two 27-mm IWKA-Mauser zannon; bomb load 19,841 lb (9000 kg)

Rockwell B-1 Lancer

United States
December 1974

When the B-70 bomber was cancelled in 1964, the USAF re-evaluated the concept of the supersonic bomber in the light of SAM development, beginning studies into an aircraft capable of low-level supersonic penetration. After various 'way out' designs were rejected, a variable-geometry wing and turbofan engines were chosen (to allow high-level transit), and a request for proposals (RFP) was issued in November 1969. In June 1970, Rockwell was selected to build five (later three flying) B-1 prototypes. The first flew on 23 December 1974 and the test programme was underway when President Carter cancelled the production **B-1A** in favour of air-launched cruise missiles (ALCMs) carried by B-52s in June 1977. Nevertheless, a revised fourth prototype flew in 1979 and did much test work that proved invaluable when President Reagan revived the programme as the **B-1B** in 1981, ordering the production of 100 aircraft, redesigned to carry ALCMs in a rotary launcher in the bomb bay.

Outwardly similar to the B-1A, the Rockwell (now Boeing) B-1B is very different inside, with sophisticated defensive and offensive EW systems (which have been known to interfere with each other) and other refined avionics. The blended low-wing/body configuration contributes to a low radar

Designed in the 1970s for nuclear strike, the B-1B eventually saw action in the conventional role in the late 1990s. (Author)

A B-1B makes a high speed pass in afterburner with wings in swept position, showing its low-level manoeuvrability. (Author)

cross-section (RCS). Three weapons bays allow the carriage of 24 ALCMs, or B26 or B83 nuclear bombs, or 84 Mk 82 bombs. Another 44 conventional bombs can be carried on the rarely used external pylons.

The first production B-1B flew on 18 October 1984. Deliveries began on 27 July 1985 with initial operational capability with SAC exactly a year later. Until 1991, the B-1B was tasked with the strategic role and is compatible with a variety of nuclear devices, which it can deliver over an unrefuelled range of approximately 7,455 miles (12000 km). A conventional munitions upgrade programme (CMUP) was begun in 1993, with block numbers denoting successive improvements. **Block D** is the current standard, allowing the use of many precision weapons such as JSOW (joint stand-off weapon) and WCMD (wind-corrected munitions dispenser), and **Block F** (to be completed in 2009) will see the defensive systems upgraded.

The B-1 saw its combat debut in Operation *Desert Fox* in December 1998. In 1999 the B-1 was used in Yugoslavia where over 100 sorties were flown and over 5,000 Mk 82 bombs dropped. In 2001 plans were announced to reduce the fleet by 30 aircraft.

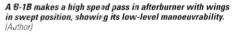

Specification: Rockwell B-1B Lancer
Type: four-engined strategic bomber
Crew: four
Powerplant: four 30,780-lb (36.92-kN) thrust General Electric F101-GE-102 turbofans
Dimensions: span (spread) 136 ft 8.5 in (41.67 m); length 147 ft (44.81 m); height 34 ft 10 in (10.36 m); wing area 1,960 sq ft (181.1 m²)
Weights: empty 192,000 lb (87091 kg); max. take-off 477,000 lb (216365 kg)
Performance: speed 823 mph (1324 km/h) or Mach 1.25; range 7,455 miles (12000 km)
Armament: payload up to 75,000 lb (34020 kg) bombs or ALCMs

Sukhoi Su-25 'Frogfoot'

USSR
February 1975

The Sukhoi Su-25 was developed during the late 1960s as a jet shturmovik, using the tried and trusted weapons system of the Su-17M-2. The **T8-1** prototype flew on 22 February 1975 with RD-9 engines and a trainable GSh-23 cannon under the nose. Further prototypes introduced the R-95Sh turbojet (a non-afterburning version of the MiG-21's R-13-300), a twin-barrelled AO-17 30-mm cannon and the upgraded weapons system of the Su-17M3.

The production **Su-25 'Frogfoot-A'** introduced enlarged engine intakes and increased armour around the cockpit and critical components. Evaluation under combat conditions in Afghanistan led to the addition of bolt-on chaff/flare dispensers, and an exhaust IR suppressor. From 1987 the R-195 engine was introduced, fitted to all two-seaters, and to 50 Su-25BM dual-role attack/target-towing aircraft. Single-seat Su-25 production ended in 1989, after 330 aircraft had been delivered, including export **Su-25K**s to Angola, Bulgaria, Czechoslovakia, Iraq and North Korea. Peru took delivery of a number of probably second-hand Su-25s, while Iran obtained ex-Iraqi aircraft during the Gulf War.

Following combat trials with the T-8 prototype, the Su-25 saw much action in Afghanistan from 1982 until 1989. Here it received the nickname Grach or 'rook'. Over 60,000 combat sorties were flown and 23 aircraft were shot down, one or two by Pakistani F-16s. The **Su-25UB 'Frogfoot-B'** trainer featured a lengthened fuselage with stepped tandem cockpits,

A Czech Su-25 is seen in an appropriate colour scheme. Thirteen of Czechoslovakia's 36 Su-25s later went to Slovakia. (Author)

and a taller tail fin. Similar **Su-25UBK**s were provided to export customers. The **Su-25UT** (later **Su-28**) had all armament and weapons systems removed and was intended for the pilot training role. The **Su-25UTG** was a carrier trainer with a strengthened undercarriage and hook.

The **Su-25T** and **Su-25TM** (briefly the **Su-34**) are extensively modernised Su-25 derivatives – single-seaters based on the Su-25UB airframe, using the rear cockpit to house avionics and fuel. To give true night capability, the aircraft have new avionics, sensors and systems, including provision for podded radars or LLLTV (low-light-level-TV)/FLIR systems. Eight Su-25Ts were reportedly built for Frontal Aviation, plus a handful completed as Su-25TMs. The export **Su-25TK** or **Su-39 Strike Shield** has also been offered to Abu Dhabi and Bulgaria.

In April 2001 Israel's Elbit and Georgia's TAM unveiled the Su-25 **Scorpion** upgrade, featuring a modernised cockpit with two MFDs, HUD and a new weapons delivery and navigation system.

The Su-25TK is based on the two-seater airframe with the rear cockpit area filled with avionics and extra fuel. This is the prototype. (Author)

Specification: Su-25K 'Frogfoot-A'
Type: twin-engined ground-attack aircraft
Crew: one
Powerplant: two 9,921-lb (44.13-kN) thrust MNPK 'Soyuz' (Tumanskii) R-195 turbojets
Dimensions: span 47 ft 1.4 in (14.36 m); length 50 ft 11.5 in (15.53 m); height 15 ft 9 in (4.80 m); wing area 324 sq ft (30.1 m²)
Weights: empty 20,944 lb (9500 kg); max. take-off 38,801 lb (17600 kg)
Performance: max. speed 606 mph (975 km/h); service ceiling 22,965 ft (7000 m); range 1,212 miles (1950 km)
Armament: one 30-mm AO-17A cannon; bomb load up to 9,700 lb (4400 kg)

Lockheed F-117 'Stealth Fighter'

United States
June 1981

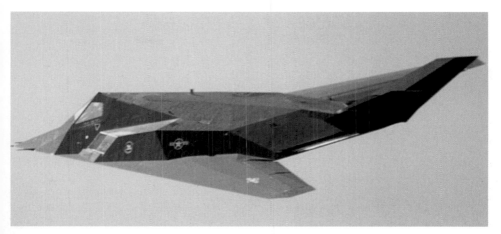

With the lessons learned from the Vietnam and Yom Kippur wars in mind, in 1974 the US Defense Advanced Research Projects Agency (DARPA) began to look for ways to build a 'stealthy' aircraft. Using a mix of radar-absorbent materials and a radar-reflective internal/external structure it was possible to dramatically decrease an aircraft's radar cross-section (RCS). Lockheed demonstrated its expertise in this field (which began with the SR-71) when the 'Skunk Works' classified projects development centre built two sub-scale 'Have Blue' technology demonstrators, which flew in 1977. They utilised a unique faceted structure to reduce RCS and, although both aircraft crashed during tests, the experience gained was sufficient to win Lockheed a contract to develop a full-scale operational tactical fighter. This was signed on 16 November 1978 and under the 'Senior Trend' code-name, Lockheed built five **F-117** full-scale development (FSD) prototypes, with outboard-canted tail fins. The first example flew on 18 June 1981 and the entire development programme and entry into service was conducted in complete secrecy.

As production of 59 **F-117As** continued at a low rate, the USAF began establishing a base at Tonopah Test Range in Nevada. In October 1983, the first unit

The F-117 entered service in 1983 but was kept secret until 1988. 37th TFW F-117s are seen in an early publicity photo. (The Aviation Picture Library)

The F-117 was based on the 1970s idea of faceted surfaces for radar dispersion. Newer stealth designs tend to use curved surfaces. (Author)

was declared operational, undertaking only night flights until November 1988, when the F-117 was publicly unveiled. The F-117 is commonly referred to as the 'Stealth Fighter', even though it is purely an attack aircraft with no air-to-air weapons or gun. Its warload is usually two laser-guided GBU-16 or -24 bombs, fewer than most tactical jets like the F-16. The official name Nighthawk has been adopted, but it is also widely referred to simply as 'The Black Jet'.

The F-117's combat debut came in 1989 in Operation *Just Cause* in Panama when it was used to drop concussion bombs near barracks. This unspectacular showing was overshadowed by its crucial contribution to Operation *Desert Storm*, when an eventual total of 42 aircraft flew from Saudi Arabia on nightly precision-attack missions, destroying the most important targets in Iraq and occupied Kuwait. The F-117 repeated this role during Operation *Allied Force* over Kosovo and Yugoslavia in 1999, when the F-117 suffered its only combat loss to date, one being brought down by an SA-3 missile.

Since the Gulf War, various upgrades have been undertaken. Two-seat and navalised versions have been proposed, but not developed.

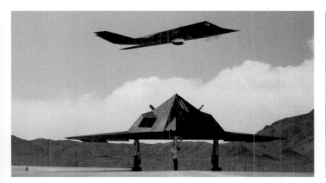

Specification: Lockheed F-117A
Type: twin-engined 'stealth' bomber
Crew: one
Powerplant: two 10,800-lb (48.04-kN) thrust General Electric F404-GE-F1D2 non-afterburning turbofans
Dimensions: span 43 ft 4 in (13.20 m); length 65 ft 11 in (20.08 m); height 12 ft 5 in (3.78 m)
Weights: empty about 30,000 lb (13608 kg); max. take-off 52,500 lb (23814 kg)
Performance: max speed 646 mph (1040 km/h); combat range 1,382 miles (2224 km) with maximum ordnance
Armament: bomb load up to 5,000 lb (2268 kg) in internal bay

Tupolev Tu-160 'Blackjack'

USSR
December 1981

The heaviest combat aircraft ever built and the largest bomber, the **Tupolev Tu-160 'Blackjack'** was heavily influenced by the Rockwell B-1A, designed to penetrate at high level, relying on performance and a highly sophisticated ECM suite to get through hostile defences. The B-1A was cancelled in 1977 and revived as the B-1B in 1981. In the interim, in fact as early as 1973, Tupolev had been working on its own, much larger counterpart. On 19 December 1981, the first prototype Tu-160 flew, having only recently been detected by US satellites.

Although similar in configuration to the B-1B, the Tu-160 is bigger in all dimensions and one-third heavier empty (and two-thirds heavier loaded weight). The airframe is much cleaner with the fuselage covered in flush antennas, with no fences or vortex generators. The four massive Samara turbofans provide nearly twice the thrust in afterburner.

The Tu-160 is capable of low-level transonic penetration and high-level supersonic penetration. The aircraft is used, however, as a dedicated cruise missile carrier with two tandem fuselage weapons bays each containing a rotary carousel for six RK-55 (AS-15 'Kent') nuclear cruise missiles, 12 Kh-15P (AS-16 'Kickback') 'SRAMskis' or free-fall bombs.

The Tu-160's variable-geometry wing and full-span leading-edge slats and trailing-edge double-slotted flaps confer a useful combination of benign low-speed handling and high supersonic speed. Its cockpit is equipped with fighter-type control columns and

A Tu-160 is seen flying with Russian Knights Su-27s. The 'Blackjack' is supersonic at low level unlike the B-1. (The Aviation Picture Library)

conventional analogue instrument displays, with no HUD. The long pointed radome houses a TFR, with a fairing below for the forward-looking TV camera used for visual weapon aiming. A retractable IFR probe endows intercontinental range. Even the unrefuelled endurance is about 15 hours on its internal load of up to 352,733 lb (160000 kg) of fuel.

The development programme of the Tu-160 was extremely protracted. Series production eventually began at Kazan in 1986 and continued until January 1992. Even after the aircraft entered service, problems continued to severely restrict operations.

Between 32 and 39 Tu-160s have been built, including prototypes. Nineteen Tu-160s were delivered to the 184th Heavy Bomber Regiment at Priluki in the Ukraine from 1987 and became part of the Ukrainian Air Force after the dissolution of the USSR. Eight have been returned to Russia to pay debts. Three aircraft were converted to launchers for satellite boosters, but have made few, if any, commercial launches.

The 'Blackjack' was formally revealed to the West during a visit to the Soviet Union by the US Defense Secretary. (TRH Pictures)

Specification: Tu-160 'Blackjack'
Type: four-engined supersonic bomber
Crew: four
Powerplant: four 55,115-lb (256-kN) thrust Samara/Trud NK-321 afterburning turbofans
Dimensions: span 166 ft 4 in (50.7 m); length 177 ft 6 in (54.1 m); height 13.1 m (43.0 in); wing area 3,660 sq ft (340 m²)
Weights: empty 260,000 lb (117836 kg); max. take-off 606,260 lb (275000 kg)
Performance: max. speed 1,243 mph (2000 km/h); service ceiling 52,200 ft (15910 m); range 9,072 miles (14600 km)
Armament: 12 ALCMs or 24 SRAMs or 99,208 lb (45000 kg) of bombs

Dassault Mirage 2000 Attack Variants

The Mirage 2000N is based on the 2000B trainer airframe with strengthening for low-level flight and retains dual control. (Dassault)

The Mirage 2000 was designed as a successor to the Mirage III and Mirage F1 and retains the delta-wing configuration of the former, albeit with fly-by-wire flight controls and sophisticated avionics. The prototype Mirage 2000 flew in 1978 and the Mirage 2000C entered service in the fighter role in 1984.

The requirement for a Mirage IVP replacement to carry the ASMP stand-off nuclear missile resulted in Dassault receiving a contract in 1979 for two **Mirage 2000P** (Pénétration) prototypes (later designated **Mirage 2000N** (Nucléaire). Based on the 2000B two-seat trainer, the 2000N has a strengthened airframe for low-level flight and considerable differences in avionics, including twin INS (inertial navigation systems), and Antilope 5 radar optimised for terrain-following, ground-mapping and navigation. It provides automatic terrain-following down to 300 ft (91 m) at speeds up to 691 mph (1112 km/h). Both pilot and weapons system operator have moving map displays. The ASMP delivers a 150- or 300-kT warhead up to 50 miles (80 km) from a low-altitude launch point. Typically, the Mirage 2000N also carries a pair of large, 440-Imp gal (2000-litre) drop tanks and two self-defence MATRA Magic AAMs. Further protection is provided by a radar-warning receiver (RWR), electronic jammers and a chaff/flare system.

The 2000D is the conventional strike version of the Mirage 2000. This example belongs to EC03.003 and is seen at RAF Marham (Author)

The prototype Mirage 2000N was flown on 3 March 1986. The first 30 production aircraft were built to **Mirage 2000N-K1** standard, without the Spirale chaff/flares equipment. The -K1 was a dedicated nuclear strike variant, and was armed with two AN52 free-fall bombs before the ASMP missile was ready for service. The second batch of 44 comprised **Mirage 2000N-K2s**, with a dual nuclear/conventional capability, and full ASMP compatibility. Mirage 2000N deliveries were completed in 1993. The 2000N-K1s have been upgraded to acquire a limited conventional attack capability.

While the Mirage 2000N is largely dedicated to nuclear strike, Dassault has also developed a similar version for conventional long-range precision-attack missions. This is the **Mirage 2000D**, which outwardly looks almost identical to the 2000N. The prototype Mirage 2000D first flew on 19 February 1991 and the last of 86 2000Ds was delivered in 2001.

The **Mirage 2000N-R2** aircraft introduced the Apache and Scalp stand-off missiles, the Samir self-protection fit, and the Atlis II laser-designation system. French Mirage 2000Ds saw action over Bosnia, Kosovo and Afghanistan.

Specification: Dassault Mirage 2000D
Type: delta-winged attack aircraft
Crew: two
Powerplant: one 21,384-lb (95.12-kN) thrust SNECMA M53-P2 afterburning turbofan
Dimensions: wing span 29 ft 11.5 in (9.13 m); length 47 ft 9 in (14.55 m); height 16 ft 11 in (5.15 m); wing area 441.3 sq ft (41 m²)
Weights: empty 16,755 lb (7600 kg); maximum take-off 37,478 lb (17000 kg)
Performance: max speed over 1,453 mph (2338 km/h); service ceiling 59,055 ft (18000 m); range over 920 miles (1480 km)
Armament: two 30-mm DEFA 554 cannon; 13,890-lb (6300-kg) ordnance

McDonnell Douglas F-15E 'Strike Eagle'
United States
December 1986

The F-15 Eagle was originally intended as a dual-role aircraft, incorporating air-to-ground capability and wired for the carriage of air-to-ground ordnance. This ground-attack role was abandoned in 1975, but later resurrected in 1982, when the second TF-15A was modified as the privately developed **'Strike Eagle'**. It was conceived as a replacement for the F-111. **F-15E** development began in February 1984, and The first production aircraft flew on 11 December 1986.

The F-15E's primary mission is air-to-ground strike, for which it carries a wide range of weapons on two underwing pylons, underfuselage pylons and 12 bomb racks mounted directly on the conformal fuel tanks. It introduced redesigned controls, a wide-angle HUD, and three multi-purpose CRTs displaying navigation, weapons delivery and systems operations. The rear-cockpit weapons systems operator (WSO) employs four multi-purpose CRT terminals for radar, weapon selection and monitoring enemy tracking systems. The WSO also operates an AN/APG-70 synthetic aperture radar and LANTIRN navigation and targeting pods. The navigation pod incorporates its own TFR, which can be linked to the aircraft's flight control system to allow automatic coupled terrain-following flight. The targeting pod allows the aircraft to self-designate LGBs. The F-15E's original F100-PW-220 turbofans were soon replaced by Pratt & Whitney's F100-PW-229 engines under the Improved Performance Engine competitive programme.

The USAF has Strike Eagles based in Alaska, the UK and the continental USA. This F-15E is from the 366th Wing at Mountain Home AFB. (Boeing)

The F-15E has been exported to Israel as the **F-15I Ra'am**, and to Saudi Arabia as the **F-15S**. Israel has acquired 25 F-15Is and the first two aircraft were delivered in January 1998. Israel's F-15Is are in some ways superior to USAF F-15Es with Elbit helmet-mounted sights and Elisra ECM, but the Saudi F-15S aircraft have been downgraded, with some capabilities deleted. The first of 72 F-15Ss made its maiden flight on 19 June 1995. In April 2002 the **F-15K** beat the Eurofighter Typhoon and Dassault Rafale to win an order for 40 from South Korea.

The USAF took delivery of 209 F-15Es between 1987 and 1994. A follow-on batch of 17 upgraded aircraft was delivered in 2000, bringing the total up to 226 aircraft, and another 10 are in production. The 'Mud Hen' flew many precision strike missions in the Gulf War. One F-15E destroyed an airborne Iraqi helicopter with a GBU-10 LGB. In Operation *Allied Force* in 1999, USAF F-15Es employed the GBU-28 Paveway III against bunkers, bridges and other infrastructure targets.

The F-15E can carry a wide range of 'iron' and precision-guided munitions. These 'Mud Hens' are loaded with 500-lb (227-kg) bombs. (Boeing)

Specification: Boeing F-15E Eagle
Type: twin-engined strike fighter
Crew: two
Powerplant: two 29,100-lb (129.45-kN) thrust Pratt & Whitney F100-PW-229 turbofans
Dimensions: span 42 ft 10 in (13.05 m); length 63 ft 9 in (19.43 m); height 18 ft 5.5 in (5.63 m); wing area 608 sq ft (56.59 m²)
Weights: empty 31,700 lb (14379 kg); max. take-off 81,000 lb (36741 kg)
Performance: max. speed over 1,650 mph (2655 km/h); combat radius 790 miles (1270 km)
Armament: one M61A1 20-mm cannon; max. bomb load of 24,500 lb (11113 kg)

Northrop Grumman B-2 Spirit

United States
July 1989

On the B-2A, fly-by-wire technology helped cure the instability found in earlier flying-wing designs. (Author)

Northrop Aircraft (today Northrop Grumman) was notable for its innovative flying wing designs in the 1940s, culminating in the piston/jet XB-35 and jet YB-49. These aircraft suffered somewhat from instability, but proved hard to track on radar. When, in the 1970s, the USAF was looking for a bomber that could penetrate Soviet airspace undetected, it turned to Northrop for a modernised version of the same flying wing concept. Fly-by-wire technology would cure the instability and various low-observable (LO) methods would make the design 'stealthy'.

Started as a 'black' programme under the codename Project Senior C J and later as the ATB (Advanced Technology Bomber), the aircraft was unveiled in November 1988 as the Northrop **B-2**, making its first flight at Palmdale on 17 July 1989. The B-2 is essentially all wing, with the payload/crew section at the apex of the leading edge. The crew consists of only two – a pilot and a mission commander, seated on zero-zero ACES I ejection seats. The trailing edge is 'W'-shaped with roll control coming from split ailerons/spoilers at the wingtips. The B-2's four F118 turbofans are non-afterburning variants of the F110 turbofan and have intakes and exhausts located above the aircraft to shield them from detection.

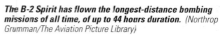

The B-2 Spirit has flown the longest-distance bombing missions of all time, of up to 44 hours duration. (Northrop Grumman/The Aviation Picture Library)

The USAF received is first operational **B-2A Spirit** in December 1993 and the last was delivered to the 509th Bomb Wing at Whiteman AFB, Missouri, in December 1997. As later aircraft were delivered, early examples were upgraded to Block 20 and Block 30 standard. Block 30 bombers have full precision-guided munitions and terrain-following capability and improved stealth measures. Total procurement, reduced initially from 132 to 75 has been curtailed to just 20 front-line aircraft due to the enormous cost of each B-2. Cost estimates per aircraft range between $1.157 billion (USAF official) and $2.25 billion. Maintenance costs are also very high due to the need to preserve the smooth, RAM-coated (radar-absorbent material) surface finish.

Although many observers thought that the USAF would never risk the costly B-2 in anything other than an all-out nuclear war, the Spirit saw action against Yugoslav forces in Kosovo in 1999. Non-stop 15-hour missions were flown all the way from Whiteman to the Balkans and back, in which up to 16 GPS-guided 2,000-lb (907-kg) JDAMs were dropped on targets such as airfields and air defence sites. In Operation *Enduring Freedom*, the B-2 flew missions of up to 44 hours duration from Missouri to Afghanistan and back.

Specification: Northrop B-2A Spirit
Type: four-engined 'stealth' bomber
Crew: two
Powerplant: four 19,000-lb (84.52-kN) thrust General Electric F118-GE-110 non-afterburning turbofans
Dimensions: spar 172 ft (52.43 m); length 69 ft (21.03 m); height 17 ft (5.18 m); wing area 5,000 sq ft (464.5 m²)
Weights: empty 153,693 lb (69715 kg); max. take-off 375 992 lb (170550 kg)
Performance: max. speed 475 mph (764 km/h); service ceiling 50,000 ft (15240 m); range 7,600 miles (12231 km)
Armament: maximum ordnance 40,000 lb (18144 kg)

Sukhoi Su-32/Su-34 'Flanker'

USSR
April 1990

With its long range and heavy load-carrying capability, the Sukhoi Su-27 offered considerable potential as a tactical strike/attack aircraft, and as a replacement for the Su-24. The **Su-27IB** fighter-bomber began life as a carrier-based trainer aircraft for Su-27K pilots, initially designated Su-27KU or Su-27KM-2. By the time the prototype was rolled out, the slimmed-down carrier programme had removed the need for a dedicated trainer, and the aircraft was redesigned as a fighter-bomber under the new designation Su-27IB. It first flew on 13 April 1990. The aircraft combined canard foreplanes with a new forward fuselage accommodating a side-by-side two-seat cockpit, with a titanium-armoured cockpit, armoured glass, and three large CRT displays. The broad, flat, 'duck-nose' led to the Su-27IB's unofficial 'Platypus' nickname, and accommodated a new Leninetz B-004 multi-function radar with a fixed phased array antenna.

The prototype was followed by four aircraft built to the planned production standard, with twin-wheel main undercarriage bogies, and a raised, thickened tail sting housing a rearward-looking tail warning radar. The first of these productionised Su-27IBs (designated **Su-34**s by Sukhoi) flew on 18 December 1993. For long-range missions the aircraft had a lavatory and a galley, with room for the crew to stand upright or lie prone between the seats. A retractable IFR probe was also provided, together with ejection seats incorporating a 'back massage' function.

The unique 'platypus' nose profile of the Su-32FN contains Sea Snake radar optimised for maritime missions. (Author)

Development of the Su-27IB has been slow, owing to funding and technical problems, and the planned in-service date of 1998 slipped by virtually unnoticed. There is still an aspiration for the Su-27IB to replace all Russian air forces' Su-24s (although not by 2005 as once announced). The programme is progressing slowly, and has not been cancelled. Eight aircraft had been produced by early 1999 and there were reports that one had been combat-tested in Chechnya. Production Su-27IBs are expected to use more powerful 39,240-lb (175-kN) Saturn AL-41F engines. The aircraft was marketed as a dedicated maritime attac< aircraft under the designation **Su-32FN** (using the third pre-production Su-27IB as a demonstrator), and as a multi-role export aircraft as the **Su-32MF**. The Su-32N's Sea Snake radar can reportedly detect the surface disturbance of a submerged submarine frcm 93 miles (150 km) away.

The basic Su-27IB airframe now forms the basis for several proposed interceptor, recce and EW variants.

The Su-32FN has been shown at several Western air shows, including Paris in 1997. The large tail pod is shown well. (Austin J Brown/The Aviation Picture Library)

Specification: Sukhoi Su-27IB

Type: twin-engined strike aircraft
Crew: two
Powerplant: Two 29,320-lb (130.43-kN) thrust Lyul'ka AL-31FM (AL-35F) turbofans
Dimensions: span 48 ft 3 in (14.7 m); length 76 ft 7 in (23.34 m); height 19 ft 11 in (6.08 m); wing area 668 sq ft (62.04 m²)
Weights: empty 41,887 lb (19000 kg); max. take-off 99,428 lb (45100 kg)
Performance: max. speed 1,180 mph (1900 km/h); service ceiling 65,000 ft (19800 m); range 1,382 miles (2226 km)
Armament: one 30-mm GSh-30-1 cannon; maximum ordnance 17,636 lb (8000 kg)

Index